Praise for

Wild Quests

'Full of terrific insights, vivaciously written and gorgeously illustrated, *Wild Quests* combines enormous passion for wild animals with some telling truths about humanity's wilful failure as guardians of our natural world.'

Phillip Adams AO,
broadcaster, writer and host of *Late Night Live* on ABC Radio National

'In *Wild Quests*, Satyajit Das takes us on a whirlwind grand tour of animal ecotourism, reflecting on what drives us to seek out exotic animals in the wild – and what we are missing in the process.'

Danielle Clode,
biologist and award-winning author of *Koala: A Life in Trees*

'A thoughtful confessional from a knowledgeable nature tourist who inadvertently became an active participant in ecocide. *Wild Quests* is a witty, honest, humble and unsparing (even to Das himself) examination of attempts to preserve wild animals.'

Paul Sullivan,
former CEO of Birdlife Australia

Wild Quests

Journeys into Ecotourism and the Future for Animals

Satyajit Das

MONASH
UNIVERSITY
PUBLISHING

Published by Monash University Publishing
Matheson Library Annexe
40 Exhibition Walk
Monash University
Clayton, Victoria 3800, Australia
publishing.monash.edu

Monash University Publishing: the discussion starts here

Wild Quests: Journeys into Ecotourism and the Future for Animals

ISBN 9781922979575 (paperback)
ISBN 9781922979582 (pdf)
ISBN 9781922979599 (epub)

Cover design by Peter Long
Front cover image: Close up of a Tiger, Vikram1972, Shutterstock, ID 2314197851
Back cover image: King Bird of Paradise, Mongkol Rujitham, Shutterstock, ID 365823341
Author photograph by Thomas Gallane Photography
Typesetting by Typography Studio

Printed in Australia by Griffin Press

FSC www.fsc.org MIX Paper | Supporting responsible forestry FSC® C018684

The paper this book is printed on is certified against the Forest Stewardship Council® Standards. Griffin Press holds chain of custody certification SCS-COC-001185. FSC® promotes environmentally responsible, socially beneficial and economically viable management of the world's forests.

All-devouring, all-destroying
Never finding full repast,
Till I eat the world at last.

—JONATHAN SWIFT, 'Riddles',
The Poems of Jonathan Swift (1724)

CONTENTS

A NOTE ON CURRENCIES AND MEASUREMENTS

All currencies in this book appear in US dollars. Both metric and imperial measures are given and have generally been rounded up to the nearest whole figure for ease of reading. For example, the port town of Anadyr in Russia is described as 6000 kilometres (3800 miles) from Moscow; the exact figures are 6191 kilometres (3847 miles).

PROLOGUE

THE ANIMALS DO NOT WANT TO SEE US

'The animals do not want to see you.' A simple factual statement, said without emotion.

It is the northern summer of 2014 and the speaker is Nikita Ovsyanikov, a stocky man with a neat beard, who introduces himself, with typical humility, as a 'polar bear biologist'. The description does not do justice to one of the world's leading experts. Nikita is a naturalist on our expedition to Wrangel Island, in Russia's Far East. Ironically, our visit has been motivated, in part, by reading his work. It is a happy coincidence that he should be on the ship.

The setting is a stuffy, windowless lecture room in the bowels of an old Russian research vessel, converted for Arctic ecotourism. After Nikita concludes his talk on polar bears, a few of us stay to chat to him. 'The animals do not want to see us!' he repeats, his tone firm. His thesis is straightforward: nature's creatures are indifferent to humans. They go about their lives despite our presence on the planet. Lions in the Serengeti or polar bears in the far north do not spend time deconstructing their relationship with us. Yet interaction with our species is at the heart of their problems: damage to habitat, hunting, shooting, killing or persecution. Even our attempts to see them in the wild can be disruptive.

Nikita's simple eight-word formulation goes to the heart of issues that have concerned me and my partner, Jade, for a long time – in fact, since we first began travelling to see wildlife.

Our voyage is a two-week round trip to Wrangel Island from Anadyr, the administrative capital of the Chukotka region in East Russia – a nearly stateless realm that, at 6000 kilometres (3800 miles) and nine time zones from Moscow, is closer to North America than Europe. The remoteness makes logistics complicated. Passengers must travel to Anadyr across the Bering Strait on a special charter from Nome, Alaska, or on the weekly nine-hour flight from the Russian capital.

Wrangel Island (Ostrov Vrangelya in Russian) is named after Baron Ferdinand von Wrangel. Between 1820 and 1824, the German searched for the island based on historical reports and indigenous Chukchi stories, but never actually found the place. The 7600-square-kilometre (2900-square-mile) island is in the Arctic Ocean, between the Chukchi and East Siberian seas, some 140 kilometres (90 miles) off the coast. Never glaciated or submerged by rising sea levels, Wrangel has evolved largely uninterrupted for millions of years. With nearby Herald Island and the surrounding waters, it is a federally protected zapovednik – a strict nature reserve where most human activity other than for scientific purposes is forbidden. Rangers and a few scientists reside on the island year-round. Around 150 to 200 tourists visit each year. Our ship carries fifty passengers from Australia, New Zealand, America and Europe, including a German film crew tracing the expedition of naturalist Adelbert von Chamisso.

The climate is forbidding. The lengthy winters are minus 40 to 50 degrees Celsius (minus 40 to 58 degrees Fahrenheit). Summers last around a month, with temperatures rising to about zero degrees Celsius (32 degrees Fahrenheit). Some days are gloriously sunlit; others are misty and foggy. High winds and snowstorms are frequent. Fierce northern winds and rough seas prevent us from visiting the exposed north side of Wrangel.

Our route hugs the Russian coast. One stop is an ancient site on Yttygran Island known as Whale Bone Alley. Huge cetacean jawbones stretch in a line for nearly 500 metres (550 yards). Only seven remain upright. It is thought that the bones were the indigenous population's navigational markers, or supports to hold or work on their animal-skin boats. Another stop is Cape Dezhnev, the eastern-most point of Eurasia, named for the first recorded European to round its tip. There are visits to Kolyuchin Island, Kolyuchin Inlet and Belyaka Spit, all celebrated for wildlife.

Our voyage crisscrosses the International Date Line, halfway round the world from the prime meridian, the zero-degree longitude in Greenwich, England. Some passengers seem mesmerised by this arbitrary division of the Earth, seeking to photograph the ship's GPS reading at the precise moment of crossing. We pass Big Diomede Island (Ratmanov Island in Russian), separated by a short distance from the American territory of Little Diomede Island. As the International Date Line lies between the two, you can see both the past and the future, depending on your position.

The time at sea is filled with lectures from the expedition's naturalists. Some of us spend the almost twenty-four hours of daylight out on the bow deck or the bridge, keeping a lookout for seabirds and mammals. On most days, there are shore visits using the ship's five zodiacs, inflatable rubber boats with outboard motors. Walkers hike over the tundra. Botanists explore the plant life. Wildlife watchers search for animals.

At Uelen village, some visit a Chukchi community, watched over by Russian border guards. The local dance group performs for the tourists. A few travellers, in turn, provide the villagers with unintended entertainment when they attempt to join in. There is retail therapy at a museum, where carved ivory mementos are for sale.

The Chukchi live off sea mammals, carcasses or remains of which are visible in the coastal villages. The ivory is from slaughtered marine life. Conservation guidelines seek to balance traditional practices and the protection of endangered species, although it is unlikely that the indigenous people's historical customs included hunting sea mammals in motorboats with explosive harpoons and AK-47 Kalashnikovs.

In these parts, the tree-less tundra, bordered by rugged coastlines, stretches to the horizon. The lack of human inhabitants reinforces the isolation. It is the end of the world or, at least, the beginning of the end of the world.

The immense plains are dotted with frozen marshes. In summer, a carpet of wildflowers and berries cover the ground in brilliant reds, blues, purples and yellows. There are more than 400 species of plant, around twenty of which are found nowhere else. Moss and lichens cover rocky surfaces.

Plants here must withstand the inhospitable conditions. Adaptations include cushion growth, mat-like structures of dense stems and hair that trap heat, allowing the plant to maintain a temperature several degrees higher than the surrounding air. Some plants live mostly underground, with large tap roots reaching to the surface. It is a world in miniature, which one enthusiast studies in a prone position with a magnifying glass.

Seabirds travel annually to breed in the short Arctic summer before returning south. At one point, our ship is surrounded by hundreds of thousands of short-tailed shearwaters. There are waterfowl, most in their dull eclipse plumage because they are moulting, having finished breeding. Flocks of snow geese fly overhead in their familiar V formations. Wrangel is their only surviving colony in Asia, with an estimated 60,000 nests. Peregrine falcons, the Arctic variety among the largest in the world, hunt for small birds. Skuas or jaegers (German for hunters) and snowy owls skim low over the tundra in search for prey.

One of the on-board naturalists and a few passengers spot a juvenile short-tailed albatross – possibly the northern-most recorded sighting of the species. The dark-hued bird, with its prominent light-pink bill, circles the ship once before gliding away.

At the bottom of the food chain, on rocky slopes, there are pika, short-limbed rodents with rotund bodies, rounded ears and no tail. Small furry lemmings forage on grass, leaves and shoots, constantly on the alert for predators.

There are muskox, tundra-adapted herbivores, standing up to 1.5 metres (60 inches) at the shoulder and weighing as much 400 kilograms (900 pounds). Their thick coat – a mixture of black, grey and brown, with long guard hairs that almost touch the ground – makes them appear even larger. The wool is prized for its softness and warmth.

Arctic foxes steal the show. A young animal plays with a piece of felt, pouncing on and shaking it like a domesticated puppy, pausing occasionally to look in the direction of his audience of photographers as if inviting them to join in. The adult foxes are hunting. We watch one fox catch and swallow several lemmings with ruthless efficiency.

On Belyaka Spit, an Asiatic brown bear appears on the other side of the inlet. The animal stands upright, scratching his back on a whale bone, a rare pleasure in the treeless terrain.

Grey and humpback whales are visible from the bridge. In Anadyr harbor, we could see white beluga whales, spotted and bearded seals. But the highlight for many on the trip is the walrus, a highly social pinniped (eared seal) with prominent tusks, whiskers and bloodshot eyes. The adults weigh up to 2000 kilograms (4500 pounds). On Kolyuchin Island, around 1000 walruses rest on the shore in two rookeries.

Taking care not to frighten them, we observe from a distance. The walruses in the water bob up and down, watching us with a mixture of wariness and curiosity, their exhalations audible.

The animals are skittish due to continued native hunting. The only exception is on Wrangel itself, where hunting has been banned since 1976. But the usually large walrus rookeries there are empty, probably due to the lack of sea ice.

The main attraction of this trip is the polar bear. Standing more than 1.3 metres (50 inches) at the shoulder and up to 3 metres (10 feet) in length, large males can weigh up to 700 kilograms (1500 pounds). Its scientific name, *Ursus maritimus*, means maritime bear.

On the southern side of Wrangel, we come upon polar bears feeding on a whale carcass. We are able to witness these normally solitary animals in a communal setting. There are around fifteen individuals, varying in age. Some are eating; others are resting or awaiting their turn. Most have full bellies and blood- and blubber-streaked faces. Nearby, there is a female with a cub. Two males playfight, lit up briefly by a shaft of sunlight. The zodiacs approach the bears from downwind, allowing us to get within a few metres. A big male notices us and walks to the edge of the surf to investigate, forcing us to withdraw.

Nikita has spent more than thirty years researching polar bears on Wrangel. He and his wife, Irina, spent time on Herald Island in the 1990s, where they recorded the greatest concentration of polar bear dens ever found in the world: twelve dens per square kilometre. The steep cliffs, terraced top, proximity to the sea and surrounding ocean conditions were ideal for polar bears to hunt and come to breed. Today, the warming climate and shrinking sea ice has resulted in fewer females denning on Herald Island. By autumn, when they would normally come ashore, the ice has retreated too far from land for them to reach it easily. Dens have fallen by 90 per cent over the last three decades.

Polar bears occupy a narrow evolutionary niche. Their heavily insulated bodies are adapted for the cold. They are designed to hunt calorie-rich seals, living off fat reserves when food is scarce. The loss of their sea-ice hunting platforms, due to climate change, and declining prey populations mean that the bears struggle to find enough calories. Fewer cubs now survive, and adults regularly appear underfed and stressed. Increasing stretches of open water strain the bears' endurance.

Polar bears are highly adaptable, having evolved over hundreds of thousands of years, during which large-scale climatic events occurred. But today their ability to adjust is curtailed by human impact, including pollution, disturbance and increased conflict with people. As if to underline the threat, on our return to Anadyr, we learn of a polar bear shot when it came too close to humans.

The 2022 Global Living Planet Index, a biennial World Wildlife Fund study documenting the state of the planet, recorded an average 69 per cent fall in monitored populations of mammals, birds, amphibians, reptiles and fish from 1970 levels. More than 35,000 species, a quarter of those assessed, face extinction. One in four mammals and one in eight bird species are threatened. Numbers of large fish, sharks and stingrays have fallen sharply. Insects, those little things that run the world, are in sharp decline. Three-quarters of the world's flowering plant species are at risk of disappearing.

Iconic animals are in danger of extirpation. African savannah elephants now number about 350,000, compared to an estimated population of three million in 1979. Forest elephants are critically endangered, having declined by perhaps 80 per cent – the Asian elephant has suffered a 50 per cent population decline over the past sixty to seventy-five years. Most of the remaining number are in India, where they are in constant conflict with the country's growing population. African white and black rhinoceros populations have fallen by 90 per cent over recent decades. The Indian sub-species clings on in a few protected reserves. Javan and Sumatran rhinos are nearly extinct. Once common, African rhinos are now difficult to see outside of private reserves, where armed patrols guard individual animals against poachers. But even here, they are not safe. In Singita, a luxury private game reserve bordering South Africa's Kruger Park, you could once see dozens in the space of a few hours, but now only a handful are left.

The decline in predators is drastic. Lions have disappeared from more than 90 per cent of their historic range. Numbers have halved since *The Lion King* premiered in theatres in 1994. There may be only 20,000 African lions remaining in the wild; there are only around 500 Asiatic lions, all located in a single Indian national park. The global wild population of tigers is now below 3000, marking a 97 per cent decline over the last century, and the Sumatran and Siberian varieties have all but vanished. There are perhaps no more than 60,000 jaguars and 50,000 pumas left. Wolves, once abundant, are scarce: there may be 300,000 globally. The number of African wild dogs, the second-most endangered carnivore in Africa after the Ethiopian wolf, has plunged to around 5000. Large packs, which once reached 100, are rare. Dholes, Asian wild dogs, are ferocious predators known to take down tigers when hunting in a group. There may be no more than 2000 left.

Even species regarded as conservation successes, such as gorillas and whales, remain vulnerable. Thanks to protection, the population of mountain gorillas has increased from 600 individuals in 1989 to around 1000 today. But the overall state of primates is poor: 75 per cent of species are in decline and 60 per cent are threatened with extinction. The populations of great whales remains low. There are probably no more than 10,000 blue whales, the largest animal to ever inhabit the

Earth, where once there were around 250,000. The species has been hunted to the brink of extinction.

The poignant image of a polar bear on an isolated ice floe in an expanse of ocean has become a staple portrait of the effects of climate change. The Living Planet Index would be better titled the Dying Planet Index.

The Russian Far East was a waypoint in our travels, which began in 1991, when Jade and I travelled to Africa to see mountain gorillas and the continent's plains animals on little more than a whim. Three years later, an unexpected opportunity allowed us to undertake a semi-circumnavigation of Antarctica. Unwittingly, we had completed two of the most popular journeys on the average person's bucket list.

Looking back, our motivations for those trips remain opaque. There was a frustration with ordinary tourism, the allure of others' travel stories and of nature documentaries, and a desire for novelty – but mostly it was serendipity that led us to these wild places. Our planning and preparation was rudimentary, especially by our current standards. We did not know what to expect. But those experiences came to have a lasting influence on us. The primal simplicity, the unvarnished beauty and the subtraction of the unnecessary trappings of modern living proved irresistible. Over time, the search for wildlife in their natural setting became the gravitational centre of our lives. Everything came to revolve around our travels. We worked to make these quests possible.

Over three decades, good fortune has allowed us to see many different mammals, reptiles and nearly half of all bird species in their natural habitats. Our travels coincided with the rise of ecotourism, allowing us to be both observers and participants in its development and machinery.

In the beginning, the animals and locations provided us with an uncomplicated joy. Every trip was anticipated eagerly. But over time, other emotions intruded. Evidence of the loss of wilderness and wild animals contradicted the omnipresent images of unspoilt nature in documentaries. We were witnessing a dying world up close. In all probability, we would be one of the last generations to see these places and animals in anything close to their original state. The environmental destruction and our contribution to it weighed on us. The inherent compromises underlying our desire to encounter animals troubled us more and more.

On the bow deck in the Arctic, scanning the ocean hour after hour, I ruminated over these issues that shadowed our journeys. The exhilaration of witnessing wild animals in their natural environment is impossible to explain to those who do not share this passion. Seeing animals' displays and natural behaviours firsthand provokes wonder. The moments are special, possessed of a now uncommon character. They also provide a retreat from the self-absorption of modern life.

Our journeys have come to shape our understanding of the world and our place in it. The humbling beauty provides purpose and meaning to our existence. Wilderness has become our sanctuary in disordered times.

But the ambiguity of our position is unavoidable. Our pursuits originated in the belief that ecotourism would help preserve the planet's special places and amazing creatures. It held out the promise of offering disadvantaged local communities a decent livelihood from sustainable and less invasive activities. Although there have been some notable successes in this regard, on the whole these goals have proved difficult to achieve in practice.

The travels Jade and I undertake are part of the insatiable human consumption damaging the Earth's natural state and biodiversity. The carbon imprint is staggering. Human presence changes the landscapes and affects the animals that live there, rarely positively. Ecotourism's contribution to conservation is doubtful.

Concern and sadness about the avaricious consumption of planetary resources now dog our explorations. Our awareness of what ethicist Peter Singer described as the tyranny of human over non-human now dominates. Jade and I are active agents in ecocide. We are trapped in the contradictions of our pursuits.

Wild Quests is a literal and metaphorical record of our travels and the questions they raise.

Chapter 1, 'Natural Fetishes', looks at ecotourism: what it entails, the travellers and their motivations. Chapter 2, 'World of Wounds', examines the history and politics of humanity's relationship to nature as well as the evolution of conservation.

Chapters 3 to 6 explore the psychological aspects of ecotourism. Chapter 3, 'Wild Wish Lists', examines our obsession with particular species, while Chapter 4, 'Show Times', explores how wildlife encounters are sometimes staged for ecotourists. Chapter 5, 'Freudian Slips', analyses the anthropomorphism fundamental to ecotourism, in which human preoccupations and anxieties are projected onto nature. Chapter 6, 'To the Ends of the Earth and Beyond', describes how ecotourists now venture into remote and fragile environments, such as the polar regions and deep oceans, because it is technically feasible, disregarding the damage it may cause.

Chapters 7 to 9 examine the commercial aspects of ecotourism and the profits being mined from nature. Chapter 7, 'Show Me the Money', looks at the business of ecotravel, especially tourism operators, manufacturers of specialised travel or optical equipment and pharmaceutical firms. Chapter 8, 'The Attenborough Effect', considers how portrayals of animals in wildlife documentaries and the media can mispresent nature and create a distorted sense of our connection to nature. Chapter 9, 'Greenwash', analyses environmental NGOs (non-government organisations) that have made saving nature into a profession.

Chapters 10 and 11 focus on the factors underlying the loss of wilderness and animal populations, as well as its implications. Chapter 10, 'Biotic Attrition', outlines the root causes behind the bleak prospects for many species. Chapter 11, 'Click Here to Save the Planet', examines the implications of loss of ecosystems and explores individual and collective actions that could be taken to mitigate and perhaps reverse the damage.

Written from the perspective of an ordinary traveller and based on first-hand knowledge, the book is part travel narrative, taking the reader inside encounters with wild animals, and part examination of the complicated passions and tensions intrinsic to the activity of wildlife tourism. Ultimately, it interrogates people's unreciprocated desire to connect with wild animals who want little to do with us and questions the real consequences of our attempts to pursue one-of-a-kind 'experiences'.

There is no boundary between humanity and nature. We are part of and reliant on a system that requires us to coexist alongside other living things, rather than exercise mastery over them. Humans have the ability to destroy the Earth as we know it. We can also choose to protect it. The choices made will determine the fate of many species, including our own, giving an existential imperative to understand humankind's inseparable bond with wild places and the creatures that inhabit them.

As the *Spirit of Enderby* sails away, Wrangel is bathed in bright sunlight. Lenticular clouds, a series of ascending spirals resembling UFOs, hover in a piercing blue sky. There is snow on the distant hills. Leo Tolstoy's words from his novella *Hadji Murad* reverberate in my head: 'What a cruel and destructive creature man is. How many different living creatures and plants he has destroyed in order to support his own life.'

1

NATURAL FETISHES

The Ecotourism Phenomenon

Venezuela's Llanos is 250,000 square kilometres (96,500 square miles) of flat, swampy grassland. Like its southern counterparts, Brazil's Pantanal and Argentina's Iberá wetlands, it is noted for wildlife. The Llanos is known for its green anacondas, among the world's largest snakes.

Living in swamps or slow-moving streams, anacondas are ambush hunters. Eyes set high on the head allow the snake to see while remaining hidden just beneath the water's surface. When prey approaches, an anaconda strikes, coiling its body around the victim, suffocating it by constriction. They take mainly fish and aquatic birds, though large individuals may consume deer, tapir (horse-like herbivores with short trunks), capybara (the world's largest rodent – about the size of a large dog) and caiman (a form of alligator). Despite tall tales and film plots, there is no evidence that anacondas are 'man-eaters'.

Anacondas are olive green with black markings along the length of the body and distinctive orange-yellow striping on the sides of their narrow head. Females grow much larger than males and can reach 5 metres (16 feet) in length and weigh up to 70 kilograms (150 pounds). Breeding involves multiple males attempting to copulate with a female, forming breeding balls that can stay in position for weeks. Unusually for a reptile, they give live birth – to up to eighty young, after a six-month gestation. As they do not eat during pregnancy, it is common to find emaciated females after they have given birth.

Jade and I spend a week at Hato El Cedral, a large cattle ranch that caters for tourists. We time our visit for the dry season, when the property is a patchwork of isolated pools, holding the snakes. Our guide, Ramon, is a frequent background figure in documentaries about anacondas. The diminutive, shy septuagenarian has worked at Cedral all his life. His knowledge of its animals is priceless to scientists, to filmmakers and to us.

Ramon looks for tracks, following them to fresh muddy protrusions – potentially casts of earth around a snake. He looks for nostrils poking out. When he finds an anaconda, he digs it out carefully. The cold-blooded reptiles, sluggish until warmed by the sun, are easy to handle. Afterwards, Ramon puts them back, replacing the mud to prevent the snake from drying out. During our stay we find three individuals, all around 3 to 4 metres (10 to 13 feet) in length.

The Russian guests we encounter favour a different approach. Each morning, they head out with their guide to tramp barefoot in the swampy lagoons. Dr Jesus Rivas, a biologist featured in *National Geographic*, pioneered the technique of using unshod feet to locate anacondas. Once you step on a snake, you work out where the head is, grab the reptile firmly behind the skull and pull it from the water.

This is not without risk. Anacondas have inward-sloping razor-sharp teeth. If you are bitten, you must – counterintuitively – reach further into the snake's head to free yourself. When the anaconda loosens its grip a little in order to get a firmer hold, you must quickly pull your hand out. The snake could also coil itself around your body and apply pressure of up to 90 pounds per square inch (620 kilopascals) – equivalent to an elephant sitting on your chest. The lagoons also contain sharp-toothed piranhas and electric eels able to deliver shocks of up to 600 volts.

The Russians are desperate for a giant specimen. Legends of anacondas 20 metres (65 feet) in length remain unverified. In 1910, Theodore Roosevelt offered a $1000 reward for a live snake measuring at least 10 metres (over 30 feet). Today, the Wildlife Conservation Society offers an inflation-adjusted $50,000.

For those with the financial resources, leisure travel is now an accepted part of modern life. But for most of human history, people's lives played out within a short distance of their homes. Animal-powered transportation limited the distances travelled. Natural barriers, such as water and terrain, were not easily overcome. Preoccupied by the fight for survival, most did not have the time or money to travel widely. Even today, most of the planet lives in this way.

Even as technological advances made travel easier, hardships and risks meant that only necessary journeys were undertaken. Explorers set out to search for new areas to settle and commodities to support growing populations. Armies travelled to conquer. Merchants voyaged to trade. Wandering monks spread theologies or made pilgrimages. Christopher Columbus sought new sea routes to the Far East to profit from the riches of India, China, Japan and South-East Asia. King Ferdinand and Queen Isabella of Spain financed him, seeking commercial gain and to extend their empire.

A major change in the evolution of travel was the concept of the Grand Tour, which developed in the late sixteenth century. Young European aristocrats and wealthy individuals undertook pre-planned, multi-year journeys in Europe – especially Italy and France – and the Holy Lands of the Middle East. Exposure to different civilisations, culture, fashion and arts were intended to prepare aspirants for successful lives and careers, completing their academic and spiritual education.

By modern standards, the journeys were demanding. Nicolas T. Parsons' *Worth the Detour* records that one guidebook warned that all meat and fish in Spain were likely to cause illness to foreigners, and the waters of the Tigris, constipation. A recommended travel accessory was a portable mahogany-rimmed chamber pot (disguised as a bonnet box). Prospective travellers were advised to make testamentary arrangements before departure.

Leisure travel and associated terms such as 'sightseeing', 'tourist' and 'tourism' first appeared in the eighteenth and nineteenth centuries. Initially, it was the preserve of the wealthy because travel required money and free time. Before mechanisation and the internal combustion engine facilitated fast, reliable, safe and affordable transportation, even short distances took days or weeks to traverse. Jules Verne's Phileas Fogg circumnavigated the world in eighty days; today, jet aircraft makes it possible in a little over a day.

In the early nineteenth century, Karl Baedeker's travel guides provided reliable information for the aspiring tourist, such as maps, routes, transport options, accommodation and descriptions of noteworthy attractions. *The Atlantic Monthly* disapproved, objecting to the German's attempt to reduce sightseeing to a science.

By the mid-nineteenth century, railways had facilitated rapid and convenient travel. Agencies and tour operators catering to all levels of society appeared. Class distinctions did not disappear. The British publication *Punch* joked that ticket collectors asked first-class passengers, 'May I trouble you for your tickets?' Second-class passengers were asked, 'Tickets, please.' Third-class passengers faced a less civil interrogation: 'Now, then! Tickets.'

After World War II, postwar prosperity allied to the development of commercial air travel, built on a surplus of aircraft and pilots, accelerated the industry's growth, especially in North America, Britain, Europe and Australia. According to the World Tourism Organization, in 1950 there were twenty-five million international tourist visits, rising to

166 million in 1970 and 435 million in 1990. Before the 2020 Covid-19 pandemic, this had reached around 1.8 billion trips annually.

There are the stated motives for leisure travel. It is a break from work, providing physical and mental rest, improving wellbeing and health and allowing recovery from stress or trauma. Journeys offer learning, exploration and the potential for unusual encounters. For Elizabeth Gilbert, the protagonist of *Eat, Pray, Love*, travel alleviates unhappiness.

Then there are the unstated reasons. Travel allows people to transcend mundane lives. It provides interesting anecdotes and becomes a marker of one's adventurousness and originality: 'Last year in [insert location: France / Venice / Beijing / the Okavango Delta / the Pantanal].' It is also a signifier of wealth. Like birds showing off their plumage, certain travellers displayed their economic power to their peers. Spending on non-essential goods and services reinforced their social status. Narcissistic expenditure gratified their hedonic expectations. Economist Paul Nystrom termed it the philosophy of futility.

Originally, conspicuous consumption described the behaviour of wealthy or high-income people. In a trickle-down world, new groups, with more to prove, embraced these behaviours. As travel democratised, a good life became synonymous with a well-travelled one. It has become such a marker of achievement that one woman, Alexis Alford, aka Lexie Limitless – the daughter of travel agents – was awarded two Guinness World Records for visiting all 196 countries before the age of twenty-one.

In 2023, the inaugural Most Travelled People conference, catering for competitive travellers, took place in Equatorial Guinea. Enthusiasts wanted to visit as many places on Earth as possible – at last count around 1500 countries, regions, territories, dependencies, island groups and so on. Travellers logged places visited to ascend the pecking order. The current leader has been to nearly 1400 of these spots.

Tourism has become a complex and changeable undertaking. Journeys are enmeshed in rituals and recurrent motifs, signs, connotations and readings. They are charged with real or attributed social, anthropological, historical and philosophical subtexts.

For those in developed societies, travel is one way to overcome the dissatisfaction of being ordinary, but over time it turned out to be devoid of significance. For some, it was a chore or a rite of passage, an obligation. Eighteenth-century English writer Dr Samuel Johnson held that a person who had not travelled was conscious of his inferiority, having failed to do what was expected of him.

The Grand Tour began as a quest for knowledge. Over time, it became a way to demonstrate superiority and class snobbery. The journey reinforced preconceptions and stereotypes. Everything abroad was terrible but had to be seen in person. An unpleasant present had to be tolerated in exchange for touring a place's ancient treasures. In his 1869 satire *The Innocents Abroad*, Mark Twain recorded the disappointments of tourism. Everything was spoilt by its apparatus. Everywhere was crowded. The traveller was besieged by mendacious operators, guides and hangers-on after baksheesh.

For others, it was a licentious party away from the strictures of home. The antipathy was reciprocated by locals, who thought tourists vulgar and noxious. By the late nineteenth century, terms derived from groups of animals, such as herds or flocks, were being used to describe tourists. Cheaper travel meant popular places were overrun. Piers Brendon, in *Thomas Cook: 150 Years of Popular Tourism*, cites a description of Egypt's seasons around that time: first, flies; second, mosquitoes; third, flying bugs; and fourth, tourists. In many places, tourism is now the only season.

Today tourism is a succession of what French anthropologist Marc Augé called non-places, such as airports and hotel rooms. Once a tourist has adjusted for the backdrop of location, climate, language and ethnicity, every place looks familiar. In a globalised world, architecture, fashions, shops, eateries and cultures merge into a stultifying sameness. The more you travel, the greater the boredom and sense of déjà vu. Overexposed gems of antiquity and lost civilisations feel fake. The traveller, already in possession of points of reference, ticks the box of seeing a treasure in person, but the emotional charge of wonder is absent. Fiction and fact blur. New Zealand, where *The Lord of the Rings* was filmed, is for many a literal representation of Tolkien's Middle Earth. Dubrovnik's old, walled town is King's Landing, the main city in *Game of Thrones*, for some. To a certain unimaginative tourist, Pile Gate is where rioters threw excrement at King Joffrey's head, rather than the formidable entrance to a fortified city used to welcome or deter visitors for more than 500 years.

The explosion in travel has led to an overrated roster of places claiming touristic value. It recalls Don DeLillo's 1985 novel *White Noise*, in which 'the most photographed barn in America', a vaunted shrine of consumerism, can't be perceived outside of the system of signifiers in which it exists: 'We're not here to capture an image, we're here to maintain one. Every photograph reinforces the aura.'

It is what ethnographers call staged authenticity. In many visited places, all is geared to the visitor's perceived needs and prejudices. The sought-after culture shock of the foreign is unobtainable. Guides and experts are agents of reductionism and fabrication. Attempts to discover different cultures are fraught, as the visited live much like the visitors, at least for the most part. Travel becomes a game of Pokémon GO, a mindless race from one location to another with little appreciation of what is seen. You visit, sip a coffee at a café, take your snaps and leave. This discord manifests in the digital pantomime of selfies with the traveller's back to the object of the visit. The illusion is that precious leisure time has been well spent.

Travel today is less about place than an investigation of self: who you are, where you have come from, your disorientation and discontents. It is the world of always moving neurotics seeking something unspecified and beyond reach. Instead of freedom, travel is a means of containment. It reminds Eric Leed, writing in *The Mind of the Traveler*, of prisoners pacing a cell along the grooves made by previous captives. Travel has become work, and sometimes work is more fun. As the titular character played by Richard E. Grant in the 1987 cult classic film *Withnail and I* confesses: 'We've gone on holidays by mistake.'

The chasm between the fiction and reality of travel was predictable. Robert Louis Stevenson thought that there were no foreign lands, only the traveller who is inherently out of place. In a similar spirit, fearing that his mental image of London would be compromised, Jean des Esseintes, the hero of Joris-Karl Huysmans' 1884 novel *À Rebours*, cancels his travel plans. Visiting could not give him anything that he had not already gained from Baedeker and Dickens.

Unsurprisingly, by around the late twentieth century, the search for novelty and authenticity drove a demand for alternatives. It was the desire to conquer unfamiliar territories, not dissimilar to the impulse that inspired ancient armies and Grand Tour participants alike. There were colonial connotations as travellers pushed into more distant, less developed lands.

Some turned to nature. It could be a simple secluded location away from civilisation. It could involve exploring the natural history of Africa, Latin America, Asia or the icy ends of the Earth. Ecotourism – the fetishisation of wilderness and animals in their natural habitats – became a thing. With cheap travel increasingly available to the aspirational inhabitants of developed countries, it soon became one way to distinguish the true traveller from the bovine tourist. This was fear of *rattrapage*, French for catching up. It was the anxiety about one social class catching up with another, identified by Italian social theorist Marco D'Eramo.

Wildlife tourism has an added cache. It is the opportunity to see something finite, to glimpse a disappearing world before it is gone, as the title of a book by *Hitchhiker's Guide to the Galaxy* author Douglas

Adams, *Last Chance to See*, makes clear. In it, he and biologist Mark Carwardine recorded their search for threatened species.

Academic Claus-Dieter Hetzer is credited with the neologism 'ecotourism'. The idea combines wildlife watching and the preservation and sustainable use of wilderness with economic opportunities for local communities. While theoretically sound, in practice combining ecology and tourism has proved awkward.

Ecotourism traditionally involves visiting specific locations to watch animals, either independently or with a commercial guide. The definition of ecotourism, always vague, has become increasingly elastic over time. Some argue that it is about the intent of the individual or organisation involved, and many businesses now use the term to include visiting zoos or animal rehabilitation centres, hunting, fishing and even staying at resorts with nearby wildlife. It overlaps with adventure activities, such as trekking or kayaking, or cultural heritage and wellness tourism.

Originally glorified holding pens where wild animals were kept in appalling conditions, zoos have rebranded themselves as conservation arks. Most visitors to Australia will see the continent's distinctive wildlife in this setting. The absurdity deepens when you consider that many overseas travellers could have seen them in a similar facility in their home country.

The attraction of zoos and wildlife parks reflects the difficulty of seeing some species in the wild and the time or travel distances required. Australia's platypus, a semi-aquatic egg-laying mammal, is a case in point. It resembles a mole but has a duck's bill and webbed feet, with clawed digits. The males also have poisonous spur on their hind legs. Europeans initially believed that the platypus was a hoax created by a taxidermist by sewing a duck's beak onto the body of a beaver-like animal. Now threatened, its nocturnal habits make it hard to observe in the wild. It took Jade and me more than a decade to see one. We did not see it in pristine wilderness but at a sewage pond.

Like others, Jade and I 'graduated' into ecotravel. Dissatisfied with familiar locations, we drifted away from the crowds and into journeys that were focused on nature. It was a natural progression for two animal lovers like us. But escape into nature does not allow you to avoid your fellow human beings entirely. We discovered the inescapable stereotypes and clichés. The location and details may change, but human nature does not.

Peru's Manu National Park is among the most pristine Amazonian habitats left. It has around 160 recorded species of mammals and 1000 recorded avian species. In 1997, it was still considered off the beaten track. Our party included six elderly bridge-playing American women who had chosen the Amazon for their annual vacation because it sounded adventurous. But Manu's privations were unexpected, given its expense. There were the lacks: flushing toilets, hot water, laundry facilities and electricity. Then there were the haves: ants, spiders, other biting insects, rats and poisonous snakes. Our companions were taken aback and did not know what to do while there, except for their nightly bridge sorties. They found themselves, like Woody Allen, at two with nature.

There are those ecotourists whose bucket list includes a safari. For some, failure to see a desired species can necessitate return visits. The list can expand: *we've seen snow monkeys, what about gorillas? We've done Africa, maybe Alaska?* This is the effect of excess time and money, the need to maintain parity with peers.

Birdwatchers are locked in a frantic juggle of time, money and mortality to see every one of the nearly 11,000 species of avian life. There are amateur naturalists, men and women knowledgeable about natural history who see themselves as citizen scientists and can provide, if you are interested, an excellent free education in botany, geology and biology. Then there are boors, whose pernickety pedantry leads to friction with guides or other amateur naturalists.

There are also the professionals, for whom ecotourism is business. Agents exploring new places or scrutinising operators. Guides or tour leaders undertaking reconnaissance for new itineraries for clients. Professional photographers building up stock photo collections. Journalists and authors researching stories. We once met a scout reconnoitring film locations. Some are pseudo professionals, who run travel-related side hustles to transform the costs of leisure into tax-deductible business expenses.

Companionability of ecotourists varies. Pros make undesirable travel companions. Their concentration on outcomes makes for sharp elbows. They try to monopolise the best guides or trackers, the best transport and the best trails. On boat rides, drives or walks, they will think nothing of pushing you out of the way to get a better look or a photo. Such is the unwelcome collision of commerce and hope.

Definitional complexities mean that the exact number of ecotourists is uncertain. To give an example: in 2019, the US Fish and Wildlife Service estimated that 45 million, or 18 per cent, of Americans were birdwatchers. To be counted, you had observed and tried to identify birds around the home or taken a trip of at least 1.6 kilometres (1 mile) to observe birds. Around six million Britons identify as birdwatchers, and the UK Royal Society for the Protection of Birds has around one million members. Sales of field guides and membership of birding organisations suggest much smaller numbers. There are 2.5 million members of BirdLife International, a global partnership of NGOs seeking to conserve birds, across 116 country partner organisations. eBird, a popular birding website, has only half a million active users worldwide.

Whatever the exact number of travellers and how far they go, ecotravel makes up a fraction of the total leisure tourism market, which is worth around $5 trillion in total, or about 5 per cent of global output, according to the World Travel and Tourism Council, the industry's peak body. However, the segment is growing rapidly, much more than the overall tourism growth rates of around 3 to 4 per cent.

Ecotourism is significant business, especially for countries with high biodiversity. In 2019, Costa Rica earned $6 billion from all tourism, of which around 40 per cent, or $2.5 billion, was from wildlife watching. In that year, Uganda generated $1.6 billion, around 70 per cent of that from gorilla tracking. In comparison, Egypt received close to $30 billion from all tourism, chiefly its archaeological sites, Nile river cruises and its Red Sea beach resorts.

As most visitors are foreign, ecotourism is a major source of valuable foreign exchange earnings for many countries. Governments derive income from ecotourism through access to protected areas, operator permits or licence payments, charges for leasing concessions, and taxes. The economic benefits theoretically provide an incentive for conserving wilderness and animals, but the distribution of income is problematic.

A pillar of ecotourism is that it provides employment opportunities for locals, increases availability of basic services and raises standards of living, sometimes from abject poverty. In reality, the local community, especially in less developed countries, rarely has a major stake in wildlife tourism developments, which are promoted by governments, NGOs or private operators. These communities frequently lack the education levels, technical skills and funds to capitalise on the opportunities.

Ecotourists are generally educated, affluent and older. They stay longer than other visitors and spend more money, which should set off a multiplier effect through the broader economy, creating employment opportunities. Seeing a lion, gorilla, rare bird, whale or penguin is not cheap, requiring substantial expenditure on transportation, accommodation, food and beverages, park entry permits and guide fees, as well as equipment costs. The economic structure is that of an inverted human pyramid: instead of more and stronger people at the bottom, with progressively fewer individuals at each level, the traveller is at the bottom, supporting progressively larger numbers of people on his or her shoulder – tour operators, transport and accommodation providers, guides and park authorities. International operators do better than local ones. Local communities, not to mention the animals themselves, are unlikely to be major beneficiaries.

The amount of income accruing to locals is often concerningly small. In many parts of Africa, tourists pay between $400 and $1500 per person to see gorillas. Yet communities living around the forests receive only around 10 per cent of permit fee and a small percentage of park entry fees. Payments are often late or not passed on. But locals bear the long-term costs, which are not fully offset by any additional income or jobs. Host communities can face displacement, dispossession of their lands or loss of access to resources. Wild animals raid their crops. The treatment of host communities sometimes spills over affecting travellers: in Papua New Guinea's Central Province, a dispute over sharing of tourist payments barred us from seeing the blue bird-of-paradise, whose distinctive early morning calls we could hear.

There are successful community-operated ecotourism operations. In Uganda, we visited a village near Bigodi, where a small area of forest had been preserved and could be visited for a fee. It yielded an elusive papyrus gonolek, a stunning crimson bird with a bright yellow cap, in the tiny patch of swamp. In Columbia, at the Otún Quimbaya Sanctuary run by the local community, we saw a rare mountain tapir and several difficult-to-find birds. In Ghana, our trip supported village communities, helping protect endangered birds and animals. Unfortunately, such projects are the exception, not the rule.

Income from ecotourism accruing to private interests or governments is not always spent wisely. Revenues are not consistently used for improvements in habitat, anti-poaching operations, feral animal management or ensuring sufficient rangers and equipment. In many emerging countries, protected areas are routinely in disrepair. Staff are paid poorly, when they are paid at all. They rely on tips from visitors or help from friends and family.

Some locals continue to protect the animals. Despite not being paid for years, rangers in war-ravaged Democratic Republic of Congo's gorilla reserves have continued to try to protect their charges, at risk to their own lives. Others turn to hunting or poaching to survive, reversing their job descriptions. Nothing about ecotourism is ever straightforward.

While visits to areas of ecological significance have grown, ecotourism remains a minority pursuit. Its modest deprivations restrict its appeal. Travelling to wilderness areas no longer requires multi-year voyages and scurvy, but getting to distant locations still presents challenges. It can involve long drives on dusty, corrugated roads, boat transfers or flights in small bush planes, of the kind a traveller on one of our trips refused to board because it had only one engine. Comforts such as privacy, hot showers, good food, electricity and the internet are not always available.

The accommodation at Kirindy Reserve in Madagascar was primitive. On our first night, Jade and I were awakened by a persistent rustling. Torchlight revealed a wonderful surprise – a Madame Berthe's mouse lemur, the smallest primate in the world, around 8 to 9 centimetres (3 inches) long and weighing around 20 to 30 grams (1 ounce).

During our stay, there was a commotion. A newly arrived American woman was lying on the bed in her hut, reading, with the windows open. A large rat jumped up on the bed. Her guide explained that this was a jungle: wild animals were to be expected. Clearly uncomfortable, the woman demanded to be taken to the nearest hotel, some 200 kilometres (160 miles) and a day's drive away. She ended up spending the hot night locked in a car with the windows up until someone would drive her the next morning.

With many remaining wilderness areas located in unstable countries, safety can also be an issue. Our journey to Madagascar was delayed on two occasions due to conflict over disputed elections. In Southern Ethiopia, we were stopped at a crude barricade staffed by unemployed Oromo youth. While the real police stood by watching, the youths searched our car. Without the diplomatic skill of our driver, Tade, we would have been robbed, or worse. Shortly after, Ethiopia's simmering tribal differences erupted into full-scale civil war.

Located in the highlands of Papua New Guinea, Ambua is an award-winning lodge surrounded by montane rainforest that contains more than 200 avian species, including thirteen different types of birds-of-paradise. On arrival, we found ourselves in the middle of a tribal war between the villagers, the lodge staff and the constabulary over some festering dispute whose obscure dynamics we never quite grasped. Vehicles were stoned, huts set on fire. From the lodge, where we sheltered, we could hear gunfire exchanges between villagers and police; a number of locals were killed or wounded. The lodge was closed for a lengthy period, inflicting great hardship on the local employees.

While we were awaiting evacuation – complicated by the fact the villagers had dug up the lodge's grass airstrip – Ambua produced a consolation: a majestic Papuan harpy eagle flew past us before disappearing into the forest. With its 1.6-metre (5-foot) wingspan, the bird is one of four large forest eagles in the world. Phil, our Australian guide, who visited New Guinea regularly, had not seen a specimen for five years.

Searching for wild animals is not easy. Extremes of temperature, humidity, rain, storms and mud are regular companions. In many places, biting insects and blood-sucking leeches are a hazard. Brief sightings of marine mammals in the open ocean mean long hours on the vessel's deck or bridge, a routine sacrifice of meals and rest. Travel of this sort requires effort. Jade and I are generally out before sunrise, as animals and birds are most active at dawn. Often, we are out again late at night, looking for nocturnal species.

It can be frustrating, as no amount of effort guarantees that you will see what you hope to see. Antiquities, buildings and museums are always where they are meant to be. Wild animals do not follow the same rules. In the Llanos, our guide tells us an American woman not particularly interested in wildlife has recently seen a jaguar and a puma in a single night. We have to make do with a close miss: on a 4.00 am drive, a jaguar crosses the road a few minutes after we pass, its tracks clearly visible over our tyre marks. The wildlife deities are cruel.

Leisure travel should be simple, but like most human endeavours, it is not. Ecotourists like Jade and I just want to see wild animals and wilderness areas as they once were or should be. Our motivation is to help them survive. But our quests are tangled in a web of complex and constantly shifting meanings, perspectives, interpretations, needs, emotions and anxieties. They are shaped by a specific history and limited by the strictures and practicalities of travel. Ecotourism is neither authentic nor inauthentic, but now defines how we see, know and understand the natural world. Unless you can turn the clock back or are willing to embark on a true expedition into the unknown, there is no other way.

At Hato Cedral, the Russians did not find the giant anaconda they sought, leaving without having accomplished their goal. It was not for a lack of enthusiasm or effort, but because of the assumptions and expectations of the ecotourist.

2

WORLD OF WOUNDS

The Birth of Conservation and the Redefinition of Wilderness

Nature's effect on individuals can be profound.

Alfred Russel Wallace is credited alongside Charles Darwin as the author of the theory of evolution and natural selection. Lacking privilege and financial means, Wallace, a working-class orphan who left school at thirteen, collected specimens for museums and private hobbyists to finance his explorations of Amazonia and the Far East. His eight years in Asia alone yielded around 128,000 items. A bronze statue of Wallace, erected on the centenary of his death, stands in London's Natural History Museum, which holds part of his collection.

Writing in *The Malay Archipelago*, Wallace's record of his first sight of a birdwing butterfly in the wild betrays uncontrollable excitement:

> I found it to be as I had expected, a perfectly new and most magnificent species, and one of the most gorgeously-coloured butterflies in the world ... more than 7 inches across the wings, which are velvety black and fiery orange ... The beauty and brilliancy of this insect are indescribable ... my heart began

> to beat violently, the blood rushed to my head, and I felt much more like fainting than I have done when in apprehension of immediate death.

Wallace's reaction was that of a naturalist delighted at seeing a coveted species. It is also of its time.

Today, a proliferation of images has contributed to an erosion of that sense of wonder about animals. Overfamiliarity and indifference too often shapes our relationship with nature. In addition, for travellers seeking wildlife in their natural setting, unavoidable evidence of the deteriorating state of the planet coexists with the beauty.

Conservation and its curious handmaiden, ecotourism, are poor palliatives. At the heart of both is a philosophy that suggests humans are not part of nature but its overlord. This dichotomy was always present and has become more pronounced over time.

In 1991, Jade and I travelled to Zaire, now the Democratic Republic of Congo, to see mountain gorillas. We were startled to find that Kahuzi-Biega National Park was a small enclave encircled by farms right up to the boundary fence. Today, decades of war and conflict mean that the park has been degraded by clearing, poaching and lack of protection.

The Congo is not unique in this. In Malaysia and Indonesia, the cultivation of palm trees for their oil, used for cooking and food production, has resulted in mass deforestation. The endangered proboscis monkey is a large, reddish-brown primate now found only in north-east Borneo. The male has a penis-like long nose or proboscis, which hangs over the mouth, amplifying sound and allowing for the loud vocalisations that seemingly impress females during mating season. We found a group at dusk, preparing for the night, in a thin line of trees along the Kinabatangan River. Behind them was a vast palm oil plantation. Despite the area's status as a reserve, cultivation and logging meant that only a tiny fraction of the original forest remained.

Orangutans once ranged throughout South-East Asia and south China. The critically endangered great apes are now found only in the rainforests of Borneo and Sumatra. The animals are largely arboreal, but the dense rainforest, with its canopy and overlapping large trees, has all but disappeared. Large adult males, with distinctive cheek pads or flanges, are rarely seen. The only male we have ever seen was on the ground, making his way to the next patch of forest. Astonishingly mobile and elegant in the trees for an animal its size (an adult male can weigh 75 kilograms, or 165 pounds), it moved clumsily across the ground. It was demeaning for the magnificent creature.

Travellers visit nearby Halmahera, one of Indonesia's fabled spice islands, in search of the standardwing bird-of-paradise, first described in 1858 by Alfred Russel Wallace. Males have a glossy violet and lilac crown, an emerald-green breast shield and two long white plumes coming out from the bend of the wing that can be raised or lowered at will. At the lek, an area where male standardwings gather, engaging in competitive displays and courtship rituals to entice visiting females, the background sound was chainsaws.

Across the globe in South America, land clearing for slash-and-burn agriculture or industrial farming has decimated forests. Over the last four decades, the Amazon – once home to half of Earth's tropical forests and one-tenth of the world's species – has been reduced by a quarter. Satellite imagery revealed that from 1985 to 2021, deforested area has increased from 490,000 square kilometres (190,000 square miles) to 1,250,000 square kilometres (485,000 square miles).

Ethiopia's Awash National Park covers 756 square kilometres (292 square miles) of acacia woodland and grassland. There, we chanced upon an eastern paradise whydah, a brood parasite that lays its eggs in the nests of other birds. During breeding season, it grows a tail up to three times longer than its own body. This makes the bird appear to dance in the air when flying. It was once possible to see more than 350 avian species in Awash. When we visited, the park was dusty, grassless and largely devoid of life due to locals grazing their domestic animals within the protected area.

Geladas are sometimes called bleeding-heart monkeys, a reference to the distinctive bright red patch of skin on their chests. Once common across Africa, the Mediterranean and Asia, they are now only found in the higher elevations of Ethiopia's Simien Mountains, a popular trekking route. On our visit, we found the camping grounds littered with rubbish and trekkers feeding the geladas to get close enough for selfies.

One of Ethiopia's greatest attractions is its eponymous wolf. Less than 500 individuals are left. On a bitterly cold but sunny day, we climbed 4000 metres (13,000 feet) to the Sanetti Plateau in the Bale Mountains to search for them.

The Ethiopian wolf's skull morphology features an elongated head, a long jaw and widely spaced teeth, ideal for hunting the big-headed African mole rat, its favoured prey in the Afroalpine habitat. We saw one wolf motionless near a network of burrows, waiting for a rat to emerge to forage. Once it spots a victim, the wolf tries to pounce on the rat. The prey typically darts into the nearest burrow. The annoyed wolf starts to dig violently, trying to extract the fleeing rodent. Finding the rat in the honeycomb of holes and tunnels is difficult. The process is repeated over and over until the wolf catches one.

On the plateau, there were large flocks of sheep and goats, accompanied by shepherds and their dogs. We saw two large domestic canids spot and chase a wolf off. The incursions by herders, risk of interbreeding and the transmission of rabies and distemper are obvious. Outbreaks have resulted in the loss of 75 per cent of the known population of wolves. Since our visit in 2018, wolf numbers have fallen further due to a combination of these pressures.

Human interference is both direct and indirect. In Africa, North America and Russia, hunting poses a major threat. In addition to legal quotas, baiting to tempt large carnivores such as bears, lions and tigers outside legally protected national parks is common.

Fishing in international waters is poorly regulated, with agreements difficult to police or enforce. In 1997, on a visit to the Galápagos Islands, made famous by Darwin and now a nature reserve, we observed the effects of overfishing. Fernandina, the westernmost of the islands, is famed for its flightless cormorants and marine iguanas. On any day, to the west of Fernandina you could see fishing boats from Taiwan, China, Korea and Japan extending across the horizon just beyond the 20-nautical-mile (37-kilometre) territorial limit. In 2020, Ecuador, which has sovereignty over the Galápagos Islands, discovered a huge fishing fleet totalling over 260 mostly Chinese vessels in international waters just outside its exclusive economic zone. Overfishing has seriously damaged the delicate marine ecosystem. Populations of sea lions, fur seals and seabirds, such as blue- and red-footed boobies, have declined sharply due to reduced fish stocks.

In poor countries, wild animals are a food source, just as they were once in advanced economies. In Papua New Guinea's Sepik River, a local teenager walked past us on a trail, attempting to hide a large slingshot he was using to hunt birds.

Many birds, especially wading shorebirds, make huge, hazardous migrations. Until relatively recently, the disappearances and re-appearances of migratory birds was a mystery. It was brutally solved in the nine teenth century when a white stork that arrived in northern Europe was shot and killed. It had a long stick through its neck, which was identified as a spear from tropical Africa, providing proof of avian migrations.

Arctic terns, which weigh a petite 110 grams (4 ounces), make an annual round trip of 71,000 kilometres (44,000 miles) between

Greenland and Antarctica. Sooty shearwaters travel around 65,000 kilometres (40,000 miles). Many aspects of the migrations, such as navigation and routes, remain poorly understood. The waders follow flyways with stops, typically wetlands, where the birds rest and feed to build up energy reserves. Many of these areas have been destroyed by development. Wader populations have plummeted by 80 per cent over the last quarter of a century. Fifty species that use the flyways are currently at risk of extinction.

Prehistoric humans lived at the mercy of the environment and in fear of large predators. Over time, the development of tools, especially fire and weapons, gave them a measure of control. It allowed for modification of the environment and use of nature's resources. This permitted the transition to agriculture, domesticated animals and, ultimately, industrial society, powered by fossil fuels.

Over the past 100,000 years, human populations grew and dispersed across the planet, altering the ecological balance. Palaeontology provides evidence of extinction and environmental degradation. The best-known of these prehistoric episodes involved the disappearance of mastodons, ground sloths, giant camels, giant beavers and other large mammal species between 12,500 and 10,000 years ago. The process has accelerated in line with human development.

The drive was survival and propagation of the species. It was also grounded in a specific worldview – nature's inexhaustible bounty and humanity's entitlement to exploit it. In North America, early investigations of new regions, sparsely occupied by indigenous peoples, provided a misleading view of available resources. Meriwether Lewis and William Clark's nineteenth-century expedition recorded American plains teeming with bison and other animals. It encouraged profligate use of this abundance. In 1831, Frenchman Alexis de Tocqueville observed that Americans were generally insensitive to nature's wonders and largely ignored forests except to cut them down.

Homo sapiens saw themselves as special. The Greek sophist Protagoras declared humans the measure of all things. Shakespeare's Prince Hamlet thought our species the paragon of animals. In *The Tempest*, Prospero's treatment of Ariel and Caliban is premised on the notion of humanity overcoming nature.

This belief often drew on religious dogma. In Genesis, the Bible asserts that the Christian god awarded humans dominion over all the Earth, including the fish of the sea, the birds of the heavens and livestock. It was a view shared by Saint Augustine and Calvin. Philosophers, including Kant, believed that humans, by dint of reason, were the titular overseers of nature. Even Marxist dogma of limitless scientific progress asserted homo sapiens' primacy. Without humankind, the Earth and all other life forms had no independent existence or value.

Some native peoples had alternative belief systems that recognised our dependence on the natural world. They sought to balance human needs against the environment's capacity to meet those needs. Over time, these concerns found their way into Western thinking.

Conservation combines an idealised view of nature and science. The Enlightenment and Romantic movements found beauty in the natural world. People sought escape from the bleak living conditions and Dantesque horrors of industrial civilisation, captured by William Blake's image of 'dark Satanic mills'. In contrast, scientists focused on resource management. The developing fields of forestry, agronomy and aquaculture recognised the need for long-term sustainability.

In his 1864 work *Man and Nature: Or Physical Geography as Modified by Human Action*, George Perkins Marsh, arguably America's first environmentalist, identified the interconnectedness of humans and nature, expressing a remarkably modern concern about biodiversity: 'All Nature is linked together by invisible bonds, and every organic creature, however low, however feeble, however dependent, is necessary to the well-being of some other among the myriad forms of life.' Writing in 1877, natural historian Stephen Alfred Forbes in *The Lake as a Microcosm* saw an organic complex in which it was impossible to study any life in isolation from the other species upon which it depends for its existence, and the conditions upon which these depend.

Interest in conservation drew on voyages of exploration into new worlds. It reflected the tales of explorers and settlers, native peoples and the exposure to new landscapes and exotic species. Records of the journeys of Alexander von Humboldt, Charles Darwin, Alfred Russell Wallace and others proved popular.

There were philosophical, literary and artistic foundations. Ralph Waldo Emerson, Henry David Thoreau, poet William Cullen Bryant and novelist James Fenimore Cooper exalted nature. In *Walden*, Thoreau glorified living a simple life in harmony with the environment. Painters and photographers, such as Ansel Adams, celebrated nature's splendour.

Conservation history is filled with myths. Thoreau was certainly far from a misanthropic hermit. The house at Walden Pond was not isolated in the wilderness but close to the railroad and the main road into Concord, which he walked to regularly to visit family and friends. The legend of an experiment in simple, pure living and solitude better fits the narrative.

From the start, environmental philosophy accepted that human activity affects the ecosystem and recognises that scientific methods must underpin conservation. It assumes a responsibility for maintaining the planet for future generations. The practical impetus came from US President Theodore Roosevelt, a man with extensive farming and outdoor interests. The President and George Bird Grinnell, a close ally, were concerned about uncontrolled logging and hunting, which had brought many North American game species to the edge of extinction.

Roosevelt placed conservation on the political agenda and highlighted the need to preserve wilderness areas. He advocated reform, believing that unregulated market forces and the laissez-faire approach of the government were wasteful and inefficient. The solution was a long-term plan for management of wild places devised by experts to maximise the economic benefits. Roosevelt helped create the United States Forest Service and several national parks, a project made easier by the fact that much of the affected land and natural resources was state property.

In 1903, Roosevelt travelled west to California to tour Yosemite with naturalist John Muir. Seen now as a pivotal moment in environmental history, the occasion obscured differences. Roosevelt, a hunter, wanted to conserve places because of the value of natural resources for food, water and recreation. Muir believed in their sanctity and value for its own sake. He did not think Roosevelt's brand of conservation, which emphasised human use, would protect the natural world adequately. That conflict remains to this day.

In the 1960s, conservation gained impetus from an unlikely bedfellow – affluence. The first half of the twentieth century was calamitous: two world wars and the Great Depression. The second half began better. Living standards, especially in the West, improved dramatically. Portions of society enjoyed better health, superior employment opportunities and greater access to material goods than in earlier eras. A by-product was interest in conservation. More free time, rapidly expanding travel or leisure opportunities and greater disposable income facilitated this shift: with physiological, safety and personal needs in Maslow's hierarchy largely satisfied, attention shifted to esteem and self-actualisation. Against a background of overdevelopment, pollution and industrial damage, conservation morphed into environmentalism. The term became an amorphous label covering a wide range of concerns: environmental protection, preservation of species and creating a sustainable balance between humans and nature.

American biologist Rachel Carson's 1962 book *Silent Spring* was pivotal. Mixing science and polemic, it sold millions of copies globally, described the environmental damage caused by the use of chemicals, especially the insecticide DDT (dichlorodiphenyltrichloroethane), in agricultural production, when those using them had little understanding of their side effects. These 'elixirs of death' entered the food chain, poisoning fish, birds, larger animals and, ultimately, human beings. The book took its title from poet John Keats: 'The sedge is wither'd from the lake, and no birds sing.' Carson wrote movingly about chemicals silencing birdsong. *Silent Spring* emphasised that all living things are related: 'In nature, nothing exists alone.'

Carson's timing was perfect, reaching a diverse constituency of the public and policymakers. Over time, works such as Paul Ehrilch's *The Population Bomb*, the Club of Rome's *Limits to Growth*, E.F. Schumacher's *Small is Beautiful* and James Lovelock's *Gaia* would also prove influential.

From the beginning, environmentalism subsumed different philosophies, ideologies and politics. The core of biophilia, care for nature and animals, was easy to accept. The contradiction – affluence as the cause of the destruction that conservation sought to address – was overlooked. Caring about the environment did not, for most, entail major alterations in behaviour or a reduction in living standards. Environmentalism became a call to action, producing citizen action groups and NGOs and supercharging the growth of existing organisations, such as the Sierra Club and the Audubon Society. Placing limits on development, reducing industrial pollution and preserving natural habitats became part of the political conversation.

Public concern led to the creation of the US Environmental Protection Agency in 1970 and subsequent bans on the agricultural use of DDT in America in 1972. The United States enacted the *National Environmental Policy Act* (1970), the *Clean Air Act* (1970), the *Clean Water Act* (1972) and the *Endangered Species Act* (1973). The actions were duplicated around the Western world. Recognising the cross-border scope of the issues, countries ratified the Convention on Wetlands of International Importance (the Ramsar Convention, 1971), the Convention on International Trade in Endangered Species (CITES, 1975), the International Convention for the Conservation of Migratory Species of Wild Animals (the Bonn Convention, 1978), the United Nations Convention on the Law of the Sea (1982) and the United Nations Convention on Biological Diversity (1992).

Environmentalism spawned political movements, such as Germany's Green Party, which entered the Bundestag in 1983, a mere four years after its formation. In other countries, similar parties emerged. Over time, conservation issues were subsumed into broader social justice platforms. The Greens began to spout the turgid business-school language of modern politics: *manifestos*, *goals*, *targets*, *assets*, *systems*, *value maximisation*, *resource management*, *sustainable economic development*.

The politicisation of the environment had to balance the unquenchable material needs of citizens, the insolubility of many conservation concerns and changing voter constituencies. Green parties everywhere benefitted from the apathy of existing political parties on environmental issues. Their initial appeal, the high point of which was the 1970s and 1980s, was their narrow focus and moral clarity. But given that few people would willingly reduce living standards, it was always going be easier to debate environmental problems than to solve them.

Green, unsurprisingly, became code for environmental values. The colour is used for digital manipulation in computer-generated imagery. Chroma key technology requires isolating a single colour or brightness value in an electronic image. In post-production, this value is made transparent, allowing another image or footage to be placed where colour has been blanked out. Green is used because it doesn't match any natural skin tone or hair colour, meaning no part of an actor will be edited out. Environmentalism was the chroma key. Each group projected their agendas onto the green background.

Joni Mitchell's song 'Big Yellow Taxi' is a remnant of this era. Written against a background of environmental angst, Mitchell's sombre lyrics warn against taking precious things for granted. It remains the anthem for familiar, unresolved debates.

Saving wilderness required money. Some came from governments. Wealthier interested nations provided funding, either bilaterally or through international institutions, to countries with more limited resources. There was private money from NGOs, wealthy foundations and donors who funded specific projects, such as Dian Fossey (gorillas), Jane Goodall (chimpanzees) and Biruté Galdikas (orangutans).

The idea of financially self-sustaining conservation emerged. Ecotourism was the obvious answer to insufficient state and private funding. Wildlife films, documentaries and nature magazines had increased awareness of wilderness habitats; it was a short step to travelling to see them firsthand. Revenues from ecotourists would help finance the preservation of wild areas and wild animals.

Costa Rica came to be seen as ecotourism's poster child. The Central American country's land area is 51,000 square kilometres (19,700 square miles), the size of the US state of West Virginia or the European state of Denmark. Despite its compact dimensions, the country has diverse features – mountains, volcanoes, valleys and plains. The Pacific Coast is a disproportionately long 1290 kilometres (800 miles) because of extensive inlets and bays. Sea frontage on both the east and the west adds an inter-oceanic element. There are a variety of habitats, ranging from arid areas, beaches, mangroves and rainforests to high-altitude cloud forests.

The topography drives great biodiversity. Costa Rica has more animal and plant species than the United States and Canada combined. It has jaguars, tapirs, sloths and a variety of monkeys. It is home to a wide variety of reptiles and insects, especially butterflies. Turtles nest along the coast. Around 850 different types of birds, 8 per cent of the world's total avian species, can be seen. The fact that it is part of the land bridge linking North and South America allows free mixing of species from both regions.

It is a go-to place for the resplendent quetzal, venerated by the ancient Aztecs and Mayans, who thought it the god of the air. In sunlight, the bird glows an iridescent green-gold or blue-violet. The male has a helmet-like crest and a long tail streamer about double its body length. Jade and I saw a pair in the cloud forest, but only the tails were visible, the rest of the bodies hidden by foliage.

In the 1980s, the Costa Rica government prioritised conservation, supported by funding from agencies such as the World Bank. A scheme rewarded private landowners for keeping forests intact. Today, the land covered by forests has reached around 50 per cent, up from 20 per cent in the 1980s.

Costa Rica simultaneously developed its tourism industry. Normally, around three million foreigners visit the country each year, about 60 per cent of its five million population. Books such as Sterling Evans' 1999 *The Green Republic: A Conservation History of Costa Rica* celebrated its environmental credentials. Studies and articles promoted the Costa Rican model of tourism conservation. The reality was more nuanced.

Costa Rica benefitted from certain special characteristics. Development was difficult due to geography: invading Spaniards had found it inhospitable and difficult to access. As the land was not ideal for agriculture, European settlement did not result in the extensive deforestation that occurred elsewhere in the Americas. Despite its name meaning 'rich coast', there was no gold or other minerals prized by the colonisers. The major industry was coffee, which began in the mid-nineteenth century. The terrain encouraged small family-owned farms, *cafeteras*, not industrial coffee monoculture, which helped limit large-scale destruction of forests. These farmers proved more responsible stewards of the land and responsive to conservation initiatives.

There was relative social and political stability. Costa Rica avoided the protracted post-independence civil wars and chaos of its neighbours. The lack of a substantial land-owning elite was one factor. The abolition of the army in 1948 removed another common source of instability in many new nations.

Costa Rica has a small population. Investment in health and education is high. It regularly rates highly on the UN's Human Development Index among countries in Central and South America. The record of continuous, orderly constitutional government, good governance and solidity reinforced foreign investment and interest in its model.

The adulatory view of Costa Rica's conservation efforts is misleading. In lieu of fossil fuels, the country relies on hydropower for around 80 per cent of its electricity. The dams displaced indigenous communities as well as being detrimental to local flora and fauna populations. Most foreign tourists come for the tropical weather, sandy beaches and low-cost resorts, not the biodiversity. Large tourist numbers are increasingly damaging the environment. An influx of North American retirees seeking a cheap, warm and safe refuge with affordable healthcare has led to overdevelopment.

Manuel Antonio is a small national park on Costa Rica's Pacific coast 130 kilometres (80 miles) from the capital, San José. Established in 1972, it now caters to around half a million visitors annually. It is an ideal place to see sloths and several types of monkeys. The abnormal rise in numbers of these species is due to the disappearance of their main predator, harpy eagles, primarily as a result of hunting and deforestation.

Costa Rica's focus on ecotourism was also not revolutionary. Wildlife safaris were already part of the tourism sector in Africa and, to a lesser extent, India, where it initially coexisted with and ultimately replaced hunting. Colonial-era protected areas for the elite became the basis of today's extensive network of national parks and private ranches. But every movement needs a success story, and the mantle was bestowed on the Central American nation. As the 2020 pandemic would expose, it made many developing nations, including Costa Rica, overly dependent on tourists from developed economies.

Environmentalism was always a luxury, available to those in wealthier, developed countries. The emergence of ecotourism focused attention on the global North–South fault line, synonymous with economic, social and political divisions between rich and poor nations.

For emerging nations of the South, the priority was development, using whatever resources they possessed. Under colonialism, these developing nations – many simple subsistence economies – produced raw materials for the benefit of colonial powers. The money received bought manufactured goods from the colonisers. After the end of colonialism, the system continued under the tutelage of the World Bank and the International Monetary Fund, albeit with differences. Economic and cultural imperialism replaced direct military and political authority. Mass media cultural seduction was used to elicit demand for Western-manufactured goods, and trade became more multilateral.

This colonial heritage affected conservation. The North had already destroyed much of its own natural history and, during colonisation, parts of the South. In an act of monumental hypocrisy, developed nations now wanted less-developed countries to preserve what remained. Wealthier countries deployed selective bribery to further this objective. Advanced economies would continue to farm, mine and harvest in the South where it suited them. A parallel flow of money was set aside to conserve certain areas for their natural values. Aid and debt forgiveness were conditional on agreement to preserve selected zones. This, in theory, benefitted all, but in practice the denizens of advanced nations benefitted the most.

The South saw conservation as a barrier to economic progress. Against the history of politically and economically repressive colonialism, environmental NGOs, most based in developed countries, were seen as eco-imperialists. Protection of biodiversity ignored the prospects of poor nations and the effects on livelihoods. As the director of a private reserve in Argentina told us: 'This is conservation without humans. Nature, flora and fauna, are being prioritised over indigenous people.'

The fears are well founded. Historically, governments worldwide used conservation as an excuse to remove or simply exterminate indigenous groups. Estimates suggest that there are tens of millions of conservation refugees today.

In the 1990s, Botswana removed the San and Bakgalagadi people out of the Central Kalahari Game Reserve, originally created to safeguard wildlife as well as allow indigenous peoples to live and hunt unmolested inside its borders. The decision was ostensibly based on declining wildlife populations but suspected of being designed to secure access to their land. We saw the indigenous peoples unhappily resettled into camps, dependent on government handouts. In East Africa, 70 per cent of national parks and game reserves are on Maasai land. Local peoples have also been killed or forced out over decades in the United States, India and Indonesia.

Stung by criticism, NGOs now seek to involve locals in ecotourism initiatives. The results are mixed. Many facilities are owned by foreign investors and corporations who capture the majority of profits, while employment prospects in tourism for locals are often at the lowest levels, providing meagre wages. Local ethnic groups become a backdrop, another form of wildlife to be seen and photographed. Worse, tourists can encourage the development of destructive markets in wildlife souvenirs, such as wooden or coral trinkets and animal products, contributing to illegal harvesting and poaching. Overdevelopment and lack of regulation results in environmental degradation, damaging grazing land.

Conservation schemes can promise indigenous communities immediate wealth. The economic benefits from ecotourism ventures, handicraft and other small-scale commercial enterprises, or payment for ecosystem services programs, generally take time or may never be realised. In the meantime, the establishment of protected areas can result in local people losing homes and being forced onto marginal lands. The lack of long-term compensation causes resentment. There is a reversion to environmentally unsound activities. The continuing lack of economic opportunities creates ongoing damage as locals find it difficult to sustain an income. Rich foreigners can undertake trophy hunting, now termed bioprospecting, even for endangered species. In contrast, locals trying to save crops or feed their families are branded poachers. The environmental footprint of ecotourists is justified on the ground of uncertain investment in conservation and local communities. Critics see the process as whitewash for racism and territorialism.

Near Lake Langano in Ethiopia, our car is inadvertently left unlocked for a short time while we are bird watching just off the road, very close to our vehicle. Some local children steal my backpack. There is nothing of great value, just my bird guide, notes, water bottles and an old Swiss army knife.

Our driver travels to the nearby village and asks the elders to intervene. Some money changes hands. It takes hours, but he recovers the backpack. In *The Wretched of the Earth*, Frantz Fanon writes of the poor, driven by lack and envy, turning on those seemingly richer than them. The theft expressed the children's dream of possessions and rebellion against their fate.

German biologist Ernst Haeckel coined the word 'ecology' in 1866. Historically, it focused on documenting and studying the natural world. Norwegian philosopher Arne Naess and Hackel differentiated between shallow and deep ecology, echoing the schism between Roosevelt and Muir. Shallow ecology takes an anthropocentric view. It views nature as a resource to be used sustainably. Rejecting this viewpoint, deep ecology pursues the preservation of the web of life of which humans are part. Nature does not need saving; it needs to be left alone.

Writing in 1933, American environmentalist Aldo Leopold observed that conservation sees wildlife as a renewable resource to be harvested scientifically. Expanding on his philosophy in his 1949 essay *The Land Ethic*, Leopold rejected shallow ecology, urging an emphasis on the integrity and beauty of nature for its own sake. He saw humans as merely members of the biotic community, not its masters.

Ecotourism is one of conservation's foundation myths, based on shallow ecology. Without this fairytale, wildlife tourism is simply short-term mining of the resource and has no role in a modern sustainable society.

Slick marketing slogans present New Zealand to the world as '100 per cent pure', untamed wilderness and pristine wide-open spaces. That adulatory view is incomplete. Picture of turquoise waters and crystal-clear glacial flows from snow-capped mountains belie that fact that New Zealand's freshwater rivers are among the most polluted in the developed world. A 2020 government report found nearly 60 per cent of the country's rivers have unacceptably high levels of pollution. Intensive agriculture and the country's dairy industry have contaminated 95 to 99 per cent of rivers in pastoral, urban and non-native forested areas.

Early explorers described New Zealand's immense woods and lofty trees. Much of the country's forests have since been logged and replaced by farms or pine plantations. Successive waves of immigrants have decimated the country's original and highly distinctive wildlife.

In 2009, author David Quammen restated the need to leave wilderness alone. Visiting the Kronotsky Reserve in Russia's Kamchatka Peninsula, he celebrated the vast landscape of volcanic mountains, tundra, forest, river valleys and coastline. The area is home to brown bears, wolverines, eagles, gyrfalcons, Steller sea lions, several types of salmon and steelhead trout. Acknowledging the impact of his own visit, Quammen thought the Kronotsky Reserve too good, too fragile and too special to be invaded by people.

But there is little support for deep ecology. The economic cost is too great. Conservation must pay for itself, even if it only through tourism revenues. Despite its laudable aims, ecotourism is merely another way to exploit the planet.

Located in the Southern Kalahari, Tswalu is South Africa's largest private game reserve, covering an area of over 110,000 hectares (270,000 acres). It was created by English entrepreneur Stephen Boler's purchase of existing farms. The project had a controversial side under Boler: an exclusive hunting reserve called Takuni, justified as a means to control population numbers and generate income to support the reserve.

When Boler died in 1998, his will gave the right of first refusal on Tswalu to Nicky Oppenheimer, a member of one of Africa's richest dynasties with interests in De Beers diamond operations. Oppenheimer purchased the reserve. Hunting was stopped. Some existing farms and fences were removed. Over time, purchases of uneconomic bordering properties allowed for expansion.

Tswalu's high rainfall compared to other parts of the Kalahari creates varied habitats – rolling dunes, grasslands and a mountain range. The reserve contains around eighty-eight mammal and 240 bird species, many threatened. It is home to black-maned lions, cheetahs, rare antelopes, giraffes, buffalos, zebras and the world's largest population of black rhinoceroses. Tswalu's role in tourism and conservation was recognised when Nicky Oppenheimer and his wife Strilli were awarded the 2007 World Wildlife Fund Lonmin Award for nature conservation.

As a private reserve, Tswalu's guests can go off-road, and no areas are off limits. They have their own dedicated vehicle, with guide and tracker. Spending time as they wish, they enjoy the feeling of exploring the property alone. This experience is complimented by Tswalu Kalahari, one of *National Geographic*'s Unique Lodges of the World, which was built on the reserve. The luxurious space accommodates around thirty guests. Food is prepared by an accomplished team of chefs, complemented by the best libations from South Africa and the world.

Magnificent though it is, Tswalu reveals the nuances of modern conservation. Visitors may not realise that many species are introduced. Numbers, especially of large predators, must be restricted by capture and relocation or culling, to maintain an artificial balance. Electric fences keep the animals in and poachers out.

A main road cuts through the reserve, splitting Tswalu into two distinct sections. The lions are confined to one part, to separate them from the cheetahs and rhinos. Young male cheetahs restlessly pace the fence lines, eager to seek out new territories. They have to be traded or killed when their numbers increase too much. Some meerkats are habituated to allow guests to get close to these entertaining creatures. Animals are radio-collared to make them easier to locate for guest viewings.

In the Tswana language, Tswalu means new beginning, but it also signifies an end. The name captures the reserve's considerable conservation achievements, but it redefines the idea of wilderness entirely.

Every journey now reminds Jade and me of the ravaged state of wild places; it is unavoidable. In Ingeniero Juárez in north-west Argentina, we search for the rare Chaco owl, which inhabits the dry woodlands of Southern Bolivia, Western Paraguay and Northern Argentina. With few visitors to this region, our guide, Mario, has not been here recently. The patch of forest where the bird used to be found has been cut down for firewood. Despite this, we decide to wait till dusk in case.

As the sun drops below the horizon, Mario plays the bird's call, a distinctive dry rattling hoot. There is no response.

Suddenly, something flies into a nearby tree. We turn our torches on. It is a Chaco owl. Within seconds, its mate appears. We have brief but clear views. Then the owls fly off.

They are still here. The next time Mario returns, the chances of the birds being there are slim.

Writing in *A Sand County Almanac back in 1949*, Aldo Leopold saw a world of wounds, some obvious and others where the damage was invisible to the casual spectator. He thought an ecological education required hardening to make believe that the destruction and suffering was not your problem. The alternative was to cast yourself as a witness to the slow death of a planet that believes itself to be well and a population that refuses to acknowledge otherwise, irrespective of the evidence.

Over the last thirty years, Jade and I have been spectators to and active participants in a war – homo sapiens versus the rest. As much as the obliteration of wilderness is painful to see, the fact that we have come to expect it is even more so.

3

WILD WISH LISTS

Our Preoccupation with the Dangerous, the Cuddly and the Colourful

Asked for her favourite animal, Jade's surprising response is always 'skunk!' Coming upon our first specimen – the hog-nosed Latin American variety, she literally danced around, overcome by its perfect black-and-white design and impossible resemblance to Pepé Le Pew, the amorous French-accented cartoon skunk. To most, it is a common pest, whose noxious spray will penetrate so deeply into your clothes you would do best to burn them. Her choice is not typical.

The planet has around 6400 species of mammals, 11,000 types of birds, more than 11,000 amphibians and reptiles, 330 marsupials and three monotremes. There are nearly 400,000 plant species. There are more than 900,000 types of insects. Despite this abundance, most ecotourism concentrates on a few animals – primarily mammals, birds and some reptiles.

Ecotravellers belong to separate tribes, each with their own wish list of animals they want to see in the wild. There are mammal watchers and birdwatchers, although interests sometimes overlap. Mammal-watching ecotourists want the dangerous, the cute and the cuddly:

charismatic predators and primates. Big cats, gorillas and chimpanzees top the list. Birdwatchers or birders can have a monomaniacal focus on numbers, expanding their list of species seen. Jade and I enjoy watching birds although, to date, we resist taking an adding machine out into the wild to tally the numbers.

Whatever the motivation, the result is the same: just as the spectrum of colour visible to humans is a thin sliver of a continuum of radiant energy, wilfully limited ecotourists prioritise seeing certain types of animals over others – and this has implications for conservation.

Shortly after arriving in East Africa, even the neophyte will be raving about the Africa's mammalian Big Five – the must-see list of lions, leopards, elephants, buffalo and rhinoceroses. After seeing all five species in a morning in a South African private reserve, one traveller we encountered, booked in for a week-long stay, lamented, 'Now what am I going to do?'

The list is based on what hunters consider the most dangerous animals to hunt on foot. Ironically, it mainly consists of herbivores.

The elephant's appeal is obvious. The Earth's largest land animal is an odd collection of body parts: a massive frame, huge stumpy legs, large fan-like ears, long tusks, a sensitive trunk and expressive eyes. The world remains enamoured of Elephantine Indian gods, Babar children's stories and pachyderm-branded products. That fondness brings misery, with some 3500 elephants kept captive in India alone, used for work, temple rituals, political processions and rich children's birthday parties.

Scientists are beginning to understand the elephant's intelligence and social patterns. Herds, consisting of females and young led by a matriarch, protect and raise calves, a process that takes four years. While male offspring leave at maturity, around the age of twelve, females usually remain together throughout their lives. Individual families have relationships with wider clan groups. An elephant may have 100 and 200 acquaintances, a number not dissimilar to humans. They seem to mourn their dead, visiting carcasses, sniffing them and vocalising what might be grief.

Rhinoceroses are heavily armoured. They are either grazers (the white or square-lipped rhinoceros) or browsers, which feed on leaves, soft shoots or fruits of shrubs (the black or hook-lipped variety). Solitary, short-sighted and famously cantankerous, their resemblance to unicorns might explain their allure. Their distinctive single or double horn, which can grow up to a metre (3 feet), is keratin, the stuff of human hair and nails. Demand for the horns, which are carved into dagger handles for Arab tribesmen and used in traditional Eastern medicines – despite having no proven therapeutic value – has led to poaching on an immense scale.

While they resemble cattle, African buffaloes were never domesticated. They are large: 1 to 1.7 metres (3.3 to 5.6 feet) at the shoulder, a head-and-body length between 1.7 to 3.4 metres (5.6 to 11.2 feet), and weighing up to 870 kilograms (2000 pounds). The adult male African buffalo horns typically join to together to form a shield known as a 'boss' that can deflect bullets. In Africa, buffaloes and hippopotamus kill more people than carnivores. Walking in the bush, the sight of a group of notoriously volatile male buffaloes causes the guide to arm his rifle as a precaution.

Beyond this charismatic few, vegans appear to be defined by a certain cud-chewing lack of magnetism.

Jade and I are not immune from a fascination with predators. Each is superbly equipped for killing. Sitting atop the food chain, they also perform important ecological roles: regulating prey populations, eliminating weaker or old animals to improve gene pools and help manage the demands on the land, and scavenging carcasses to limit disease outbreaks.

Seeing a predator in the wild provides a sense of excitement missing from ordinary life. The appeal may be simple thrill-seeking – an encounter with a wild predator raises the same emotions as standing near a moving train, teetering on the edge of a precipice or handling a loaded gun. It may also be a backhanded tribute from one apex predator to another.

Some predators – such as lions and cheetahs, which occupy plains, where sightlines are good – are relatively easy to see in the wild. Lions live in prides, making them simple to find. Like all felines, they sleep for much of the day, usually in favourite spots. In Kenya's Masai Mara, each lion probably sees hundreds of tourists every day. Forest-dwelling tigers, leopards, jaguars and smaller cats present greater challenges – the animal must cross a trail or be on the side of a water course to be visible. Many species are mainly active at night.

Zambia's South Luangwa Park is known for its leopards. Our stay coincided with a full moon, when the animals are less active because the light makes them more obvious to prey. Despite many long evenings in the park, we didn't spot a single leopard, but paw prints showed they had patrolled their territories near our lodge.

Seeing predators is not enough for many. Some crave the sight of a hunt, preferably one that is brutal and bloody.

We have seen lions at kills, but never a successful hunt. In East Africa, especially on private concessions where it is possible to drive off-trail, you can see cheetahs hunt. Those who have witnessed it express disappointment. The explosive action is best seen on film, where slow motion makes the details of the chase clear.

We have seen African wild dogs kill. Hunting by sight during the day, they make no effort at concealment. Herbivores are approached at a steady trot. When the prey runs, the dogs pursue at speeds up to

60 kilometres (35 miles) per hour. The alpha male or female identifies the target, perhaps because it is slower or more vulnerable. The pack lines up behind. Wild dogs are slower than most antelope and rely on stamina to tire out their victim.

As soon as the lead dog catches up, it pulls the prey down if it is small or slashes at its rump if large to slow it down until the pack can join in. At the kill of a kudu, we saw their social interactions. The current year's litter, perhaps experiencing their first hunt, wandered about, unsure of what to do. Their musical calls and excited whines were audible.

In Uganda, just outside our lodge, spotted hyenas killed a 60-kilogram (130-pound) kob, the primary antelope species of the region. Often derided, these dog-like animals are striking, with their high shoulders and their powerful forequarters sloping down to the hind legs. Sandy brown in colour, the species has dark spots on the back, flank, rump and legs. They are noted as scavengers. The Maasai people of Kenya and Tanzania leave their dead to be consumed by hyenas. But the animals are also intelligent hunters, who work as a group to isolate a herd animal and kill them.

The kill had taken place minutes before our arrival. The three hyenas at the carcass were still panting from their exertion, muzzles dripping with fresh blood. Other members of the pack loped in. We heard the laugh-like calls that give them their nickname, laughing hyenas. Consuming the kob took hours. Lower-ranked animals, subadults and young, waited respectfully until called for their turn to eat. Between turns at the carcass, they rested nearby, stomachs engorged. The hyenas left nothing for the vultures that had waited, not even the bones, which had been crushed and eaten. As always in nature, nothing was wasted.

Jaguars top the ecotourist's wish list in Central and South America. Mayans believed that the jaguar – the name in native languages means he who kills with one blow – was a symbol of darkness, the ruler of the underworld.

Up 1.80 metres (6 feet) from head to base of tail, standing around 70 centimetres (2 feet) at the shoulder and weighing up to 100 kilograms (220 pounds), jaguars are the largest native cat species of the Americas and the third-largest overall. They look similar to leopards but have stockier limbs and a squarer head. The yellowish coat is covered with a pattern of rosettes, which differs in each individual. Adept climbers, they inhabit forests, woods and swamps. Good swimmers, they are well adapted to water.

Jaguars are stalk-and-ambush predators that hunt capybara, tapirs, giant anteaters, deer and peccaries, a type of wild boar. In aquatic settings, they will take caiman, fish, tortoises and reptiles. Their powerful bite can even pierce crocodilian armour. Adults can drag up to three times their own body weight up a tree. Related to Asia's clouded leopard, the jaguar's predecessors crossed over the Bering land bridge in the Arctic and worked their way down the Americas, all the way to southern Argentina. Classified as near threatened, they have been largely exterminated in the United States and can only be found south of Mexico.

Despite their size, jaguars are difficult to spot. More humans are watched by a jaguar, unaware they are under surveillance, than see the animal. A researcher we know tracked a radio-collared individual to within a few metres but could not see the animal.

After unsuccessful attempts in Costa Rica, Venezuela, Columbia, Peru and Ecuador, Jade and I arrange to visit Brazil's Pantanal, considered the most reliable place to see jaguars.

The Pantanal (Portuguese for swamp or marsh) is one of world's largest wetland areas, covering 195,000 square kilometres (75,000 square miles). It is far from pristine, consisting mainly of agricultural and cattle properties. We travel south about 150 kilometres (90 miles) on the Transpantaneira Highway in the Northern Pantanal to the Cuiabá River. Material dug out for construction of the road has left large depressions on the sides, which become a source of water during the dry season, attracting birds and animals.

We stay at several pousadas (inns) to explore the grasslands, gallery forests and waterways. There are primates – black howler monkeys and black striped tufted capuchin monkeys – as well as marsh and brocket deer, peccaries and agoutis, large rodents. Waterholes overflow with caiman. Capybaras are everywhere. We see tapirs, the largest land animal in the Americas, which is part-horse, part-rhinoceros and part-hippopotamus. There is a mother with young; a male crosses a stream, totally submerged in the water. We record more than 250 species of birds. But jaguars prove elusive.

On a drive between two lodges, a brownish feline shape crosses the road ahead. When we reach the spot, the only evidence of the cat is the alarm calls of birds and monkeys.

Our last chance is Porto Jofre, where tourists in motorised boats search for jaguars along the Cuiabá, Piquiri or Three Brothers rivers. The cat has to be on the riverbank to be seen. If the animal retreats into the jungle lining the river, it is invisible.

After an unsuccessful day on the river, we discover that everyone else has seen a jaguar, or two or three. Feigning equanimity and polite disinterest, we smile while contemplating mass murder, as our own predatory instincts stir.

On the second day, we get word that a jaguar has been sighted on the Piquiri. It will take us about forty-five minutes to get there, by which time the animal may have moved. As we contemplate our options, a passing fisherman tells us of a jaguar on a sandbank a few hundred metres away. Steering to the place, we spot the individual swimming across the river. The basketball-sized head is only a few metres from our boat, which sits low in the water.

Mounting the opposite bank, the jaguar rests on the side of the river. Within minutes about twenty boats arrive, jostling for position. Eventually, irritated by insects, the male, nicknamed Borboleta – Portuguese for butterfly, after the distinctive pattern on his forehead – continues his patrol, spraying urine to mark his territory. We follow until he turns into the forest, out of sight. He passes within touching distance of a group of local fisherman on the riverbank, who do not seem concerned by his presence.

The impetus to see the cute and cuddly underlies primate ecotourism. Biology comes into play, as the animals remind us of babies, which we are programmed to take care of. Visual cues trigger a euphoric brain response. There is also the evolutionary link. In the nineteenth century, Charles Darwin correctly surmised the linkage between African apes and humans. DNA studies of gorillas, chimpanzees and bonobos have confirmed the lineage. Donna Haraway, in her book *Primate Visions*, argues that the interest in and study of primates reflects the continuous and varied search for similarities and differences between humans, be it in appearance, intelligence, behaviour, reproduction patterns, sexuality, race, dominance or social and individual lives. Primatology serves, in part, as a domain for thinking about what it is to be human.

Primates are not only gorillas and chimpanzees. They include prosimians, the best known being Madagascar's lemurs, which originally arrived from mainland Africa. After the island separated from the continent around 160 million years ago, the animals adapted to its different habitats. Lemurs are endemic to the island (that is, a species found in a single defined geographic location). Differing in size, diet and habits, they all have soft fur, big bright round eyes, kid gloved hands and – in most cases – dog-like noses. Their star quality makes them the backbone of Malagasy ecotourism.

There are more than 100 species of lemurs. Mouse lemurs weigh only a few grams and are among the smallest primates. Indris are the largest species, at about 64–72 centimetres (25–28 inches) in length and weighing between 6 to 9.5 kilograms (13 to 21 pounds). They look like black-and-white stuffed toys. Indris sing from the treetops. A typical song consists of a several-second-long roaring sequence, followed by descending shorter notes. The wails progressively become lower-pitched. The calls, which can be heard up to 4 kilometres (2.5 miles) away, maintain contact or advertise territorial claims.

Sifakas have smallish arms but long powerful hindlegs, making it possible for them to climb and leap easily. They travel with incredible speed, covering hundreds of metres in a few seconds. They move in precise bounding leaps from tree to tree, one thorny bough to another, or between the sharp rocks of the Tsingy (limestone karst formations). Their build makes them awkward on the ground. They bound sideways on their hind legs between trees in a gait that inspired Monty Python's John Cleese to create the Ministry of Silly Walks.

Ring-tailed lemurs are named for their striking black-and-white tails. They live in large groups, led by a breeding female. They inhabit the dry scrub and deciduous forests of South Madagascar. Ring-tailed lemurs bask in the sunshine on the ground or in trees. They sit upright with hands on knees in their sun worship posture. The sight of them walking in single file with their raised tails is a staple image of wildlife photography.

Simians are deeply embedded in human culture. Indian mythology records the heroic actions of Hanuman the Monkey God. The Chinese calendar has the year of the monkey. They are a staple of children's stories, comics, films, video games and literature. The creatures of popular imagination are generally macaques that inhabit Asia and North Africa.

But the simian world ranges widely, from tiny pygmy marmosets, which fit into the palm of a human hand, to larger monkeys.

The forests of Asia contain many species, including gibbons, the most agile and fastest of all tree-dwelling primates. Their wrist is like a ball-and-socket joint. This reduces the amount of energy needed in the upper arm and torso and the stress on the shoulder joint. It also allows biaxial movement (movement along two planes) and, combined with long hands and feet, brachiation (motion where the suspended body swings by the arms from one hold to another). Gibbons swing through forests in a fluid, continuous manner, as if they are flying. Their distinctive hoots can be heard up to 1 kilometre (0.6 mile) away. An enlarged throat sac acts as a resonating chamber, enhancing the volume.

In Africa, baboons patrol open grasslands, gallery forests and arid thorn scrub insouciantly. Reclusive red-, blue- and lavender-faced Mandrills are native to West Africa.

Well adapted to human settlements, vervet monkeys are common around East African lodges, usually on the lookout for food. In the forest, grey-cheeked mangabeys make a whoop-gobble call. Troops of red colobuses, with their colourful orange caps, feed in the canopy. Black-and-white colobuses show off their dramatic white-hair mantles and long, plume-like tails.

The rainforests of Central and South America are particularly rich in primates. Tool-using white-faced capuchins clamber through the trees energetically. With black hands and feet, distinctive sideburns and a triangular head marking, tufted capuchins signal other members of their troupe with calls, grimaces and head-shaking. Spider monkeys dangle nonchalantly from branches using their prehensile tail. In Peru, a large group of tiny squirrel monkeys, numbering in the hundreds, took nearly an hour to pass us.

Night or owl monkeys have enormous eyes, adapted for seeing in low light. White-faced saki have a prominent white mask. Red uakaris have a crimson face and are quite bald. Tamarins have bold decorative patterns of facial hair; the emperor tamarin has a drooping moustache. Found only in Colombia, cotton-top tamarins have a striking white crown. Golden-headed lion tamarins have a reddish mane. The golden-handed tamarin has bright yellow hands and feet. Increasingly difficult to find, many of these species can only be seen by visiting a field camp where biologists are studying them.

The Feliciano Miguel Abdala Private Reserve in Brazil, named after the landowner who fought to protect this patch of Atlantic Forest, is home to a small population of muriqui, or woolly spider monkey, the largest primate in the Americas. Once widespread, there are now less than 1000 left. Our local guide finds the muriquis high in the trees. They have a greyish-brown coat, long limbs and a prehensile tail. The lines and contours of the face are human-like. In the treetops, a mother helps her infant move through the canopy 30 metres (100 feet) above the ground. She holds two branches, using her body to create a living bridge allowing her young to cross from one tree to another.

Among our favourites are marmosets, around 20 centimetres (8 inches) long. Black-tufted marmosets have dark tussocks of hair around their ears that resemble the payots of orthodox Jewish men. Marmosets live in the upper canopy of forest trees, feeding on insects, fruit, leaves, tack, sap and gum.

At the Feliciano Miguel Abdala Reserve, we search for the rare buffy-headed marmoset. It was heard a few days ago in one part of the forest. In the late afternoon, we wait, listen and scan the forest. As we are about to admit defeat, a group of five or six individuals are spotted 200 metres (650 feet) from us. They resemble gremlins. The tiny monkeys have orange-yellow fur on their heads and cheeks, and similar tufts of hair around their ears, which contrast sharply with their black and grey bodies. Like all marmosets, they have claws instead of nails, enabling them to cling to trees with ease. They are gouging holes in the trees to encourage the flow of sap, which they will come and drink later. Then, they are gone. The next day, there is no sign of them.

An increasing proportion of ecotravellers are birders, with their penchant for lists. Birdwatching grew out of trophy hunting or collecting birds' eggs, feathers and skins. Recording a sighting with a photograph or a listing may substitute for these now prohibited activities.

The innately competitive practice provides pleasure. The ability to distinguish between similar species makes us feel clever – identifying subtle physical features, songs and calls provides a sense of superiority over other birders, as Jade and I can attest. It demonstrates affinity and provides a sense of ownership, even if this is metaphorical, conferring value and status. There is also an aspect of legacy. Tracing the footsteps of adventurers, like Wallace, to search for rare birds may bring today's traveller closer to bygone eras of true exploration.

Anthropologists suggest that listing provides a sense of order. Evolutionary theorists have speculated that collections, even in list form, might be a way for individuals to signal the ability to accumulate resources to attract potential partners – much like Australia's male bowerbirds, who build elaborate nests filled with bric-a-brac to increase their appeal to females.

The limited need for equipment and the ease of access to birds means the activity crosses socio-economic groupings. Even in built-up urban environments, it is possible to see hundreds of species. A 2012 documentary, *Birders: The Central Park Effect,* celebrated the number of wild birds that can be seen, especially during migration season, in what Dutch architectural theorist Rem Koolhaas called the synthetic arcadian carpet grafted onto Manhattan's grid.

Birding has ecotourism's most distinctive vocabulary. Binoculars are bins. Telescopes are scopes. You 'work a trail', 'maximise the species list'.

It is important to cover ground. You bushwhack, searching dense brush for elusive birds. Identification is by giss – general impression, size and shape. Notta birds or pseudo birds are bird-like shapes that bins or a scope reveal not to be an avian life form. A spark bird is a species that triggered your interest in birding. A lifer is a bird that you are seeing for the very first time. Birders have nemesis or jinx birds, species that defy attempts to seek them out. A birder's tally is the number of birds seen. A tick is a new bird. A mega tick is a rare or special bird. When you cannot find the species you are looking for, you dip out. If another birder finds the bird, they have gripped you off.

Birding superstition dictates that you never go looking for a species, especially a rare one. Akin to the thespian's fear of speaking the name of Shakespeare's Scottish play, it is unwise to say the bird's name aloud. Avoid birding with someone who has been looking for that species for years without success. Rather, chances are enhanced by being accompanied by a non-birder.

Serious birders keep lists. There are lifetime lists: all the birds seen. Geographic lists record species seen in a particular country or place. Annual lists detail birds encountered in a calendar year. Trip lists note species seen on a particular journey. Some even record the number of specimens viewed. On organised group tours, ticking off species seen that day is a nightly ritual.

Until recently, Jade and I resisted keeping a list. We found that listing detracted from the enjoyment of birdwatching. It eventually became necessary to keep track of what we had seen to answer the guide's inevitable question: 'Is that a lifer for you?'

Listing creates issues. Underemployed ornithologists, armed with the latest DNA-sequencing technology, taxonomic studies and driven by the need to publish erudite papers, split or regroup species constantly. The red-bellied pitta is an attractive bird with a green-blue band above its red belly. When we first looked for it, it was one species. Subsequently, it was split into ten on the basis of minor physical differences and location. We saw the bird on Sulawesi. If so inclined, we could pursue the newly created others to expand our list. If we had seen the same bird on a different island, we would have increased the number of species seen – termed an armchair tick.

Serious birders want to see every one of the around 11,000 extant species, although few birders manage to see more than 7000 species. A more modest aspiration is to see a representative of all 250 families of birds, a substantial goal in itself. The obsessive nature of listers is captured in a joke. When two birders get taken hostage by insurgents, the question is, did they see the Cundinamarca Antpitta before they were captured?

There is a related question we could ask: what happens to the birder when the list is complete? Retired US Foreign Service officer Peter Kaestner holds the world record for most species seen. He has a life list of more than 9800 species and a personal goal of 10,000. Phoebe Snetsinger, a well-known female birder, saw around 8400 species, allegedly spending her inheritance on the quest. Her travels to remote locations involved significant personal risk: she survived being raped in New Guinea, and eventually died in a road accident in Madagascar.

Listing is a combat and sometimes a contact sport. One event is twitching, the pursuit of a rare vagrant, allegedly named for the nervous behaviour of Howard Medhurst, a British birdwatcher. Twitchers or chasers (the American equivalent) routinely travel long distances to tick off a bird appearing outside its normal range, despite having seen it before in its usual habitat. Cheaper travel and digital birding tools disseminating sighting information have fostered the practice.

In 2017, the unexpected sighting of an Aleutian tern, a shorebird that typically spends the summer in Indonesia, saw hundreds of birders travel from far and wide to a small Australian coastal town. In 2023, many American species were blown by a hurricane to the British Isles, prompting a mega-twitch. Such birds are disoriented vagabonds, generally without ecological or conservation value. Most vagrants die, unable to return to their normal range. Twitching's sole purpose is the bragging rights and adding to the list.

Listing reveals some of ecotourism's contradictions. Birders' lists are commonly a record of the number of species *shown to them*. Outside their own environment, birders rely on local guides, guidebooks and devices to attract birds. Without specialist assistance, fewer species would be seen.

Seeing is also not always seeing. In Colombia, we heard a powerful woodpecker, a bird similar to the now-extinct North American ivory-billed variety. It was atop a branch directly above us, with only its legs and toes in view. Jade and I do not regard ourselves as having seen the bird, but others may count it. Some birders even regard hearing a call as seeing the species.

Birding in a group is an exercise in osmosis. One guide we know adopted a democratic solution – a bird was seen if a majority of the group had glimpsed it. Another guide led each bird list session with the words: 'I saw ...' 'Seen by guide' is for some a tick.

Most lists are approximate, as misidentification is common. Many birders claim to have seen the extremely rare buff-breasted button quail. Recent scientific work suggests that the birds seen are the more common painted button quail. Some birders are outright mendacious. In Columbia, a leading world lister claimed to have seen a rare chestnut-bellied cotinga. He was alone. There was no photographic evidence. There were no known records of the bird in that location. There is something sad about a birder falsifying a list – it's like cheating at Solitaire.

Birding can also bring out the worst in individuals. In groups, if a sought-after rarity is spotted, the person may not share the information with the guide or others to ensure that no one else can claim it. English nature journalist Bill Oddie, in his *Little Black Bird Book*, exhausted derogatory adjectives in describing birders: tense, competitive, selfish, shifty, dishonest, distrusting, boorish, arrogant, pedantic, unsentimental, envious.

Ultimately, serious birding, like all ecotourism, is a privileged activity, as it is about time and money. The degree of difficulty in adding to the list increases exponentially as you see more. The species you want are rarer, found only in highly specific, often inaccessible or remote locations and not especially cooperative. You might be after the elusive antpitta or the invisible rail, and both prefixes are accurate descriptors of the task.

The cost per new species mounts. Tony, our Finnish guide, once took a famous American lister solely to see a Siberian jay, a common bird widely distributed in the coniferous forests of North Eurasia, which was absent from the individual's lengthy list. The missing species was duly ticked off at a cost of several thousand dollars.

If you do the sums, seeing each bird species probably costs, on average, \$300 to \$500. In essence, \$3 to \$5 million and an awful lot of time is required to see all the planet's birdlife. It also demands a singular dedication. Historian Steven Gelber in his study of culture pointed to the contradiction of taking a leisure activity and turning it into work. Serious listing requires forsaking a normal life in pursuit of a singular passion.

If much ecotourism is about the frisson that derives from rarity, or the difficulty in seeing an animal or a landscape, travel to remote areas only increases the attraction. For example, grizzly bears are easiest to see in late summer or early autumn, when they congregate near rivers with salmon runs. Accommodation is limited and expensive. Visitor numbers may be restricted, in some cases allocated by ballot.

The focus on the uncommon underlies unsurprising demand for spectacles. Perhaps the best-known is Africa's annual plains migration, where almost two million wildebeest and plains animals migrate from Tanzania's Serengeti to Kenya's Masai Mara in search of grazing land and water.

The migration has remained unchanged for millions of years. The earth trembles and great clouds of dust rise as massive herds of grazing animals, many with newborn calves, approach the Mara River. Predators, largely lions, hyenas and jackals, trail the herds. Birds of prey and vultures circle overhead. At the river, there is a lull as the herds mill about. Then, with no apparent warning, animals slide down the banks and leap into the water. The momentum means that those in front are pushed from behind. Many are trampled and injured, sometimes fatally. The noise and confusion is deafening. Large Nile crocodiles move in, jaws snapping to catch prey. Thousands of tourists pay top dollar to see the event. In 2020, with travel to the region impossible due to the pandemic, a disappointed traveller seriously insisted that the migration itself would have to be cancelled due to the lack of tourists.

Arguably the greatest spectacle on Earth involves insects, not a traditional focus of ecotourism. Each year, millions of monarch butterflies winter in Mexico before migrating north. On a sunny day, when the light catches them, the fluttering insects provide one of nature's great sights.

Such enormous aggregations might reassure us about our stewardship of wild places. Once, abundance was common – flocks of passing passenger pigeons or migrating birds blotted out sunlight; bison and caribou crowded the plains as far as could be seen; rivers were solid with migrating salmon. Ironically, as animal numbers decline and examples of nature's plenitude become scarcer, the sight of a single rare animal becomes prized.

Ecotourism is shaped by travellers' most-wanted lists. It means that the industry is concentrated in certain locations, which bear the brunt of our love for animals and natural places. These include East and Southern Africa (which offers safari-style viewing of large cats and megafauna), North America (large mammals and birds), Central and Southern America, including the Galápagos Islands (rainforest wildlife and birds), India (tigers and birds), South-East Asia (more birds) and Australasia (marsupials and birds).

Wildlife tourism is led by the amount of biodiversity, the degree of accessibility and the infrastructure. The top-visited areas are determined by the total number of species in a location, the mean number of species per square kilometre or mile, and the percentage of endemic or threatened species. Columbia, Peru and Indonesia score highly among birders due to uncommon diversity, very high concentrations and high endemism.

This means that enthusiasts overburden small pockets within a few countries. The presence of so many humans inevitably has a detrimental effect on the area and its wildlife. Meanwhile, other parks and reserves are neglected.

The higher economic value of prized species creates a disproportionate emphasis on conservation of certain animals at the expense of the ecosystem as a whole and its biodiversity. For example, there is exaggerated demand to protect birds that are the sole representative of a particular family or genus, which allow birders to add to their list of families seen.

One of birding's holy grails is the monotypic shoebill stork, also known as whale-headed stork. The large grey bird stands up to 1.5 metres (4 feet) high, with a wingspan up to 2.5 metres (7 feet). The name comes from its massive shoe-like bill. Jade and I saw the prehistoric birds in Uganda standing motionless on the side of channels, waiting for their preferred prey – lungfish. When a shoebill spots a target, it pounces, using its massive bill to engulf the fish. Razor-sharp edges of the mandibles and a large hook at the tip decapitate its prey. Alongside gorillas, the bird is central to Ugandan ecotourism, despite its other biodiversity.

Demand to see specific species can sometimes take on extravagant dimensions, such as a three- to four-weeks voyage to Heard Island, a group of mostly barren volcanic rocks about two-thirds of the way from Madagascar to Antarctica, to tick off two birds – the Heard shag (a cormorant) and the black-faced sheathbill – found nowhere else. The quest to see the rare can appear little more than a game of one-upmanship, with ecotravellers consumed by ticking off sightings of animals rather than appreciating them.

Over time, my interest and Jade's has drifted away from the most-wanted list. Quality has come to matter more, as the rush for numbers detracts from the sight itself. We do not assume we will see all the animals present in the location. We are grateful to enjoy whatever is there, irrespective of whether it is common or rare, old or new.

This less-trodden path can be rewarding. In the Pantanal, our fellow travellers, unable to conceive of anything other than jaguars, are bemused by our decision to travel four hours up the Piquiri River in hope of spotting a yellow armadillo. We are rewarded by giant river and neotropical otters, as well as myriad birds. We enjoy superb views of a king vulture, the largest New World vulture other than the condor. Predominantly grey and white, its head and neck is a colourful melange of yellow, orange, blue, purple and red. Amid the wrinkled folded skin, there is an irregular golden crest above its orange-and-black bill. A close view of a king vulture is rarer than that of a jaguar.

Native to the grasslands and rainforest of Central and South America, the giant anteater is a large insectivore, around 2 metres (6.5 feet) in length and 1 metre (3 feet) in height. The elongated snout, extended bushy tail and distinctive coloration make it instantly recognisable. Despite its size and its claws, capable of ripping apart a rock-hard termite nest, giant anteaters, sometimes called ant bears, are typically placid, posing little threat if left alone. While they have poor eyesight and hearing, their sense of smell is acute, forty times more sensitive than that of humans. It is possible to get very close to them by remaining quiet and downwind.

At Brazil's Upper Canastra Park, our guide, Fred, spends long days scanning the grasslands for giant anteaters. Eventually, he thinks there might be something. We get in the car and drive about a kilometre. After a frustrating half-hour search, we are forced back to the vantage point to check the exact location. It appears that we went to the wrong spot, an easy error in a landscape without distinctive markers. We double back and begin searching through the tall grass.

Two giant anteaters materialise mysteriously metres from us. Close up, it is obvious why they are so difficult to see. The grey-and-white body and the brown tail blend perfectly into the grasslands. The coat hairs and stiff mane have the texture of dry grass, completing the camouflage. Fred had been searching for a vague dark line, the blackish stripe along the anteater's back, moving slowly in the tall grass.

The proximity reveals every detail. Their necks are extremely thick, bigger than their heads. The anteaters walk slowly on their knuckles, keeping their elongated claws out of the way. They move their 60-centimetre (2-feet) tongues in and out of their tube-like mouths, lapping up termites and insects. Trapped in a thick, sticky saliva, prey is swallowed, crushed against the anteater's palate and digested with formic acid.

We follow them for an hour until they disappear into the tall grass.

Ecotourism must accommodate a consumerist preoccupation with accumulation and entertainment. But patience and effort allows you to sometimes get close to the animal's world. The encounter with the giant anteaters remains one of our most precious memories, a reminder of what ecotourism truly offers its disciples: the power of surprise.

4

SHOW TIMES

Engineering Our Encounters with Wild Animals

To see mountain gorillas you must visit the Virunga Mountains, the name meaning 'isolated mountains that reach the clouds' in the local language. The range spans three countries – Congo (formerly known as Zaire), Rwanda and Uganda. Our plan was to travel to the Rwandan side, but conflict forced us to travel instead to the Congolese Kahuzi-Biega Park.

At the time of our visit in 1991, thirty-two daily permits, each costing $100, were available. Low visitor numbers meant you could turn up on the day and get one. Today, the permits cost as much as $1500 per one-hour visit, and high demand means that they must be arranged months in advance.

The process is now regimented. On the morning of your trek, you arrive at the ranger station for a briefing. At the time of our visit, this was just a casual chat with a ranger. Now, you sit in a hall and are given a formal in-person or video orientation. Then, you are separated into small groups of around eight and allocated a guide. Trackers armed with machetes cut paths through the forest. Porters are available to carry your belongings for a fee.

Our guide carried an ancient Lee–Enfield rifle, ostensibly to make a loud noise to discourage errant elephants. Today, guards armed with semi-automatic weapons are mandatory for protection, mainly against local militias. Over the years, a number of Western tourists have been taken hostage when they stumbled across the wrong gorillas.

The animals can be near or far away. You usually start at around 2300 metres (7500 feet). Your assigned gorilla family can be above 3000 metres (9800 feet). The densely vegetated terrain is steep and muddy. Uganda's aptly named Bwindi Impenetrable Forest indicates the challenges. In a concession to tourists, rangers triage according to age and fitness: younger visitors get the harder hikes; older ones are allocated more accessible groups.

The trackers start near where the gorillas were seen the previous day. They look for their night beds, crude platforms in trees made from twigs and leaves. They follow a trail of broken bamboo saplings (a favourite food) and faeces, the temperature of which allows estimates of when they were there. Once the group has been located, the guide makes a series of shrieks and low-pitched grunts, to warn the animals of human presence. Heartbeats quicken and mouths dry in anticipation.

And then, inexplicably, the gorillas suddenly appear. The rules are simple: you must be quiet and maintain a minimum distance, you must adopt a submissive pose and eye contact is forbidden. If a gorilla charges, then you must hold your ground.

We visited two separate gorilla families on successive days. Each family is headed by a silverback, named for the white hair on the back of an adult male. A fully developed male is around 150 kilograms (330 pounds) and 1.5 metres (5 feet) tall. The group consists of the dominant male, a number of females, their young and older juveniles.

The first family's silverback was Maheshe, who featured on the country's 50,000 zaire banknote until the mid-1990s. The family were foraging and feeding. Up close, the sizeable silverback's powerful muscles and thick, coarse hair were obvious. A mouthful of yellowing teeth stripped bamboo trunks as if they were celery stalks.

There were several females carrying young on their backs or clinging to their chests. The infants were surprisingly small. A boisterous youngster clambered up a thin sapling. Releasing his hold to pound on his chest, producing the distinctive soft drumming contact sound, he tumbled down nearly on top of us. The adults took no notice.

The second family was led by silverback Mushamuka. They were resting and grooming one another while the young played when we found them. The group contained two juvenile males, who would soon leave to start their own families. One reclined on his back in a hollow, a few metres from us. He propped himself up on one arm in an approximation of Auguste Rodin's *The Thinker*. He looked directly at us with an open and inquiring gaze. Our eyes locked, both sides ignoring the rules of engagement.

Chimpanzees are considered our closest living relative in the animal kingdom. We are also more distantly related to bonobos. Biologists speculate that the human race might have been less violent and kinder had we evolved directly from them.

In Uganda's Kibale Forest, tourists can visit two habituated groups of chimpanzees. In 2015, Jade and I tracked them, led by guides who had been working with the animals for more than two decades. We started at dawn to reach the group, which numbered about 150. They were already active by the time we caught up with them, after an hour of tracking. We heard the chimpanzees before we saw them; their pant-hoots echoed eerily through the forest. It started with breathy, low-pitched hooting that got quicker and higher-pitched, building to a loud climax. The vocalisations establish contact, express emotions and serve as greetings or self-identifiers.

They were feeding in a tall, fruiting tree. We waited for them to come down, being careful to avoid falling fruit, the occasional golden shower of urine or something more substantial. After two hours, they suddenly descended. We found ourselves surrounded. They scattered into the forest, moving unpredictably but with great agility and speed through the dense vegetation. We followed as best we could.

On the ground, their resemblance to humans was evident. Adult chimpanzees are around 1.2 metres (4 feet) tall and weigh up to 40 kilograms (90 pounds). Their arms are longer than their legs, reaching below the knees. Their hands have long fingers with short thumbs and flat fingernails. The black or brown hair covering their bodies is sparse. The face, fingers, palms of the hands and soles of the feet are a hairless pink or brown.

There were mothers carrying and feeding their tiny pink offspring. Two older males groomed each other and shared a jackfruit, to reinforce allegiances. Another older animal – once a high-ranking member, we are told – perched in a tree eating abrasive leaves that help with digestion and parasites. In chimpanzee society, deposed males live peacefully within the group under the suzerainty of the new leader.

Individual personalities were on show: cheeky youngsters, coy nubile females, bossy matrons, dominant males, plotting leadership pretenders. Toti, a tetchy male well known to the rangers due to his hand, deformed from a fight, staged a mock charge. We did not move. He rushed past us, stopping to grab and shake a tree before walking away.

On a trail, the alpha male with his Praetorian guard passed by us. They knuckle-walked on all fours. I could reach out and touch them. They moved confidently, without once looking at us, and disappeared into the forest.

Above us, two black-and-white colobus monkeys, sometimes hunted by chimpanzees for meat, watched silently. It is a reminder of the duality of our relatives. Edgar Allan Poe's 'The Murders in the Rue Morgue' features a murderous rogue orangutan. A chimpanzee might have been more suitable.

A gorilla or a chimpanzee trek suggests adventure. In reality, the outcome is assured, with visitors virtually guaranteed to see the primates. The wild animals seen are habituated – rangers have spent years making them comfortable with humans. Even when there are no tourists, each group is visited daily to ensure that they remain accustomed to people.

We have never seen an unhabituated gorilla. We chanced across a wild chimpanzee at Kibale. He bounded away shrieking at the sight of us, despite the fact that we were some distance away in a car.

Given their highly choreographed nature, the emotional charge these visits have speak to the hold these animals have on the human imagination.

Alongside habituation, a variety of techniques borrowed from hunters, including feeding, baiting or tracking, are used to allow ecotourists to find the targets on their wish lists.

The practice can be overt. Maned wolves, the largest canid in South America, regularly visit Brazil's Caraca Monastery to feed on meat left for them by the monks, a long-standing practice. We saw them there, surrounded by hundreds of hyperactive schoolchildren. Their gait, which sometimes led them to be described as foxes on stilts, resembled the catwalk sashay of fashion models. They have elongated legs, an adaptation for the long grasslands of the Cerrado (savannah). This enables them to stalk small mammals, usually attacking with a spectacular pounce. We heard their curious roar-bark vocalisation. Ambivalent about staged wildlife encounters, we had gone to Caraca because it was already difficult to see the very few maned wolves left in the wild. Today, it is much harder.

The practice can also be covert. Chile's Torres del Paine National Park, a stunning landscape of snow-topped mountains and aquamarine lakes, is the best place in the world to see a puma. An ancient species and a contemporary of the long-extinct sabre-toothed cat, it ranges the mountain spine of the Americas from Alaska to Tierra del Fuego. Adult males can be up to 3 metres (10 foot) from nose to tail and weigh as much as 100 kilograms (220 pounds). Agile and powerful, they are supreme predators. At Torres del Paine, over several days, we see an adult pair at a guanaco kill (guanacos are camelids closely related to llamas), a sub-adult and, unforgettably, a female with her cubs.

Tour operators introduced puma tracking in the park, a pursuit geared to wealthy tourists eager to photograph them. Unregulated, it expanded rapidly, with groups walking across fragile Patagonian landscapes and harassing the animals. Park authorities eventually suspended the practice, insisting that tourists stick to the roads and a few designated trails.

This did not stop the activity. Torres del Paine is surrounded by farms, across which the pumas range freely. Tour operators purchased exclusive access to adjacent private ranches. For farmers, income from puma tracking far exceeds that made from livestock. Baiting or allowing predation of domestic sheep is allegedly now used to encourage the cats onto these private properties for the benefit of ecotourists.

In the Pantanal, a ban on hunting and decades of motorboat fishing on the rivers has habituated jaguars to human presence. Increasingly, operators leave food on the riverbank to lure them onto sandbanks so they can be more easily seen. Similarly, cattle ranchers now routinely allow their cattle to be predated in order to entice jaguars onto their land for tourists.

The more difficult an animal is to see in the wild, the greater the impetus to provide ecotourists a view. Wolverines, small, weasel-like predators, are solitary animals always on the move across their large territories. You usually stumble across them accidentally. In eastern Finland, wild wolverines are baited with food in front of viewing hides to maximise that chance. The bait is strategically placed on the ground or in a tree, depending on the desired photograph.

Sometimes feeding is used to make the animals perform. Japan's Jigokudani (Hell's Valley) is famed for its snow monkeys, Japanese macaques who use the hot springs to warm themselves. It is thought that one monkey discovered this practice, and others imitated. Today, tourists and guides perpetuate this behaviour by dropping food into the water for the macaques to ensure everyone gets the photographs they have come for.

In many places, putting out insects, fruit, grain, seeds or other food to attract birds is common. Hummingbirds – hummers to birders – are brilliantly coloured living jewels that most visitors will see at feeders. Named for the sound of their beating wings, there are about 350 species, with the Andes home to the largest variety. The names are as dazzling as the birds: hermits, incas, brilliants, sapphires, emeralds, coronets, sun-angels, star-frontlets, sun-gems, sylphs, lancebills, sabre-wings, jacobins, awl bills, caribs, coquettes, coronets, plumeleteers, mountain-gems, hill-stars, puff-legs, mountaineers, metal-tails, visor-bearers and wood-stars.

Some fit comfortably into the palm of a child's hand. The great sapphire-wing is large enough for individual wingbeats to be visible to the naked eye. Booted racket-tails have white boot-like feathers on their legs and an elongated tail with a teardrop-like blue racquet at the tip. The male red-tailed comet's green-gold back ends in a distinctive shimmering crimson tail. The sword-billed hummingbird has a bill longer than its body for feeding on flowers with long corollas. The bird cannot preen with its long bill and must use its feet instead.

Advanced photography has revealed details of the hummingbird's breathtaking aerobatic manoeuvres, which include climbs, plunges, dives, swoops and hovering. The wings beat up to 100 times per second. Their hearts beat above 1000 beats per minute, the highest rate among warm-blooded animals. Each day, the birds must consume around 60 to 70 per cent of their body weight in nectar or insects to survive.

Hummingbirds are difficult to see in the wild as they continuously zip and dart through the forest between flowering patches. Suspended feeders stocked with a sugary liquid mixture that mimics nectar are used to attract them so paying visitors can see or photograph them.

Antbirds, antpittas, tapaculos and pittas are skulkers, living in low, dense, scrubby bushes where it is nearly impossible to see them. Antbirds follow ant swarms, feeding on disturbed insects. Shadowy glimpses can be seen of them as they flit through the forest understorey. Skilled guides can manoeuvre these birds briefly into the open using playback, a technique where pre-recorded signature vocalisations are used to attract the animal. The practice originates from indigenous hunters mimicking animal sounds to entice prey into killing range. In Brazil, our guide, Fred, enticed a Brasília tapaculo out of the undergrowth. It literally hopped past my boots.

In many parts of South America, rangers and guides have habituated antpittas and tapaculos using mealworms. These normally shy forest dwellers are now lured out for tourists, allowing for good views. In Asia, enterprising landowners have habituated colourful and traditionally hard-to-see birds, such as pittas, partridges and pheasants, with a mix of feeding and artificial ponds during the dry season. Birdwatchers and photographers now jostle for the best slot at the bird hide, rather than seeking them out in the wild.

Identifying dens or nests is another technique guides use to increase the possibility of ecotourists seeing otherwise difficult-to-find wildlife.

Owls have a flat facial disk, excellent night vision and sensitive hearing. A great grey owl can detect prey under 50 centimetres (20 inches) of snow over 100 metres (330 feet) away. The wings are baffled along the front edge to reduce air disturbance for silent flight. Superbly equipped with sharp, strong talons and a curved beak for tearing, owls are efficient hunters of small mammals or fish. They can turn their heads 270 degrees, creating the appearance of the cranium spinning around completely, like Linda Blair in *The Exorcist*.

In Greek mythology, an owl accompanies Athena, the virgin goddess of wisdom, symbolising erudition, wisdom and perspicacity. In some cultures, owls are symbols of art and longevity. In others, owls are bad omens, portents of death.

Most owls are nocturnal and difficult to see well in the wild. Finding a nest site increases the chances of a good view. The sites may be artificial nest boxes because of the lack of suitable hollows due to the felling of trees.

In early spring, owls gather in the forests and woodlands of Scandinavia to breed. All through one northern winter, Jade and I are in constant communication with the guides tracking the population of voles, small rodents. The higher the numbers of the rodents, the better the chances of seeing owls.

We saw great grey, northern hawk, Ural, Tengmalm's, pygmy and short-eared owls. Unknown to us, a Eurasian eagle-owl, the largest European species, was nesting a few hundred metres from our hotel in downtown Helsinki, attracted by a large population of former pet rabbits that had colonised parks.

Ural owls are uncommon visitors to Finland, only appearing when voles are plentiful. With their beautiful pale buff colours, straw-coloured beaks and black eyes, they look deceptively gentle. Our guide checked a nest box, using a branch to make a scraping noise. If in residence, the bird usually pokes its head out to determine whether the noise heralds a predator. Without warning, a large Ural owl flew out of the box and perched briefly on a nearby branch. Then, it dived towards us, passing within a few inches of our heads. Heeding the warning, we exited, maintaining a safe distance from the nest.

Harpy eagles were named after the winged spirits of Greek mythology that carry the dead to Hades. The larger females weigh up to 9 kilograms (20 pounds). Only the Philippines and Steller's sea eagles are larger. Our stay at Serra das Araras in the Brazilian Pantanal was planned to coincide with the bi-annual breeding cycle of a known pair. Even then, a sighting was far from assured. On arrival, we discovered that the chick had already fledged. The nest, made from twigs, sticks and branches, 30 metres (100 feet) above the ground in a Cambará tree, was empty. Around dusk, the pale chick flew into a nearby tree, but the parents did not appear.

Next morning, we made one last hopeful attempt at the nest. The chick was there but there was no sign of the adults. Just as we were getting ready to give up, the female landed in a dead tree only metres from us. Every feature was visible – the slate blue-black upper feathers, the white belly, the broad black band across its breast, the pale grey head, the double crest, and even the grey-brown eyes. The yellow talons, at 15 centimetres (6 inches), were bigger than those of a grizzly bear. They are so sharp they can stab through monkeys and sloths. Responding to a call from its chick, the adult bird took off for the nest, revealing its 2-metre (7-foot) wingspan.

The nest was in a tiny patch of forest cleared on all sides to improve viewing and photographic opportunities. The farm had a small population of sheep. They probably provided food for the eagles, compensating for a lack of sufficient natural prey in the vicinity. It ensured that the eagles return to breed, supporting lucrative ecotourism.

Tourism operators sometimes go much further to guarantee views. In Madagascar, we saw around half the island's lemur species, but not the aye-aye. Thought to fit the evolutionary niche filled elsewhere by woodpeckers, it has an elongated, extremely thin middle finger. This is used to probe gnawed-out holes in trees, extracting insects from within. The aye-aye's grotesque gargoyle-like appearance is considered by the Malagasy to be an ill portent.

Nocturnal and shy, they are difficult to see. Even guides may only see one or two in their careers. Today, tourists can see them at a small, privately owned island in the middle of the Mananara River, where about fifteen relocated aye-ayes are confined. A sighting is all but certain on a night tour. You are taken to a spot where food is placed to lure them to the forest edge. The positioning provides good photo opportunities, unlike normal sightings in the wild. The exercise is defended on the basis that the animals come to feed of their own free will.

Ensuring predictable tourist outcomes can undermine the purpose of ecotourism – the preservation of biodiversity. Practices that increase the possibility of a view, especially one that will yield a photograph, largely ignore the welfare of wild animals. It has changed the behaviour of grizzly bears in North America, kangaroos and dingoes in Australia, birds and monkeys throughout the globe. The long-term impact on individual animals and eventually populations and ecosystems is considerable.

Wildlife watching, especially the desire for greater proximity, can easily disrupt patterns of feeding, hunting, breeding and movement, potentially weakening animal populations, making them more susceptible to disease or predation. Many birds or small animals desert nests. Disruption drives wild animals out of protected areas, increasing their risk of being hunted or killed.

Jade and I have seen cheetahs forced to hunt in the heat of the day to avoid tourists, who generally retire to their lodges and swimming pools at that time. It reduces their chances of success, as they cannot sustain their breathtaking speed in high temperatures. Tourist vehicles attract lions and hyenas, who take over cheetah and leopard kills. Disturbance can lead to abandoning a hunt or a carcass. The reduction in food can be highly consequential during periods of shortages in prey or high energy demand, such as breeding.

Conversely, ecotourists may deny animals respite during the hottest part of the day. In Sri Lanka's Yala Park, noted for its Asiatic leopards, a sighting of a resting cat in a tree attracted hundreds of cars, as drivers alerted by SMS messages arrived to snap photos of the beast.

The disturbance is greatest for nocturnal animals, such as owls and nightjars, who sleep during the day, camouflaged by their cryptic plumage. In Malaysia, we found a local guide kicking the tree where a Javan frogmouth, a type of nightjar, was roosting, to get the bird to open its eyes for a livelier photo for his client. On night walks, the use of high-intensity spotlights instead of filtered infrared light can damage the sensitive eyes of night birds, mammals and marsupials.

Feeding alters diets and can introduce exotic diseases or non-native bacteria or plants. Lions, hyenas, coyotes, foxes, raccoons, skunks and birds of prey are known to converge around tour groups in search of food. The best place Jade and I found to see brown bears in Kars, a city in north-east Turkey, was the local rubbish dump. Animals who associate humans with food may become aggressive or a nuisance. It can lead to loss of hunting habits, reliance on unnatural food sources and overbreeding, altering the natural ecological balance. An abrupt termination of feeding can be fatal.

The use of call playback was once infrequent and generally used only for skulking, difficult-to-see birds. One reason was the practical difficulty, which has reduced over time due to the proliferation of handheld devices such as smartphones, which can be used to play bird calls at will. Excessive use, common especially among photographers and guides, can cause immense stress to birds. It is sometimes done during breeding season, when birds have their most beautiful plumage. The practice distracts them from feeding their young or identifying real predators.

Inconspicuous, secretive birds such as crakes and rails are elusive. They are only vocal when they turn up, unpredictably, in certain areas to breed. Birders' eagerness to add to their list of seen species has encouraged operators to offer special tours to look for them, which inevitably involve the use of playback. The effect on the reproductive success of species, many of which are poorly known and whose conservation status remains undetermined, is ignored.

Jade and I use playback, but only on a restricted basis: never where there is concern about the bird's welfare or during breeding seasons. Some birds have learned to distinguish between genuine calls and playback and do not respond – a case of feathered brains trumping birder brains. Sometimes, it leads to the comedy of two birders chasing each other, having mistaken the recording for the genuine thing.

Wildlife tourism risks introducing human diseases to primate populations, who lack immunity. This exposure increases as the pursuit of animals extends into previously untouched areas.

Habituated animals can become trusting of humans, making them prone to predation and poaching. In Uganda, Rafiki, one of the world's best-known silverback gorillas, died after being speared. The killer was a local who claimed self-defence, although was found to be carrying hunting equipment, including the spear and rope snares. Accustomed to humans, the gorilla might have not been concerned about the hunter. In the local language, 'rafiki' means friend.

Some Indian national parks institutionalise cruelty in the officially sanctioned tiger show. Rangers set out on domesticated elephants to track a wild animal. If found, the rangers use the pachyderms to contain the tiger in a small area. Then, they conduct visits on elephant back for a fee. The tiger is usually a female, as larger males are likely to attack the elephants. The animal has usually made a kill and is reluctant to abandon its hard-won prey. They confine the tiger, denying the animal the opportunity to drink, despite their need for water, especially when eating. The animal may be contained for several days. The activity ensures that visitors see a tiger.

Tarsiers are found in the forests of Indonesia and the Philippines. Their fame comes, in part, from the resemblance to the *Star Wars* character Yoda. They are the only entirely carnivorous primate, feeding on insects and lizards. Tarsiers are small, ranging from 12 to 38 centimetres (5 to 15 inches) in length. Their name comes from their highly elongated tarsus, the bones of the ankle and upper foot, which gives them the longest legs relative to body size among primates. This physiology allows them to leap up to 5 metres (16 feet). The human equivalent jump would be around 30 metres (100 feet) – the world record for a long jump is around 9 metres (30 feet). These attributes make them superb nocturnal hunters.

Their most striking feature is enormous eyes, the biggest relative to body size in the animal kingdom. Each weighs more than the animal's brain. Tarsier eyes are fixed but the animal can rotate its head almost 360 degrees. Like many nocturnal creatures, they are hard to see in the wild – their irises don't reflect light, making them difficult to detect even with spotlights.

We saw a group of tarsiers at a nesting tree in Tangkoko National Reserve in Sulawesi. At dusk, they emerged to hunt. As camera flashes went off and people crowded in for photos, they bounded away on their nightly forage. They seemed to ricochet from branch to branch, tree to tree.

We passed the place at midday on another day. A guide and a tourist were prodding the resting tarsiers to get pictures. When stressed, the animals can die. They are one of the few species that commit suicide by holding their breath or banging their heads in cages when held captive.

Few ecotourists can undertake the eighteen expeditions over eight years that ornithologist Edwin Scholes and biologist Tim Laman needed to document every bird-of-paradise for *National Geographic*. Engineered wildlife sighting are concessions to the time-limited ecotourist's sense of entitlement. Jade and I must constantly reconcile our desire to see a species, its welfare and the ethics of wildlife viewing. Above all, we recognise it is not about us but about the animals.

Trying to see wild animals requires patience and stoic acceptance that it will not always yield the desired results. But when it succeeds without artificial incitement, the moment possesses a casual genuineness and an element of surprise that can be overwhelming.

In Uganda's Kibale Forest, in pre-dawn darkness, we hear the *prrrrp* of the green-breasted pitta's display, but the invisible bird moves away from us, dashing our hopes. After another hour, we chance upon a mother on the path. The bird is green, with a red belly, a black head and a broad golden stripe that runs from the base of the beak, above the eye, to the rear of the head. She is feeding her chick. Our guides have never seen this behaviour.

In Colombia's Páramo, an alpine tundra, we search for the tiny helmetcrest, a hummingbird uniquely adapted to survive the harsh high-altitude environment. A day-long search in Sumapaz, near Bogatá, turns up nothing. At Parque Nacional Natural Los Nevados, located in the Cordillera Central of the Colombian Andes, we climb to over 4000 metres (13,000 feet) at dawn, struggling with the thin air, to be rewarded with a brief view of a buffy helmetcrest.

The fiery topaz, another hummer, has brilliant orange-red iridescent plumage and two elongated tail feathers. In the Amazon, at dawn, we visit a river where they are sometimes seen. Army conscripts performing their morning ablutions scare away the bird, which we have travelled half a world to meet. Yet our visit coincides with sighting of a Stygian owl, a medium-sized bird with a blackish face and a whitish forehead. The owl has two distinctive dark feathers, ears that unusually bend inwards. We never expected to see this sought-after species.

In Iceland, we watch merlins hunt down a plover and a meadow pipit. In Namibia, a lanner falcon streaks past to snatch a quelea, a small, sparrow- or finch-like seed-eating bird that often occurs in large flocks. Off the Baja Peninsula, a diving peregrine hits an eared grebe waterbird, stunning it, circling around to grasp the dead bird in its talons and flying off in a single uninterrupted motion. But near the ruins of Tikal in Guatemala, the ornate hawk eagle, which many regard as the most beautiful bird of prey, cannot be found around its usual perch. At Montezuma in Colombia, on our way up the mountain, we startle a large raptor. The loud repeating whistling calls are of an ornate hawk eagle. It drops into a deep valley, eluding us. It remained our bogey bird for many years.

In Malaysia's Royal Belum State Park, we watch what appears to be a monkey feeding on a fruiting tree. Our boatman suddenly asks why the monkey is not using its hands. Close scrutiny reveals that it is a binturong or bearcat, a rarely seen native of South-East Asian forests. Our guide has only seen the species once before. It was the first time for the boatman and us.

On a spare day during our visit to Turkey's Taurus Mountains for Caspian snowcocks, rare bulky, long-necked partridge-like birds, we stake out a valley before dawn in freezing conditions. The hours go by. Some mountain goats seem nervous. Suddenly, from behind a rock, a Eurasian lynx emerges and saunters across the valley before disappearing into a ravine. Our Turkish guide has only seen lynx three times in more than twenty years.

Walking near Alaska's Kukak Bay, our guide notices a grizzly bear grazing on sedge grass a short distance away from us. Grizzlies can be up to 4 metres (12 feet) from nose to tail and weigh up to 600 kilograms (1300 pounds). The bear has a large hump over the front shoulders, the muscle mass used to drive the front limbs. This individual is nearly fully grown.

The bear ambles closer. About 30 metres (100 feet) from us, he turns a little to one side, rolling his shoulders in an aggressive posture. Our guide does not carry a gun or even capsicum spray, the only point of which, in any case, he told us, is to spray yourself in the face so that you can't see the approaching bear.

The bear closes the distance and then changes direction slightly, walking by us. Then he sits down barely 3 metres (10 feet) away. At close quarters, his power and size are clear. The tousled wet fur glistens. The bear's steely claws glint in the sunlight, their tensile strength evident. After twenty minutes or so, we back off carefully. The bear too gets up and wanders off along the shoreline without once looking back.

A quarter of a century after our visit to Congo, we travel to Bwindi in Uganda. Jade and I decide not to trek for the gorillas; we do not want to recapture the past. Near the park, we are on the lookout for birds: the Narina trogon (which we find) and the Fraser's eagle-owl (which we do not). Returning gorilla trekkers pass us, flushed with excitement.

In the early afternoon, with rain threatening, we retrace our steps. Suddenly, we hear the distinctive staccato grunts of a gorilla nearby. In front of us on the trail, three animals emerge from the forest onto the path. Soon we are surrounded by eight gorillas. A huge silverback is less than a metre from me. The surprise seems mutual.

The group appears to be crossing the trail to forage on the western edge of the park. The guides are concerned that the gorillas could travel over the nearby border into the Congo, where poaching is prevalent, so the head ranger, who originally habituated this group, is summoned.

It occurs to us that the apes manipulate us. In all likelihood, the gorillas feed in this area regularly. Trekking is over in the morning, leaving the rest of the day to continue their activities free from human interruption. It is as if they calibrate their movements around their human visitors.

With the chimpanzees, we noticed that on both days a young male, a different individual each time, remained on the ground to provide the tourists with close views and photo opportunities. It was as if the group rotated this assignment to allow the rest to go about their daily routine away from visitors. Michel de Montaigne worried that it was not he who played with his cat but the other way around.

Waiting for the ranger, I reflect on the unflattering differences between us and our close relatives. On our first visit to see gorillas, civil disturbances forced us to fly to Bujumbura, the capital of Burundi, and drive from there to Cyangugu in Rwanda, where we crossed over to Bukhavu in the Congo. The border is marked by a wooden bridge across a stream.

In 1994, during the genocidal civil war between Tutsis and Hutus, Rwanda's two main ethnic groups, the bridge appeared on the television news. On the Rwandan side, there were desperate Tutsis fleeing the advancing Hutu Interahamwe (meaning those who kill together). Perhaps a million people, mainly Tutsis, were killed. Uganda and the Democratic Republic of Congo have been racked by conflict for decades, resulting in the deaths, injuries and displacement of millions. The Congo has been ruled by a succession of despots. Despite great natural riches, a small group of people have siphoned off the wealth while the majority live in abject poverty. Gorillas seem able to live in greater harmony with each other, their environment and animals other than humans.

Eventually the head ranger arrives on a motorbike to corral the group and move them back into the safety of Uganda. As we resume our walk, I turn around to look at the gorillas, knowing that the opportunity will not reoccur. Humans strive to sift signal from noise, to draw meaning from events. Why can't we watch wild animals on their terms rather than ours?

5

FREUDIAN SLIPS

How Human Anxieties Shape Ecotourism

In *Life on Earth*, British broadcaster David Attenborough filmed the mountain gorillas being studied by Dian Fossey in Rwanda. He reclines in the grass very close to an adult female. Suddenly, she stretches out a hand and touches him. Surprised, Attenborough speaks seemingly spontaneously: 'There is more meaning and mutual understanding in exchanging a glance with a gorilla than any other animal I know.' Was the emotion shared? Was Attenborough's interpretation an accurate reading of the moment?

Western cultures romanticise animals. American poet Wallace Stevens wrote about thirteen ways of looking at a blackbird, exploring the awe of nature and the ways in which perceptions of reality differ between individuals. Some works are preoccupied by the author's bond with captive birds of prey – such as goshawks, in the case of Helen McDonald's award-winning memoir *H is for Hawk*. In such works, the writer's need for connection with wild creatures is paramount. Often, the world of the animal as depicted has little to do with real life – for example, in nature goshawks are ruthless, unrelenting hunters of small birds. In contrast, indigenous writings or teachings about animals are rarely poetic, focusing instead on useful knowledge of where prey can be found or where dangerous predators lurk, reflecting a different accommodation with wildlife.

Wildlife watching, researchers have found, improves mental health by reducing stress, anxiety and depression. Many find it meditative. But there are other deeper, subliminal factors that shape humans' psychological needs to connect with animals.

Sigmund Freud explored the role of the unconscious in the strong, hidden individual and societal needs that affect our interactions. Ecotourists often seek personal transformation in their encounters, which speaks to anthropomorphic preoccupations. Our self-absorption mistakes humankind as the lens through which everything must be viewed.

Ecotourists project certain attributes onto wild animals, leading to over-idealisation. They become symbols of beauty, peace and tranquillity. At the same time, they are exploited to support human requirements. Our interactions with wild animals are, increasingly, linked to fear that our mistreatment of the planet and its non-human inhabitants will rebound on us. Conservation efforts reek of guilt and conscience-driven attempts to repay debts for the harm caused. Laced through the relationship is anxiety about the future. In wilderness, we seek to escape the debilitating succubus of our stagnant and destructive civilisation. It is not easy to avoid these mental traps, as I have found.

Perhaps more than other creatures, birds fascinate us. Their defining feature is gravity-defying flight. Noisy parrots jink through the air. A falcon or hawk peels off in a breathtaking dive, rapidly adjusting direction to track its prey. Eagles soar high in the sky, barely visible to the naked eye. Condors, the largest species of vulture, can travel more than 160 kilometres (100 miles) without once flapping their wings. Leonardo da Vinci studied birds when trying to develop flying machines. Igor Sikorsky considered the flight of hummingbirds in designing helicopters.

Birds are intelligent and known for their problem-solving skills. Corvids (crows, ravens, magpies and allies) and parrots, whose brains are unusually large relative to their body weight, use sticks, stones and feathers to complete tasks that would be impossible with their beaks and feet, such as extracting grubs or breaking edible eggs. Avian mating rites are complex, rivalling human dating and matrimonial customs. The endurance of migratory species is remarkable. Birds' capacity for song, ranging from raucous roars to whistles and intricate melodies, is unmatched in the animal kingdom. Australian lyrebirds, a pheasant-like species, are famous for mimicking other birds but also human-made sounds, such as chainsaws and sirens.

It could also be their ubiquity, being found in cities, forests, deserts and the polar regions, or perhaps their variety. There are giants, such as the cassowary and the ostrich. There are bee hummingbirds, the world's smallest bird, at around 6 centimetres (2.5 inches) long and around 2 grams (0.7 ounces). Some birds are loners while others flock in the thousands.

Birds answer the human quest for beauty. They provide visual pleasure. Their feathers draw on a palette of colours, sometimes creating optical illusions that heighten the visual effect. Vocabulary struggles to capture the subtle shades of pigment: brown, rufous, ferruginous, ruddy, russet, chestnut, bran, dusky, tawny. Blue is transformed into azure, cerulean, cobalt, navy, indigo, ultramarine or aquamarine. Black becomes slaty, jet, coal or sooty.

But not all birds are attractive. Many are nondescript – LBJs (little brown jobs), in the patter of birders. There is the sadly named drab whistler and the dull-coloured grassquit. The Anaso Track at Lore Lindu National Park on the Indonesian island of Sulawesi – a 20-kilometre (12-mile) round trip on foot – is known for its high montane birds. Starting at around 1700 metres (5600 feet), the steep trail rises to 2300 metres (7500 feet). As you want to be at around 2100 metres (7000 feet) at first light, we got up at 3.00 am and started to walk in darkness. The species Jade and I sought but did not see – the great shortwing, the geomalia and the hylocitrea – are not especially distinctive. Their rarity and the remote location are what make them prized.

Many species are visually similar. Identifying wading shorebirds requires evaluating size and the bill – straight, curved, decurved (slanting down) or recurved (slanting up). Flycatchers and warblers are distinguishable only by minor variations in appearance, feeding technique or vocalisations. Canasteros, an insectivorous New World species that make large, domed nests from sticks or grass, must be identified by subtle variances of tail pattern and streaking. Bird names can create semantic problems. Our Brazilian guide Fred's daughter Cecilia wanted to know what roadside hawks were called before there were roads.

Jade and I share a confessed weakness for looney-tunes birds – extravagant, flamboyant specimens that defy design or behavioural logic. Parrots, parakeets, parrotlets, macaws, cockatoos, lorikeets, rosellas, cotingas, turacos, tanagers and toucans are favourites.

In Australia's Far North, we see palm cockatoos, with their shaggy crests and large bills. A red, bare patch of skin on the face changes intensity depending on how much blood is flushed through it. Males use their powerful bills to eat very hard nuts and seeds as well as break off thick sticks to drum to attract potential mates. Biologists believe that each individual fashions his drumsticks differently and has highly personalised rhythms.

We stake out an artificial dam at dawn. Budgerigars, slender, green and yellow-throated, appear. Usually found further inland, harsh conditions have forced them nearer the coast in their search for food and water. Before landing to drink, the airborne birds provide a mesmerising show as the flock moves in unison, a murmuration. Golden-shouldered parrots make their way down to drink. The males are an exquisite turquoise with a reddish underside. The bird has a black crown and a golden shoulder. Photos cannot do them justice.

In eastern Colombia's white-sand forest, calls alert us to a flock of feeding red fan parrots. Also known as hawk-headed parrots because of the resemblance to birds of prey in flight, they have elongated neck feathers with purple tips, which can be raised to form a spectacular mane. Deep in the nearby forest, a frog-like call announces a tawny-tufted toucanet. The male is a jumble of colour: black below and over the head and green above, with red-and-yellow thighs, a red-tipped tail, a multi-coloured bill and tawny yellow ear tufts.

Near a lek, we find a Guinean cock-of-the-rock, a type of cotinga, colourful frugivores of Central and South American forests. It is bright orange, its strange flat head topped by a prominent half-moon crest. The outer edge of its wings is decorated by protruding silky-orange filamentous feathers. At another lek, we watch a raucous group of the related Andean cock-of-the-rock, which is redder in colour.

Close to Negele in Ethiopia, we track down Prince Ruspoli's turaco with the help of locals. It is moss-green, with a colourful punk hairdo and a tuft of red feathers on its nape. The crimson under its wings is visible only in flight. It is named after a nineteenth-century Italian aristocrat who was trampled to death by an elephant. An unlabelled feather was found among his possessions. Half a century later, in the 1940s, ornithologists finally identified the bird.

A PBS nature documentary on birds-of-paradise found in and near Papua New Guinea, *Birds of the Gods*, reveals the visual magnificence of this bird family. Not all are colourful – the crow-like trumpet manucode is black, with a red iris and elongated horn-like head tufts and loose neck feathers. But many are spectacular. Males are brightly coloured and are known for striking courtship rituals in which they perform either solo or in large groups to attract potential mates.

Found only on a few islands off West Papua, the small Wilson's bird-of-paradise is outrageous – black forehead, blue head criss-crossed with dark lines, yellow and red back, green breast, blackish rump and two elongated violet-purple extended tail feathers. The superb bird-of-paradise has a shining blue-green nape, chin and beast plate. Paradigallas have a green and yellow facial wattle. The riflebird's glossy velvet black is set off by blue-green breast feathers. To enhance his appeal to receptive females, the male stands erect, throwing up his wings. He circles with outstretched wings, and the feathers flash iridescent every time he turns his head. During his dance, he opens his mouth to show off its bright lime yellow interior.

Sicklebills and astrapias have tail feathers several times their body length. The King of Saxony bird-of-paradise has two streamers, about 50 centimetres (20 inches) long, behind the eyes. Decorated by miniature plumes, these head feathers can be moved independently through a 180-degree arc during displays. The twelve-wired bird-of-paradise has six projecting thin flank feathers on each side. Males brush the stiff shafts against the female's face before mating.

The vivid crimson king bird-of-paradise has elongated tail feathers with green saucers at its tips, which are raised and waved during courtship. On seeing one for the first time, a species he knew only by description, drawings or faded skins and feathers, an overwhelmed Alfred Russell Wallace lamented his lack of faculty to express the bird's exquisiteness.

Birds inspire legends. In Samuel Taylor Coleridge's *Rime of the Ancient Mariner*, albatrosses mediate earthly and spiritual realms, simultaneously natural and supernatural. Their ghostly form emerging from mist, sailors believed, was a good omen.

Royal albatrosses nest in the green peat bog hills of Campbell Island near New Zealand. We sit in tussock grass for hours near these birds. As the wind picks up, the hiss of air flowing over their wings as they take off is audible. Several light-mantled sooty albatrosses, with beautiful grey heads and silver bodies, wheel above us, calling to each other with cat-like meows.

In the Southern Ocean, a wandering albatross flies past, inches above the sea. Their massive wingspan, up to 3.5 metres (11.5 feet), dwarfs everything else. Masters of flight, they can glide over vast tracts of ocean without flapping their wings. The British Antarctic Survey once tracked a grey-headed albatross that flew 22,000 kilometres (13,500 miles) around the southern hemisphere in forty-six days. Adapted to an oceanic existence, albatross spend the first years of their long lives without ever touching land. For Herman Melville, a wandering albatross is regal, a white feathery thing flying on vast archangel wings. If you see an albatross, you belong to a higher order of mortals.

Yet it is whales, even more than birds, that exemplify the full tangled psychology of our relations with wild animals. That is one lesson of our fourteen-year quest to see a blue whale that has something in common with Captain Ahab's obsession with the mercurial white whale in Herman Melville's *Moby-Dick*.

It starts on Sunday 30 January 1994 in the Amundsen Sea off Antarctica. From the bridge of the Russian icebreaker *Kapitan Khlebnikov*, we see a spout from a very large whale. When the ship reaches where it was seen, the whale has sounded, diving below the waves, leaving only an impression of its flukes on the water. The enormous prints can only be a blue whale, the largest animal thought to have ever existed on Earth. The name comes from the grey-blue tones of the long body when underwater. At around 30 metres (100 feet) in length and weighing up to 200 tonnes (440,000 pounds), it is about twice the size of the largest known dinosaurs.

Everything about a blue whale is outsized. Its enormous mouth would fit dozens of humans. The tongue weighs as much as an elephant. The heart is about 180 kilograms (400 pounds); the heartbeat can be detected 3 kilometres (2 miles) away. During dives to 300 metres (1000 feet), the whale slows its heart rate to four to eight beats per minute from its normal twenty-five to thirty-seven beats to save oxygen. Blue whales communicate with deep, low-pitched sounds that may carry more than 800 kilometres (500 miles) underwater.

Whales were once considered monsters of the deep. Melville warned of the deceptive nature of the sea, where the most dreaded creatures hide treacherously beneath the azure. Over the last half-century, they have become a symbol of the fight to preserve nature, inspiring environmental crusades and cults, entwined with the different interests of conservation, entertainment, science, politics and even the military. Their ability to arouse interest and emotions is mystifying – we learned that in our pursuit to see a blue properly after that first unsatisfying encounter.

For most of human history, whales were merely a commodity.

Whaling, like warfare, mirrors technological progress. Originally, primitive weapons and human- or wind-powered craft limited hunting to shallow waters near land. In the seventeenth century, organised fleets began the industrial slaughter. Initially, whales held the advantage. The speed of fin and blue whales and their ability to dive made them difficult to catch. Some species sank when killed, making recovery difficult. Others did not fare well. Right whales, so named because they swam slowly and floated when dead, were decimated. Northern right whales are still one of the world's most critically endangered animals, with only around 400 remaining, including fewer than 100 breeding females.

Over time, the battlefield shifted. Steamships and vessels with internal combustion engines were faster and more manoeuvrable. Navigation and tracking of whales improved. In 1864, Svend Foyn, a pious Norwegian sealer, developed a mounted cannon that fired a harpoon fitted with an explosive head. Compressed air kept carcasses afloat. Powerful winches aided fast retrieval. Factory ships replaced shore stations. Stern slipways made it possible to raise the entire carcass from the water for processing on deck, allowing whalers to operate away from shore and in distant oceans.

Cetacean body parts had a variety of applications. The meat provided protein. Obtained by boiling down blubber, whale oil was used for illumination, soap, margarine and lubricants well into the 1960s. Sperm whale oil burned clearly and brightly, without smoke or odour, so was ideal for lighthouses. Its lubricating qualities were maintained at extreme temperatures. Spermaceti, a liquid wax-like matter found in the heads of sperm whales, had similar properties and was used in medicines and for wool combing.

Many whales strain food from seawater using baleen, long strips of keratin in the roofs of their mouths. Flexible and strong, these plates were used in corset stays, hoops for women's skirts, fishing poles, umbrella ribs, buggy whips and carriage springs. Ambergris, a rare wax-like substance sometimes found in the intestines of sperm whales, became part of perfume manufacture. It was thought to have medicinal properties and act as an aphrodisiac.

Nearly three million large whales were killed during the twentieth century. The primary species hunted were blue, fin, sei, grey, bowhead, sperm, humpback and right whales. Once one whaling ground was exhausted, commercial whalers moved into another region. When the population of one species fell, the focus shifted to others.

A 1926 report describes the grim scene at Grytviken on the island of South Georgia, then one of the largest whaling stations on the planet. Carcasses floated on blood-red water. Rotting flesh and macerated bones of dead whales were everywhere. Men worked with long-handled flensing knives to cut flesh from blubber. Everything was covered in a thick greasy slime. The foul smell from the rank, putrefying flesh was overpowering. It was a place of death.

Scientists working with the dead bodies acquired knowledge of whale biology. Graham Burnett, in his 2012 book *The Sounding of the Whale*, records one scientist's foreboding expressed in biblical terms: what penalty would the gods ultimately inflict on man for this sacrilege?

In the 1950s, John Cunningham Lilly, an American neuroscientist who developed the isolation tank to explore human consciousness, made claims about the intelligence of marine mammals. His shaky thesis was based on the assumed correlation between brain size, cognitive abilities and communication skills. Dolphins' brains were about one-third bigger than humans'; sperm whale brains were five times that of dolphins. Lilly advocated protecting whales and dolphins in order to exchange ideas with these intelligent animals. Similarly, a popular 1972 book by Karl-Erik Fichtelius and Sverre Sjolander, *Smarter Than Man? Intelligence in Whales, Dolphins and Humans*, argued that homo sapiens were a violent and dangerous species who needed to learn from cetaceans. The efforts at interspecies communication ultimately went nowhere, but the ideas would be referenced in the films, television shows and music of the period.

The rising interest coincided with the US Navy's investigation into ocean acoustics, which uncovered strange underwater noises that turned out to originate from whales and dolphins. Military analysts sought to understand the acoustic profiles in the hope of using them to disguise sonar or radio communications in submarine warfare. This resulted in the 1970 album *Songs of the Humpback Whale*, produced by bio-acoustician Roger Payne, which became a surprise commercial success. Many folk and experimental musicians incorporated the haunting sounds into their work. The songs were included in the gold phonograph record sent on the *Voyager* spacecraft to represent the Earth to extra-terrestrial intelligence. (Why whale descants were favoured over birdsong is a mystery.)

Around the same time, anti-nuclear activists become agitated about rumours that sperm whale oil, really liquid wax, was used in the lubrication of American and Russian intercontinental ballistic missiles. This polyglot pop-cultural fusion was perfect for the trippy, happy, out-there 1960s. Whales and dolphins were intelligent and beautiful – the songs proved their musicality and other superior attributes. Whale products were being used to support the global arms race. It all coalesced into the movement to protect whales, influencing broader conservation efforts.

On 1 July 1975, a grave Walter Cronkite on *CBS Evening News* showed millions of viewers grainy footage of a confrontation between some whale lovers, calling themselves Greenpeace, and Soviet whalers in the North Pacific. The film shows the whalers firing a 110-kilogram (250-pound) grenade harpoon into a female sperm whale. The harpoon passes close to two young protestors in a small boat trying to disrupt the hunt.

The totemic moment galvanised opinion against whaling. In fact, concern for whale populations was nothing new. From the late nineteenth century onwards, scientists had cautioned against the indiscriminate slaughter that was leading to their extinction.

In 1982, the International Whaling Commission (IWC), formed after World War II by voluntary agreement among member nations, adopted a moratorium on commercial whaling. In 1986, commercial killing was banned to conserve stocks.

Although environmentalists claimed a victory, the IWC decision was designed to save the industry, whose fate was tied to whale populations. Most whale products had been superseded by petroleum and its derivatives, such as plastics. Jojoba oil had emerged as a cheaper and more stable substitute to whale oil for high-friction lubrication applications. Sperm oil's price had collapsed by 90 per cent.

The moratorium was poorly supervised and full of loopholes. Non-member countries were not bound by it. The whaling nations themselves were responsible for enforcement. The IWC only regulated hunting of thirteen species of great whales, with no agreement regarding hunting of smaller species. The live capture of orcas and dolphins for exhibiting in aquariums continued.

The ban excluded killing for scientific purposes and aboriginal subsistence whaling – hunting by indigenous peoples in accordance with traditional customs. Intended only for first nations peoples on anthropological grounds, the provisions for aboriginal subsistence whaling have been abused ever since. Qualifications for a quota are sometimes falsified. Whale meat is sold commercially to tourists and non-native peoples. Aboriginal subsistence hunts are typically less efficient than commercial whaling. Under-powered rifles can lead to protracted, painful deaths. Struck and lost rates are high, leaving the wounded animal to suffer. Whalers use this to advance their arguments for the resumption of humane commercial whaling.

Today, Canada, Iceland, Japan, Norway, Russia, South Korea, the United States and the Danish dependencies of the Faroe Islands and Greenland continue to hunt whales in substantial numbers. With whale oil rarely used, modern whaling is conducted for pet food, human consumption, and decorative carvings of tusks, teeth and vertebrae. The catch from Japan's scientific whaling endeavours ends up in restaurants, making a mockery of its designation as research. DNA samples reveal that Japanese fish markets and stores sell meat from endangered species, in violation of international law. All great whales probably look the same when packaged in plastic.

The IWC moratorium is tenuous. Iceland, Japan and Norway want it lifted on certain whale stocks. Anti-whaling nations have offered a compromise, allowing these countries to recommence commercial whaling, subject to supervised smaller catches and a complete ban in the Southern Ocean. The IWC faces long-standing allegations of vote-buying by interested parties. The participation of land-locked members, such as Switzerland, Hungary, Mongolia and Laos, and nations with no known whaling capacity, such as Gabon, Nauru, Togo and Tuvalu, compromises its credibility.

Whale watching is one lasting legacy of the 1960s.

'Eleven o'clock!' The hours on an analogue clock indicate where a whale was spotted. What was seen is a blow, a spout of vapour as warm air is expelled from a whale's lungs when it surfaces to breathe. If you are on a whale-watching vessel, the skipper manoeuvres towards the sighting.

There might be another exhalation or two. You might see a glistening back. Then, with a flourish of its tail or fluke, the whale slips below the water. It may or may not reappear within your visual range. Even from a boat, the view will be distant, if whale-watching regulations are followed. That's all you will see, unless it is a stranding victim or in an aquarium, what John Steinbeck called whale jails. Species identification from that fleeting sight requires analysis of size, colour, markings, tail and dorsal-fin shapes.

Like other wildlife tourism, whale watching focuses on charismatic species. The humpback whale – 16 metres (50 feet) long, 40 tonnes (90,000 pounds) in weight – is the ambassador for all cetaceans. Defined by their long flippers, humpbacks are known for acrobatic performances. They slap, beating the water with their pectoral fins to create loud splashes. They spy-hop, raising their heads vertically to survey their surrounds. They breach, heaving their bodies out of the water and falling back with a thunderous splash to remove parasites, orient themselves, signal to other whales and nearby boats or, perhaps, in sheer exuberance. In contrast, enigmatic blue, fin, sei, right, bowhead, minke, Bryde's and pilot whales typically offer glimpses.

The problem is even greater with beaked whales, smaller cetaceans that resemble oversized dolphins. Many deep-diving species have never even been seen alive and are poorly understood. In Russia's Commander Islands, a young marine biologist studying Baird's beaked whales told us that months of painstaking observation have allowed him merely to establish the interval between dives. Ironically, the Earth's largest creatures elude us, spending much of their time out of view. This may be part of their allure.

Baja California is one of the best places to see whales. We join fifty travellers on a 1000-nautical-mile fourteen-day expedition around the Gulf of California – or the Sea of Cortéz, depending on your historical viewpoint.

Pacific white-sided, long-beaked common and bottlenose dolphins accompany the ship, providing hours of delight as they ride the bow wake. Off Gorda Banks, near the entrance to the Gulf, we see several humpback whales. A female travelling with her calf is shadowed by an escort who has fought off competitors for mating rights. The male has the typical white scar tissue over the dorsal fin and tail that records these battles. The ship's hydrophones allow us to listen to whale sounds. However, it is not the full signature humpback song, which changes every few years.

We see fin whales, identifiable by their tall columnar blow and dark bodies. Only slightly smaller than blues but much lighter, the sleek, fish-eating fins are capable of bursts of speed of up to 50 kilometres (30 miles) per hour. The lower jaw is curiously white on the right side. Off Isla San Marcos, we come upon a large pod of short-finned pilot whales, members of the dolphin family. We see several Bryde's whales, a non-migratory species found in warmer tropical waters.

Near a deep ocean trench off Isla San Pedro Mártir, a pod of sperm whales, Captain Ahab's nemesis, rest on the surface. They are the largest toothed whale, with a huge square head (one-third of their body length). Their blow is different from other cetaceans, angled at 45 degrees and to the side. Sperm whales are the deepest-diving mammal, capable of descending to 3000 metres (10,000 feet) in search of octopus, rays, small sharks, fish and squid, including the fabled giant variety. The ship's hydrophone picks up their clicks, used for communicating, echo location or stunning prey. They can reach 230 decibels underwater. A naturalist acquaintance came across a pod of sperm whales off the Galápagos Islands. One swam up to his kayak, using sonar clicks to investigate. The sound was visceral: 'It was like being punched.'

Near Isla San Francisco we find a bait ball, small fish tightly packed in a spherical formation as a defensive measure against predators. The sea boils as around 1000 dolphins attack the shoal. Overhead, pelicans and boobies plunge-dive to pick off fish scattered by the dolphins. Magnificent frigatebirds and other seabirds swoop down to pluck fish from the surface.

In fading light near Land's End, we see the distant towering blows of blue whales, which thunder up some 30 metres (100 feet) into the air. They swim quickly away from us.

In the Gulf itself, we finally see them close. An adult makes frequent dives to feed within metres of the ship. It is two-thirds the length of our vessel. The flat head and prominent blowholes are visible (baleen whales all have two blowholes). It takes large breaths at twenty- to thirty-second intervals and dives for periods of up to twenty minutes: its long back rolls over slowly, with the hook-like dorsal fin coming into view before its huge tail fluke is visible. It is not known why only some blue whales fluke – prominently revealing their tail out of the water when diving.

A mother and calf surfaces near the boat. The calf is 7 metres (22 feet) and 3600 kilograms (8000 pounds) at birth. We learn that each day it drinks 200 litres (50 gallons) of milk. The mother may lose a third of her body weight during this period. She will resume eating at her higher-latitude feeding grounds to rebuild fat stores.

Our odyssey is at a close, and the ending is happier than Captain Ahab's.

Baja is famed for grey whales, an ancient species. We are scheduled to travel to San Ignacio Laguna, once known as Scammon's Lagoon after the nineteenth-century whaling captain who discovered these birthing lagoons. Scammon used new shoulder-launched harpoon guns to take mothers, calves and migrating bulls. The waters ran red with whale blood. Orphaned calves circled whalers' vessels for days before dying of starvation.

Today, Atlantic greys are extinct. The western Pacific species is critically endangered. Eastern Pacific greys were nearly wiped out. Despite a 1937 hunting ban, only 18,000 animals are left.

Rough seas force us to divert from San Ignacio lagoon to Bahia Magdalena, protected on the west by a narrow island with enormous sand dunes. This late in the season the whales could have already left, so we are relieved to see blows when we arrive. A few mothers and calves are still there. These grey whales winter in Baja California, travelling in spring to their summer feeding grounds in the Bering Sea, a round journey of up to 11,000 kilometres (7000 miles). Accompanied by local guides, we take to zodiacs for a closer look. Once we near a whale, a flag is hoisted, ensuring other boats do not approach. We must maintain a specified distance from the whales, but this does not preclude the animals from approaching closer if they choose.

In 1972, a Mexican fisherman – Francisco Mayoral, known as Pachico – was fishing with a friend when he was approached by a female grey whale who began to follow them. The whale circled the boat and at one point rose under it, lifting it clear of the water. Pachico feared that the grey, once known as devil fish because of the ferocity with which the species would defend their young, might smash the boat and kill the two occupants. Then, the female spy hopped to look directly at Pachico, eye to eye, remaining for a long time. Finally, Pachico reached across and touched her tentatively and then more firmly. The whale remained, floating gently. That was the beginning of whale watching in Baja.

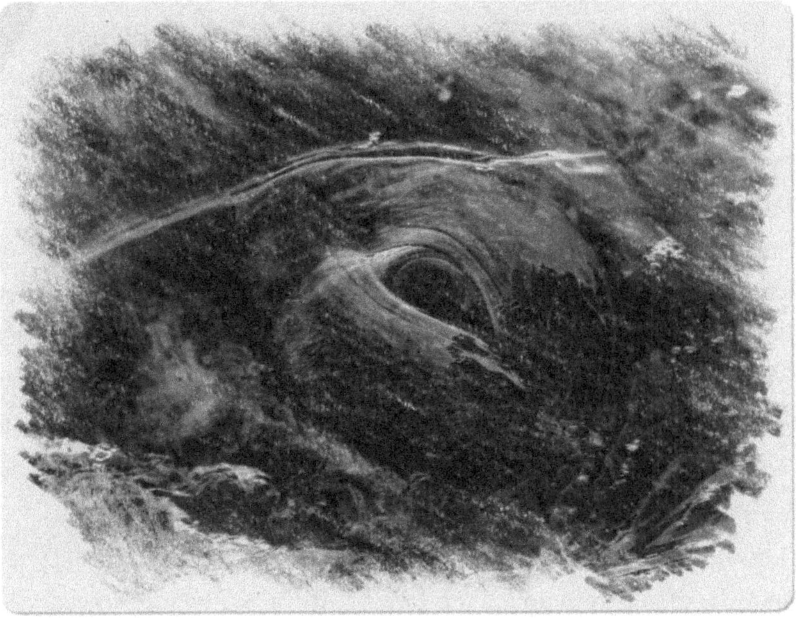

A mother and calf approach our zodiac, swimming around and under our craft, sometimes rubbing their backs on the underside. They surface alongside, allowing people to touch them, and are joined by others. The adult whales dwarf the boat. They are around 15 metres (50 feet) in length and weigh around 35 tonnes (more than 77,000 pounds). Their strength is apparent when they bump our craft: a flick of their massive tail would upend the zodiac. The pressure of the air from their loud blows is like a firehose. A mist of seawater and mucus refracts the light into rainbows. There is the rotten cabbage smell of whale halitosis.

The adults' bodies and narrow triangular heads are encrusted with barnacles and lice. Scars from attacks by predators like orcas and injuries from boat propellers are visible. The calf's skin is still shiny and smooth. It likes being touched and even rubbed, seemingly enjoying the interaction. It must be similar to the constant nuzzling provided by the mother. A huge, gentle ovoid eye fixes onto mine for a few seconds.

After a few minutes, the mother leads the calf away, directing it to deeper water. The young whales must gain hundreds of kilos each week on a diet of fat rich milk. In a few days, they will begin the perilous journey north, facing the challenges of the open ocean and waiting dangers, especially orcas.

Marine biologists dismiss the behaviour as reflexive. The greys are attracted by the sound of motors; they are looking to scratch their backs against the hulls. But many cetacean species exhibit multifaceted social patterns, intricate communication skills, cooperation, cultural transmission and tool usage. Different species have been known to come to one another's aid against predators. Whales rescued from fishing lines appear to show their gratitude to attending divers.

Some greys, who can live up to 100 years and carry old harpoon wounds, would remember the bloody history. Given the past, why Baja's greys now seek out humans, even guiding their calves towards whale watchers, remains mysterious. Whether or not we read too much into the whales' motivations, the encounters touch everybody on board deeply.

Whale watching can take on a cult-like aspect, something Jade and I found out firsthand in Argentina's Peninsula Valdés.

Orcas – killer whales – are actually the largest dolphins. Males are up to 8 metres (26 feet) long and weigh in excess of 6 tonnes (12,000 pounds). They have a prominent triangular dorsal fin about 1.8 metres (6 feet) high. Orcas live in stable matrilineal family groups. Each pod has distinctive vocalisations and sophisticated hunting tactics passed down between generations. Individual populations are specialised hunters. Some feed exclusively on fish while others hunt marine mammals. The orcas of Valdés hunt South American sea lions and southern elephant seals in shallow water, even beaching themselves temporarily to grab prey before wriggling back to the sea. Our visit is to try to see this well-documented behaviour.

We stay at a rustic estancia, a marginal sheep property with well-located private beaches where the hunt of sea lion pups is a seasonal occurrence. Upon arrival, we are greeted by the whale whisperer and his self-appointed adjutant, an intense American guest. Most of the clients, from the United States, Germany and Spain, are regulars who come every year for a month or longer. We find ourselves in a Maharishi ashram dedicated to the worship of this animal. As sceptical outsiders, we feel separate from the inner circle of true believers.

The routine is simple: arrive by 6.00 am at a beach, sit quietly till dusk for the orcas to appear. During our week-long stay, other than some playful sea lions and Magellanic penguins, we see absolutely nothing. It is *Waiting for Godot* on a loop. It appears that documented attacks have become more sporadic after the death of Mel, a famed orca who pioneered the technique. Despite this, the cult's beliefs remain unshakeable.

Mythologies persist. Whale conservation is not the success it is claimed to be. Populations have recovered but remain a fraction of pre-hunting levels. In mid-January 2021, when the first eastern grey whales arrived in the breeding lagoons in Baja California, scientists noticed that many were emaciated. The whales did not get sufficient nutrients in their Bering Sea feeding grounds, probably due to a decline in the number of amphipods, their main food, caused by warming of Arctic waters. The species may be now doomed to extinction from climate change.

Hunting for whales continues. In 2023, a cruise liner with more than 1000 passengers arrived in port at Tórshavn in the Faroe Islands, located between Scotland, Iceland and Norway in the North Atlantic, amid a bloody hunt of more than seventy pilot whales. The cruise operators apologised to the passengers, which included marine conservationists, for any distress caused. The island's government defends whaling as traditional and part of its sustainability efforts. As of July 2023, the Faroe Islands had registered over 600 whale killings for the year. More than 500 dolphins have been killed since the principality resumed its hunt in May 2023. Dolphin hunting, made infamous by the 2009 bloody documentary *The Cove*, has also recommenced in Japan.

In his 1981 treatise *Simulacres et Simulation*, French cultural theorist Jean Baudrillard examined the structure of modern society. He argued that simulation, the imitation of the world, gradually deceives humans into believing in falsehoods. Over time, simulacra, copies depicting things that are not real or no longer have an original, eliminate substance and destroy the actual things it is based on. Ecotourism is the simulacrum of the natural world.

Wildlife tourism is a play of reflections that have more to do with the watcher than the watched. Our emotional needs lead us to attempt to enter into the realm of these creatures, but entirely within a human frame of reference. Journalist and author Jane Jacobs warned that this was patronising: 'Most sentimental ideas imply, at bottom, a deep if unacknowledged disrespect. It is no accident that we Americans, probably the world's champion sentimentalizers about nature, are at one and the same time probably the world's most voracious and disrespectful destroyers of wild and rural countryside.'

In his *The Log from the Sea of Cortez*, John Steinbeck asks why human beings cannot think of themselves as just another animal species. Is it because we are afraid of what it might say about us?

6

TO THE ENDS OF THE EARTH AND BEYOND

Extreme Frontiers of Ecotourism

From fire to the wheel, agriculture, metallurgy, the use of fossil fuels, communications, medical advances and information processing, technology underpins humanity's domination of the planet. It has enabled adventure travel – extreme quests into oceans, space and the poles – once considered the stuff of science fiction.

As is often said, more is known about the surface of the moon than the deep seas on our planet. For most of history, the depths of the oceans have been beyond the reach of humans. Early surveys were conducted by boats and swimmers. The invention of scuba gear in 1942 expanded the possibilities. Today, there are around six million active divers globally, plus many more snorkelling enthusiasts. Activity is focused on littoral regions, especially coral reefs. The emphasis is on the charismatic, spectacular and dangerous – colourful tropical reef fish, giant rays and turtles, as well as predators, especially sharks.

But diving below 40 metres (120 feet) presents challenges (and to put this depth in context, the deepest known point of ocean is estimated to be 10,935 metres – 35,876 feet). Going further down requires switching between different gas blends and slow ascents to allow decompression and avoid nitrogen intoxication. The problem is water pressure, which increases 1 standard atmosphere for every 10 metres (30 feet) below the ocean surface. At 3000 metres (10,000 feet), the pressure is approximately 300 standard atmospheres, or 300 times greater than the pressure at sea level. Sperm whales can dive to these depths but most human-made objects would be crushed. Human beings can withstand 3 to 4 atmospheres.

Enter the submersible. These vessels range from small craft allowing non-divers to explore shallow reefs to submarines capable of diving to several thousand metres. Deep sea tourism is a growing industry.

While the most diverse and active creatures are near the ocean surface, at depths beyond the reach of sunlight, there is an alien world of strange creatures adapted to darkness, cold and high pressures. Some are translucent. Most are blind. Others are characterised by bioluminescence, light emitted from biochemical reactions. Many are unknown to science. But the focus of deep sea tourism is not wildlife – at least not yet – but tours of geographical features, such as the dazzling rock formations around hydrothermal vents and the deep ocean trenches, or shipwrecks, such as that of the *Titanic* or the *Bismarck*.

Humans are better at scaling heights. Mountaineers have sought to reach the seven summits (the highest mountain on each continent) or climb all fourteen of the world's 8000-metre (26,000-feet) peaks. Amateurs unable to meet the physical demands or wanting to reduce the risks increasingly use helicopter support to reach the top.

For those unsatisfied with mountains, the ultimate up is space. In 2001, American businessman Dennis Tito became the first to negotiate tourist passage on a mission to the International Space Station, at a cost of $20 million, paving the way for subsequent travellers. The catalyst was the financially strapped Russian space program's need for cash.

Commercial companies, many the brainchild of business billionaires, have sought to develop space tourism. Sub-orbital vehicles take passengers to an altitude of 100 kilometres (62 miles), the Kármán line, which defines the boundary between Earth's atmosphere and outer space. From here one can see the curvature of the planet and experience weightlessness. SpaceX's Crew Dragon spacecraft can be chartered for orbital flights or as a shuttle for stays at the International Space Station. There are plans for excursions to the Moon and Mars.

The lure of deep oceans and outer space is uncertain. The conditions are not luxurious. A deep-sea submersible involves confinement in a tiny space for up to ten hours without facilities; arduous space travel requires physical fitness and extensive training. Aircraft flights that create brief near-weightless environments are nicknamed vomit comets. Defecation in zero gravity requires the user's bottom to be exactly centred on a 10-centimetre (4-inch) hole in a space toilet.

Cost is another barrier. An hour-long submersible dive is a few thousand. A trip to the *Titanic* costs over $100,000. A sub-orbital flight is $250,000. In 2022, three individuals paid $55 million each to spend a couple of weeks at the International Space Station. The risks are also substantial – in 2023, a submersible diving to the *Titanic* was lost, with all five occupants killed.

Such extreme tourism is marketed as raising awareness of environmental issues or as citizen science initiatives aimed at gathering data. In reality, demand is linked to its exclusivity. One operator boasts that fewer people have visited the wreck of the *Titanic* than have been to space or summited Mount Everest. For those with money, the point of difference is that deep sea and space tourism is not something everybody can afford. You get to say you've done something different – even if only because you are one of few who can pay for the privilege.

For those interested in extreme tourism when deep oceans and space are out of reach, the polar regions remain more accessible. Many travellers are attracted to these hard-to-reach, cold, desolate landscapes. You can visit places that, until recently, challenged even courageous explorers, in comfort, even luxury, for amounts starting from around $10,000. But it remains an exclusive club. True adventure and disconnection from everyday life? Perhaps that's an overstatement.

From space, the Earth is a blue marble with white caps at the poles. While they share extremes of temperature and seasonal patterns of daylight and darkness, the north and south ends of the Earth are different. Antarctica is a continent surrounded by ocean while the Arctic is an ocean surrounded by continents. Both are points of singularity, where all the longitudes meet.

The north polar regions consists of the Arctic Ocean, northern Scandinavia, offshore island archipelagos such as Svalbard and Franz Josef Land, Russia and Canada's northern coastline, Alaska and Greenland. Some include Iceland, although it lies south of the Arctic Circle.

The south polar region consists of the continent itself, the peninsula that projects northwards, towards South America, and scattered sub-Antarctic islands. Antarctica existed only in the imagination for more than 2000 years, an antipodean *terra nondum cognita*, a southern land not yet known.

The poles, once magnets for explorers and adventurers, are now stops on the tourist trail. Many itineraries follow the journeys of explorers such as Sir James Clark Ross, Fridtjof Nansen, Robert Peary, Sir John Franklin, Richard Byrd, Carsten Borchgrevink, Roald Amundsen, Sir Ernest Shackleton, Robert Falcon Scott, Fabian Bellingshausen or Douglas Mawson. Their explorations anticipated today's polar tourism. The quests had little intrinsic value or scientific significance: they were mostly about personal glory, mixed with a dash of nationalism and a desire for conquest. For example, Peary did not acknowledge his companion, Matthew Henson, or the Inuit men who made his journey possible. The American made doubtful claims about reaching the North Pole first. He sought to position himself as an accomplished explorer to take advantage of endorsements, sponsorships, book deals and lecture tours.

There are cultural nuances in all of this. The British celebrate failure. Scott's expedition was poorly conceived. Rejecting the Norwegian Amundsen's strategy of dog sleds and skis, he chose the more macho but eminently less sensible option of human-hauled sleds. Instead of travelling light, Scott's expedition was weighed down by festive provisions for Christmas. Scott's death invested ineptitude with nobility. Disaster was rationalised as a divine quest and proof of Britain's greatness. The Alliance of Honour, devoted to male purity and opposed to masturbation, praised Scott's heroism on the grounds that the expedition members were not victims of, at least, that vice. Amundsen's achievement was disparaged.

On our Antarctic expedition, the vessel is trapped in a blizzard in McMurdo Sound. With the ship lodged in sea ice, the gangway is lowered on the side protected from the fierce wind. Passengers walk about on the frozen sea, experiencing something akin to the conditions that true explorers faced. Some play football against the Russian crew. The white ball blends into the whiteout. Unskilled at remaining vertical on the icy surface, the tourists are duly thrashed. Nearby, a group of British tourists sit on the ice reading aloud from *The Fire on the Snow*, Douglas Stewart's verse play on Scott's expedition. Polar myths are powerful.

The original explorers would have resented pampered outsiders like us venturing to these places. Many sought a temporarily simpler existence. Remoteness was an escape from the challenges and uncertainties of politics and wars.

The earliest known polar pleasure voyages commenced in Norway in the late nineteenth century. A shipping company, which would become Hurtigruten, carried paying passengers between Trondheim and Hammerfest in summer and Trondheim and Tromsø in winter. The adventurous could join whalers sailing from Tromsø to Spitsbergen, in the Svalbard archipelago.

During the 1920s, a Falkland Islands mail ship, which made annual visits to the whaling and sealing stations on South Shetland and South Orkney Islands, carried a small number of tourists on the round trip. In the 1930s, the Hudson's Bay Company offered cruises aboard their resupply vessel, which travelled through the Canadian Arctic from Montreal to Churchill.

Around 1966, Swedish-American adventurer and entrepreneur Lars-Eric Lindblad organised the first modern cruises to Antarctica for leisure travellers. The success of the initial voyages encouraged construction of the *Lindblad Explorer*, a 104-passenger ship for tours to the Canadian Arctic and Antarctica. The company would become Lindblad Expeditions, which in 2004 partnered with National Geographic to expand ship-based ecotourism. Others including Quark, Poseidon and Oceanwide Expeditions also helped develop polar trips.

In the 1970s, Air New Zealand and Qantas began sightseeing overflights of the Antarctic. The twelve-hour flights descended to low altitudes to allow passengers better views. On 28 November 1979, Air New Zealand TE901 crashed into Mount Erebus due to a route planning error, killing 257 people. Air New Zealand never resumed their Antarctic flights, although Qantas recommenced its Antarctic program in 1994.

Anchored off Ross Island, we see Mount Erebus and Mount Terror, named after Scott's ships. In bright sunlight and clear air, the volcanoes appear close. The site where the Air New Zealand DC-10 aircraft slammed into the side of the mountain is visible.

The end of the Soviet Union provided the unlikely impetus for polar tourism. By the late 1980s, the USSR was struggling with a sclerotic, dysfunctional economy, low oil prices and the costs of its Afghanistan war and military spending necessitated by the Cold War. General Secretary Mikhail Gorbachev's reformist policies of perestroika (restructuring) and glasnost (openness) could not reverse the trajectory. The Soviet Union eventually collapsed, bringing further misery to its long-suffering citizens.

Polar bear researcher Nikita Ovsyanikov and his colleagues were isolated on Wrangel Island. Despite enormous privations, they continued their work. Living in primitive conditions, lacking modern equipment, they were forced to survive off the land, hunting reindeer for food.

The entire Soviet Union was for sale. Industrial, civilian and military assets as well as associated expertise were auctioned off. Colombian drug cartels seeking to purchase a Soviet submarine for smuggling operations were asked whether they wanted it with or without missiles.

Amid the chaos, polar travel companies saw an opportunity. In exchange for desperately needed US dollars, they gained access to state-of-the-art icebreakers and ice-strengthened ships, staffed by Russian crews skilled in navigating ice-bound seas, which could be adapted for Arctic and Antarctic tourism. Even nuclear-powered vessels, carrying the highest ice class rating and capable of breaking through ice up to 2.5 metres (8 feet) thick, could be leased. They allowed voyages to the North Pole or tracing the North-East or North West passage, where difficult-to-penetrate multi-year ice is common. In the early 1990s, a less powerful diesel icebreaker become stuck in ice during an attempted circumnavigation of Greenland. A nuclear icebreaker had to be despatched to free it. On early trips to the North Pole, US intelligence officers masqueraded as passengers to gain information about the ships and possible radioactive leaks.

In 1994, on our second-ever wildlife adventure, we found ourselves beneficiaries of this evolution of polar travel. However, as the new Federation emerged, Russians realised that they had given away their assets cheaply. Over time, access to these ships decreased, prices increased and terms became less advantageous, forcing the tour companies to invest in their own craft.

The Arctic sees millions of tourists. The Antarctic is more exclusive, with around 50,000 to 60,000 annual visitors, up from a few thousand when we went. The difference in numbers reflects proximity to permanent human settlements, transport links, ease of access and cost. The Arctic offers a variety of land- and ship-based opportunities while, with minor exceptions, Antarctica requires expedition vessels.

The growth in visitors has been, in part, because of an increase in the size of the vessels. The Lindblad model, small ships carrying fifty to 100 passengers, was superseded. The first larger vessels used in

Antarctica carried around 250 to 500 passengers. Now, higher capacity liners are being introduced, a concession to economies of scale and to wealthy clients who demand facilities impossible on smaller vessels.

The industry has also changed in subtler ways. Pioneers of polar tourism were subsumed into or supplanted by traditional cruise operators. Intrepid individuals, seeking to satisfy their own ambition to travel to previously inaccessible places, gave way to business types.

The travellers are different. On our cruise, the majority of passengers were from the United States, the United Kingdom, Europe, Australia and New Zealand. There was a group of aged, surly Japanese, led by their guide, a young woman who spent a lot of time apologising for her charges. Their highlight was drinking whiskey with centuries-old ice chipped from an iceberg. Today, there are growing numbers of Chinese customers, who must undertake special classes prior to travel to ensure compliance with environmental rules because of a history of bad behaviour.

Our fellow travellers were a mixture of wildlife enthusiasts, adventurous souls and those bored with life or experiencing a personal crisis. Most appreciated the privilege. That honour has been diluted over time. There are now greater numbers of the rich, famous and celebrated. There is a trend to storied travellers: the influencer couple who ride their Harleys from the United States to the southernmost tip of the Americas to join the cruise; the woman seeking to be the first pole dancer to have performed on all continents.

Travel to the Antarctic and more remote Arctic regions remains based around live-on-board ships. Our ship, *Kapitan Khlebnikov*, was once a working diesel-powered icebreaker used around Murmansk and Vladivostok. It had been adapted to accommodate about 100 passengers in fifty spartan cabins. Today, ice-strengthened ships are more prevalent, in part reflecting changing itineraries. The French cruise company Ponant uses custom-made vessels which are, in effect, luxury floating hotels, offering suites and staterooms, food by celebrity chefs such as Alain Ducasse, a massage cabin, a hairdresser and multiple lounges and bars. The philosophy is that no one should have to miss their yoga or Pilates routines. There are even sleek elevators instead of the *Khlebnikov*'s endless steep, narrow stairs.

But some things are hard to overcome. True icebreakers are at home in ice. In open seas, they roll. They lack stabilisers, which would interfere with ice-breaking operations. Movement and routine actions require coordination with the ship's motion. Our semi-circumnavigation of the Antarctic continent started from the Falkland Islands (Las Malvinas) and ended in New Zealand. If there was the slightest swell, the *Khlebnikov* rolled wildly. In the Southern Ocean, the ship listed 45 degrees. Trapped in the stairwell, sure that the ship would flip over, we braced for our personal *Poseidon Adventure*. Finally, the roll slowed and the ship corrected, swinging rapidly in the other direction. No matter how luxurious the vessel, the old adage about seasickness is true. In the first stage, you think you are dying. In the second, you wish you were dead.

Polar tourism is confined to the summer, which lasts from June to September in the north and from November to March in the south. Some operators have also developed creative itineraries in Melanesia or isolated Atlantic Islands to generate revenue from their ships' repositioning voyages.

Arctic travel now focuses mainly on Svalbard, Greenland, the Canadian High Arctic, Alaska or, until the Ukraine war, the Russian Far East. You can sometimes trace the North-West and North-East passage – easier these days due to reduced sea ice in summer. Antarctic itineraries focus on the peninsula, South Georgia or the Ross Sea, Macquarie or Auckland Islands. Semi- or full circumnavigations or visits to remote parts of the Weddell Sea are rarer.

Today's programs are a concession to comfort, cost and strict timetables dictated by commercial tourism. In 2009, on an emperor penguin expedition, the *Khlebnikov* became stuck in sea ice near Snow Hill Island. Alongside tourists, a BBC crew filming for the documentary series *Frozen Planet* were delayed. In 2014, another ship, attempting to replicate part of explorer Douglas Mawson's 1912 voyage, became trapped off Antarctica. A Chinese icebreaker managed to rescue the passengers after a considerable delay, only to become stuck itself.

The itineraries are standardised. Arctic voyages start from Tromsø, Longyearbyen in Svalbard or a Northern Canadian port. Alaskan cruises leave from Seattle, Vancouver, Sitka or Seward. In the Russian Far East, you begin at Anadyr or Petropavlovsk-Kamchatsky. The vast majority of visitors to Antarctica sail from Ushuaia in Argentina, Punta Arenas in Chile or a south New Zealand port. For a premium, travellers can now even leapfrog the notoriously rough two-day journey across Drake's Passage by flying to the South Shetland Islands and boarding their ship there.

In Alaska, passengers typically travel to Johnstone Strait, the Inside Passage and Glacier Bay. A Canadian high Arctic cruise explores Nunavut, Davis Strait and Lancaster Sound. Greenland will mean Disko Bay and llulissat Icefjord, a UNESCO World Heritage Site with actively calving glaciers. You will inevitably be informed that the iceberg that sank the *Titanic* likely originated here.

In the South, travelling along the Antarctic Peninsula, you will visit Deception Island, sailing through Neptune's Bellows, a narrow gap in the wall of the semi-submerged caldera of an old volcano. There is sublime Lemaire Channel, a narrow alley full of white and luminous blue icebergs bordered by snow cliffs, some more than 1000 metres (3300 feet) high. Another stop will be Paradise Bay, with its icy peaks and glaciers. The circuits resemble the obligatory Grand Tour for the wealthy, or medieval pilgrimage routes for the devout.

Onboard, activities and amenities are designed to keep passengers entertained and occupied between scheduled excursions. A lecture program by polar historians, geologists and naturalists is a typical highlight, though celebrity speakers, mainly television and internet personalities and popular authors, are increasingly replacing experts. Outings from the ship are designed to take in scenery, wildlife, historical sights and local communities. An expanding range of outdoor activities, including camping on ice, hiking, mountaineering, skiing, kayaking or polar scuba diving, is available to tourists.

On our trip, like most, zodiacs took us to and from landings. A wet landing requires waterproof rubber boots for navigating hopefully shallow water. A dry landing entails aligxhting on rocks or a dry spot. Dry landings turn wet when plans change.

Larger vessels now launch their zodiacs from a civilised internal dock, avoiding a hazardous embarkation and disembarkation. The *Khlebnikov* and today's smaller vessels, with its fewer trimmings, require negotiating a narrow, steep gangway to the zodiacs. The driver positions the craft against the side of the ship. You hop on during the brief instant when everything is aligned. You sit down quickly on the edge and slide towards the front or rear. Getting back on board requires reversing the procedure.

Off a sub-Antarctic island in a 3-metre (10-foot) swell, the gap between the zodiac and bottom of the gangway moves ominously. The driver brings his craft in as the ship rocks. The first passenger jumps onto the gangway, helped by two sailors. As the next passenger tries to embark, the ship dips sharply, plunging the crew and the passenger into water up to their necks. Their life jackets open, triggered by immersion in water.

Waiting on the zodiac scheduled to dock next, we look on. After radio chatter between the drivers and the bridge, the ship swings around into the swell, making the transfer easier. In this temperature, you have maybe ten minutes unless you are wearing a survival suit. Hypothermia causes your core body temperature to fall and your bodily functions soon turn off.

The *Khlebnikov* carried three Soviet light-utility helicopters, a rare thing these days. On the first day of flight operations, as we wait to board, the engine on one blows up on take-off. While rudimentary, the sturdy helicopters allow us to visit spots inaccessible by zodiac, such as the Ross Ice Shelf and the top of tabular icebergs. They permit trips inland, such as to the Dry Valleys, one of world's most extreme deserts, located in Victoria Land, west of McMurdo Sound.

Ice conditions force the ship to anchor a long way offshore. The flight to the Dry Valleys is at the limit of the helicopter's range. The pilot keeps calculating and recalculating the point of no return, the position at which we would have insufficient fuel to return to the ship.

Just after take-off, the unlatched helicopter door swings open and bangs against the side. A woman in her eighties is sitting next to the door. Unbuckling her seatbelt, she calmly reaches out, grabs the door and re-latches it. Resuming her seat, she clicks in her belt and gives me a toothy grin.

There are other risks, which we have fortunately not had to deal with. In the Canadian Arctic, a group stayed at a temporary tented camp on the line of life, the edge of frozen seawater. The trip was to see – if nature cooperated – unicorn-like tusked narwhals as they swam and fed. In the middle of the night, the guests were awoken by their Inuit guides and told they were moving out in five minutes. Ice conditions had changed. The camp area was breaking up. Abandoning tents and possessions, they boarded snowmobiles and sped towards the shoreline. As they travelled away from their camp, they could hear the ice cracking and opening up. Seawater seeped through. They made it to safety after an anxious ride across the fracturing ice.

The polar regions are cold deserts largely empty of life and without, for the most part, permanent human habitation. They are ruled by an icy nomenclature.

Nilas, new thin sea ice up to 10 centimetres (4 inches) thick, bends without breaking around waves and swells. Dark nilas is thin. Thicker nilas is a lighter colour. Recently frozen ice is made up of frazil, plates or spicules of ice suspended in water; slush, water-saturated snow; or shuga, small spongy lumps of ice. Grease and pancake are crystal accumulations differentiated by thickness into grey ice and grey-white ice. Fast ice is attached to the shoreline, and its boundary marks the border with the sea. Drift ice occurs offshore, moving with currents and wind. It consists of a shear zone, a marginal ice zone and a central pack. Leads and polynyas are areas of open water within expanses of sea ice.

Where floes are driven together, compression creates ice rafts or ridges. Rafted ice occurs when one piece overrides another. Pressure ridges are lines of broken ice forced downward (keel) or upward (sail). A hummock is a hillock of broken ice that forms an uneven surface. A shear ridge is more linear than one induced only by compression. A new ridge is sharp-crested, with its side sloping at an angle exceeding 40 degrees. A weathered ridge has a rounded crest and sides sloping at less than 40 degrees.

Icebergs, some giants, are intricately sculpted with crevasses, grottos, spires and flutes. Massive tongues of ice and glaciers extend as far as the eye can see. White, grey, blue and black dominate. Brilliant shards of colour are tricks of refracting light. In mist, you might see a fog bow, an ethereal white rainbow caused by sunlight hitting the water droplets.

It is a world of silence punctuated by rumbles of cracking and moving ice or an iceberg, calving or rolling. Desolate, transient but timeless, it elicits primal sentiments. Norwegian explorer Fridtjof Nansen wrote of the incomprehensible attraction of an overwhelming luminous light. He heard silence in a way that he had never done before. The wind, when it blew, possessed a sonic force that pounded his ears. It is what George Eliot termed the roar on the other side of calm. In the *Duino Elegies*, Rainer Maria Rilke recorded a beauty where terror begins. The Arctic and Antarctic are those places.

Once the initial novelty diminishes, some find the scenery monotonous. They shuffle about taking photos and making small talk. They gorge on themed buffets or complain about the food. In this, they are not alone. Physician Mike Stroud, who tried to walk across Antarctica with British explorer Ranulph Fiennes, admitted that he didn't appreciate the stark beauty as for most of the time he was miserable.

Even in pristine polar regions, the history of human activity is everywhere. On the black cinder of Whaler's Beach on Deception Island, the ruins of an old Norwegian whaling station and British Antarctic Survey huts remain. At Cape Evans on Ross Island, you can visit the forlorn but well-preserved hut where Scott's fateful expedition based itself. Nearby, a steep volcanic cone known as Observation Hill provides a commanding view inland across the ice shelf. A cross marks the spot where Scott's companions kept a vigil for the party that had set off for the South Pole, never to return. It is a reminder of the dangers at the ends of the Earth.

These extreme climes are not devoid of wildlife, and there are large populations of some species, especially seabirds. The Arctic has terrestrial mammals – bears, wolves, foxes, wolverines, musk ox, reindeer or caribou, hares and rodents. There are only marine mammals in the Antarctic.

In the north, the polar bear sits at the apex of the food chain. In the south, it is the reptilian leopard seal. About 3 metres (10 feet long) long and weighing 370 kilograms (800 pounds), it is a powerful hunter with jaws that open 160 degrees and fangs bigger than an adult lion. Krill, fish and squid are its primary diet. In summer, it opportunistically hunts seal pups and penguins around rookeries. It sometimes toys with prey, letting it escape, recapturing it, flinging it around, and skinning it before devouring it.

The northern Pacific is home to bowhead whales, specially adapted for the cold waters they inhabit all year around. A massive bow-shaped skull over 5 metres (16 feet) long, comprising about 30 to 40 per cent of their total body length, allows them to break through thick ice with their head. Their blubber layer, up to 50 centimetres (20 inches), is thicker than that of any other whale. They use a form of echolocation to steer around icebergs and other obstructions. Old harpoon points lodged in some specimens suggest individuals may live for up 200 years. The oldest whales, around when Melville wrote *Moby-Dick*, could provide a history of humans' attempts to exterminate them.

Sea lions and seals occur at both extremities. On rocky Antarctic beaches, giant mounds of grunting, bellowing, odorous elephant seals rest. Sumo-like playfights between younger males anticipate serious and bloody contests for mating rights. Alongside crabeater and Ross seals, Antarctica is also home to the Weddell seal, the most southerly living mammal. During winter, they breathe through blow holes in the ice, which they open up with their canine teeth. Sometimes, you can hear their ancient songs beneath the ice. The north has walrus, and ribbon seals, which are distinguished by two white strips and circles contrasting with their dark brown or black fur.

There are around 100 bird species in the Arctic and forty in the Antarctic, mostly seabirds or migrants visiting feeding or breeding grounds in the brief polar summer. The Arctic has auks or alcids, the northern equivalents of penguins. In the auk family there are around twenty living species of murres, guillemots, auklets, puffins and murrelets. In the Russian Far East, we see a large flock of crested auklets wheel synchronously overhead in a spectacular show.

Clumsy flyers due to short wings, auks are excellent swimmers and divers, well suited to taking small fish. Their hunting technique becomes inefficient in warmer waters, where the fish are larger. Generally found in the open sea, they come ashore in summer, nesting in large colonies in cliffs and sea stacks. Some lay eggs that are narrow and pointed at one end. One theory is that the design prevents them from accidentally rolling off their precarious nests.

Penguins are a cosmopolitan bunch found almost exclusively in the southern hemisphere. Only the emperors and Charlie Chaplin-esque Adélies are truly polar, spending their entire lives in Antarctica or close to its shores. There are the long-tailed varieties: colourful gentoos and elegantly decorated chinstraps. There are dandies with extravagant head feathers – macaronis and royals. Snares have bushy eyebrows. Erect cresteds have twin mohawks. Rockhoppers feature wild crowns and dreadlocks. Yellow-eyed penguins have golden eyes and streaked yellow feathers. Emperors and kings, as their names imply, are giants.

In penguins, hollow, air-filled bones have given way to solid, ballasted ones. Unlike auks, whose wings are a compromise between diving and flying, their southern cousins have stiff flippers. Penguins fly in water, not in the air.

In Antarctica, you smell, hear and see penguins around guano-splattered rookeries. Despite the cacophony, each penguin can identify its mate's and chick's voice. The bonds between pairs and squabbles over real estate and stones can entertain for hours. At sea, sometimes the water boils with hundreds of penguins. Some porpoise out of the water to avoid predators.

At Cape Adare, the Adélie colony contains 250,000 birds. When we visit, it is the end of the nesting season and thousands of grey downy chicks are moulting. Waiting for their parents to return from fishing, the chicks chase any returning adult, pleading for food. The parents regurgitate a mix of krill and squid into the hungry mouths. At the gravel beach, adults gather warily. Diving in together, they swim quickly through the water to avoid patrolling leopard seals and orcas.

The living mix with the dead. In places, the snow is blood-stained. Fat brown skuas, predatory seabirds, exterminate weaker chicks ruthlessly, literally pecking them to death. They make a hole in the body to extract the flesh and organs. Petrels, ocean vultures and sheathbills (very white pigeon-like scavengers) patrol the rookeries, eliminating carcasses.

On Macquarie Island, thousands of extroverted king penguins surround our ship, trumpeting and splashing with excitement. On the beach, they follow visitors with their comical rolling gait. A woman wearing a very colourful rain jacket catches the attention of some kings. One bends his head, extends his neck and gives the woman a peck with his beak from behind. Another strides up to several large, sleeping elephant seals, pausing for a look and then, quickly and surreptitiously, gives one a violent peck on its nose before retreating.

Visitors may see the expressive behaviours as human. Yet we barely understand these creatures, as most of their lives take place at sea.

If Antarctica has an icon, it is the emperor penguin. Reaching 130 centimetres (50 inches) in length and weighing up to 40 kilograms (90 pounds), they are largest living penguins. They breed during the Antarctic winter when air temperatures may reach minus 40 degrees Celsius (minus 40 degrees Fahrenheit) and wind speeds can be 140 kilometres (90 miles) per hour.

Emperors are best seen in spring at their breeding colonies, before the chicks have fledged and the birds disperse. Our semi-circumnavigation of Antarctica is timed for the late southern summer, a concession to sea ice conditions and navigability. We do not expect to see them.

As we sail across the Amundsen Sea, a figure is spotted on the ice around midnight. The PA announcement is succinct: 'Emperor.' Sergey, the officer on watch, stops the ship in front of the floe where the bird stands. Despite the hour, passengers pour onto the deck to take photos and videos. In the twenty-four-hour daylight of high latitudes, where sunset and sunrise merge, we get good views before the bird dives into the ocean and disappears.

During the night, groups of emperors are continually spotted. By morning we have seen over fifty. Most drop onto their rotund stomachs and paddle away across the ice. Some dive into the water and reappear on a more distant floe. One bird waddles over. The black back and silvery-white breast shines. The sulphur yellow-and-orange bib is superb. Suddenly, the individual raises his head and trumpets excitedly.

Over the next few days, we see several hundred emperor penguins, surprising the naturalists on board. It seems we are passing through part of their summer range.

Later, we see an emperor penguin on the Ross Ice Shelf, the largest ice shelf in Antarctica – about the size of France. The bird is standing on the edge, looking down the sheer 20-metre (66-feet) vertical edge to the water. It may have walked there from the Cape Crozier colony, 100 kilometres (60 miles) to the west, or climbed up a collapsed snow ramp. With no obvious way to the sea, it will have to walk back or find another way to the water or it will become trapped. Polar environments do not tolerate mistakes.

There is something odd about polar visitors. In the Arctic, a cruise to the North Pole is anti-climactic. After noisy ice-bashing, you are told that the ship has reached 90 degrees north. Amid great fanfare, champagne corks pop and you take a polar plunge for obscure reasons. You climb down onto the edge of the ice floe or a hole that has been cut and have a brief dip in freezing cold water, tethered by a rope to avoid being sucked under the ice. Some do it naked.

In the Antarctic, we stop at rarely visited Peter I Island, a forlorn volcanic outcrop. The *Khlebnikov*'s helicopters spend five hours dropping off nine ham radio operators and their equipment. They will stay for two weeks, transmitting to other amateurs around the world before being picked up by another ship. The point of the exercise is lost on us.

A consumerist and technological reality increasingly mediates every aspect of human life, sometimes overwhelming us. Inventions save human labour, increase production or exploit nature. We accept their intrusions without question.

In his 1933 *In Praise of Shadows*, Japanese novelist Jun'ichirō Tanizaki highlighted a different approach. He thought that those in the East sought satisfaction in the conditions they found themselves. Darkness caused no discontent as it was inevitable. Night had its particular beauty. Westerners sought to change conditions. So from candle to oil lamp to gaslight through to electric light, they embarked on a quest to remove even the minutest shadow.

It is the contrast between a compulsion for purpose or progress and the notion of things being just what they are. Travel to polar regions, deep oceans or space is undertaken because it is feasible. There is a belief that the value of wilderness is in how humans can use it. Even if the aim is laudable, such as educating tourists about the natural world by immersing them in its beauty, we still damage ecosystems in our determination to see them.

Reflecting now on that Antarctic trip raises questions for us – queries that did not occur to us at the time, but now feel pressing and urgent. Just because we can travel to a remote location, does that mean we should? What might we be destroying in the process? How long can a wilderness remain wild once it has been discovered by humans, even those who claim to love nature?

7

SHOW ME THE MONEY

The Business of Ecotravel

The plains wanderer is a mottled brown ground bird found only in a small patch of Australia. Once thought to be related to game birds or wading shore birds, it is now in its own family, *Pedionomidae*. The bird is critically endangered due to the loss of its native grasslands, which have been largely taken over by agriculturalists. Poor fliers who rely on their cryptic colouring for camouflage, they are also easy prey for introduced foxes and feral cats.

Since the 1980s, one enterprising guide has run tours to see this enigmatic bird on a private property near Hay in south-east Australia. Birders from around the world come to see this species before it is extinct. The search takes place at night – the guide drives around in a four-wheel-drive with spotlights to try to find a plains wanderer. The process requires stamina: starting before dusk, it can sometimes end around 2.00 or 3.00 am. There is no guarantee of success. Often, you get a fleeting glimpse of the bird before it scuttles off into thick grass.

The accidental discovery of this population was the origin of the guide's business. With limited choices, the birds come back to the same area each year, despite the relentless hounding by birders seeking to add to their lists.

Ecotourism is one long supply chain. It is a major logistical undertaking. Planes, trains, ships, automobiles, horses and donkeys transport tourists to the location, where they are accommodated and fed. There is special travel attire, luggage, travel and field guides. There are cameras, optical equipment, phones and computers, replete with chargers and electrical plugs for every geography. Most tourists are inoculated and insured. Once there, guides help to find the animals and assist with identification.

It starts with an agency. For those of a certain vintage, this is a shopfront, actual people and a particular décor – maps on walls, multiple clocks set to different time zones, posters of exotic locations and glossy brochures. For younger generations, it is the dematerialised reality of websites and apps.

Cox & Kings, among the oldest travel agencies, traces its history back to 1758, when it was appointed general agent to the regiment of foot guards in India. It grew from arranging travel for British military forces posted overseas to a premium-brand Indian travel agency. In 1840, Bernardo Abreu opened his agency in Porto, Portugal, selling train tickets to Lisbon and return passage by ship to South America, as well as associated passport and visa services. Around the same time, Thomas Cook, a Baptist preacher and advocate for the temperance movement, arranged for Midland Railway to transport members to a rally. Thomas Cook & Son would become the booking clerks to the British Empire. Its successor operated as a travel agent until its bankruptcy in 2019. In the late nineteenth century, Walter Brownell founded one of the first agencies in the United States, leading travellers on European trips.

A travel agent arranges transport, transfers, hotels, restaurants, recreational activities, cruises, guides and insurance, as well as providing foreign currency services and information. They are compensated mainly by commissions, paid by the local operators who will provide the service. Over time, firms began pre-booking flights, hotels and cruises, receiving discounts for early bulk purchases. They bet on being able to on-sell tickets to customers at higher prices. Some started operating airlines and hotels and packaging tours. Today, the business of arranging travel is a complex multi-billion-dollar for-profit undertaking. Whether you like it or not, they are the gatekeepers to your journey.

The post–World War II boom created a golden age for travel agencies. Travellers had money to spend but needed help making arrangements. Information, communications, language and foreign currencies were major barriers for the uninitiated. There was fear of the unknown in what was then a novel undertaking. Agents were reassuring presences, making sure all went smoothly and expectations were met.

Over time, travellers grew more confident in making their own arrangements. Bypassing agents, eliminating agent commissions or fees, lowered costs. Airlines and hotels, eager to build brands, preferred to deal directly with customers. The internet and apps accelerated online bookings, especially for flights, hotels, conventional tours or packages.

Despite appearances, the internet DIY holiday is not what it seems. The middlemen survive behind the pixelated screens. The same package deals are sold virtually rather than via shopfronts. Bookings go through computer reservation systems or global distribution systems such as Amadeus, Galileo or Sabre. The process involves consolidators, who wholesale airline tickets, buying up seats at a discount unavailable to the public. Many online travel sites, metasearch engines and scrapers (online information retrieval tools that use web searches to extract data and produce results rebranded under their name) lack access to these booking systems. The result is that the customer is routed through multiple service providers, incurring hidden costs.

Some agents reinvented themselves. The pitch shifted to offering clients a special relationship, much like that with their personal trainer, nutritionist or spiritual advisor. Travel was presented as transformative, a shortcut to a new self, which the agent could deliver because of their intimate understanding of the client's needs. Safe and boring standard fare was repackaged into chiselled itineraries promising personalisation, adventure or exoticism. The focus was on self-actualisation, a desire for the ineffable. Incongruities thrived: a finely curated itinerary must not be rigid; a tight schedule should not preclude time for reflection, self-realisation and karmic providence.

Today, travel agencies adeptly promote their services using fear of an expensive and embarrassing DIY mistake based on misinformation and fake online reviews. No one wants to star in their own horror story. And someone needs to be ready to airlift you out at the first sign of trouble.

Like any travel agent, wildlife agents must be knowledgeable about areas and opportunities. They should be able to arrange lodging close to the wilderness sites, specialist guides and transport to get their client to and from remote locations. Accommodation is not a simple matter of booking a hotel: many wilderness areas rarely see visitors, especially foreigners. This is the world of the best available.

The infamous Green Hotel at Yabelo in Ethiopia was for many years the only accommodation near certain birding sites. It was so charmless that one birder had t-shirts printed with the slogan 'I survived the Green Hotel'. In Asia and Papua New Guinea, there is the homestay, a local village bed-and-breakfast of uncertain quality. In the Western Sahara, travellers stay in a desert camp without toilets or washing facilities. One must be prepared to 'go' behind nearby dunes. But the area holds the promise of rarely seen wildlife – fennec foxes, sand cats, golden jackals, Saharan striped polecats, desert hedgehogs and pharaoh eagle-owls.

When Jade and I began travelling to see wildlife, many state-run guesthouses in Africa required resourcefulness. We brought our own lightbulbs, rubber sink stoppers, towels and soap. Private lodges were rustic old hunting lodges or settlers' homes, sustained by the stubborn clichés of *White Mischief* and *Out of Africa*. Warthogs grazed the lawns during the day and hippos foraged at night. Today, adventure no longer means sacrificing comfort. Africa, a model of ecotourism, now offers six-star lodges, renowned for their architecture, cuisine, cellars, spas and impeccable service. Camping is glamping or flashpacking.

In 1994, on our Antarctic voyage, communication back to civilisation was via expensive radio or satellite telephones. Twenty years later in the Russian Far East, there was no mobile or internet coverage. Today, even the most remote ecotourist locations are expected to cater for social-media-obsessed, connected travellers.

True explorers would disapprove. Wilfred Thesiger, who crossed the Empty Quarter of the Arabian Peninsula on foot and camel, loathed the advent of equipment that reduced hardship and danger. Modern ecotourists are not willing to venture that far beyond their comfort zone.

Many ecotourism agencies are founded by nature lovers. An interest in animals led them to become guides or wildlife photographers, which in turn led them to start their own tour companies to monetise their passion.

Others find their way into the industry by a different route. In his book on British birdwatching, *A Bird in the Bush*, Stephen Moss recounts the story of Nigel Redman and Chris Murphy. In 1978, they undertook a ten-month journey from Britain to Nepal, covering more than 8000 kilometres (5000 miles), to see as many different species of birds as possible. They managed almost 1000. On his return, Redman was asked to become a tour leader at Birdquest – Mark Beaman, the company's founder, wanted someone with knowledge of birding sites in Asia for his birding tour company. Redman abandoned a career as an accountant and has been a tour leader ever since, seeing around half the bird species on the planet in the process.

A successful business requires scale. A few prosper growing into corporate behemoths. Larger operations bring different headaches – marketing, administration, insurance, tax, regulations, employees, contactors and, most of all, customers. Some business owners find that it leaves little time for their real interest – watching wildlife. They may choose to shut up shop and work for other operators as a guide instead. Many now use a franchise model: the operator does the promotion and marketing, arranges the logistics, and takes care of insurance and finances on behalf of individual guides.

Over time, what began as a low-key alternative to mass travel became co-opted by the mainstream. Traditional operators, sensing a lucrative new prospect, began to offer ecotourism trips with five-star luxury. The industry became the antithesis of what it aspired to be.

Businesses models vary. Inbound agencies concentrate on local itineraries for foreign customers. They theoretically cater for locals but few in developing countries can afford the cost of wildlife tourism. Outbound agencies arrange overseas trips for locals using the services of an inbound operator in the relevant country. Like many-handed Indian gods, some combine both activities. You might book with a local agent specialising in wildlife travel. They, in turn, use an inbound agent who might sub-contract to other operators, and so on.

The lengthy chain makes for miscommunication. Jade and I habitually provide detailed information on our preferences, which rarely make it to the ultimate service provider. During World War I, a British unit supposedly sent a message famous in the annals of military folklore: 'Send reinforcements, we are going to advance.' It was received at headquarters after relay by countless intermediaries as: 'Send three and fourpence, we are going to a dance.' Our communications generally end the same way.

Despite claims of customisation, wildlife itineraries are relatively fixed. Expectations of emulating Darwin, Wallace, or Lewis and Clark are unlikely to be met.

The key choice is between travelling in a group or privately. On a group package tour, you find yourself with sundry others following a script of flights, minibuses, hotels, set meals and activities. Sharing the cost of guides and vehicles makes it all cheaper. For many, the regimentation and the likelihood of being surrounded by travellers with similar aims is reassuring.

This may well be the case, but in group travel Jade and I have found ourselves teamed with travellers of different nationalities and ages, ranging from teenagers to octogenarians. Interests and intensity of focus differ, as does mobility and stamina. Some resent the pre-dawn reveilles. The importance placed on meals – breakfast, morning tea, lunch, afternoon tea, cocktails or sundowners, dinner, supper, postprandial libations – varies between travellers. Punctuality and organisation are not universal virtues. Interpersonal dynamics quickly manifest. Common or differing interests, mutual likes and dislikes, as well as personality traits, determine allegiances and antipathies. Individual acts, such as hogging favoured seats, become an exaggerated slight.

Accommodating preferences in a group tour is difficult. The unpredictable nature of wildlife viewing requires flexibility and patience. Animals rarely abide by schedules. Should a desired animal appear, not everybody can get a view, let alone a good or photogenic one. The time to linger is limited. The stage is set for acrimony and recriminations. Our friend Raffa, who runs an ecotourism business in Chile, ruefully stated about groups: 'I do not discuss. I tell them what we are going to do. We follow the plan. It is the only way!'

We started with group tours, a concession to our lack of knowledge and finances. We now favour private arrangements, the two of us with a guide and perhaps a driver. It is costly, but there is greater scope to adjust for interests and conditions. It provides a better understanding of the places and the people, and better chances for seeing wild creatures.

But you cannot avoid groups entirely. Our Baja California cruise on the *Sea Lion* was a photographic expedition organised by *National Geographic* and Lindblad. This was no ordinary journey. We would, it was drummed into us, be 'exploring'! There were fifty passengers, mostly retired Americans. Close study of our shipmates gave new meaning to the Lindblad Expeditions' slogan, 'Explore with experience'. Our presence lowered the average age significantly, which was well above three score years and ten.

They were Lindblad people. Many knew one another, having done several 'Lindblads', the founder's name doing yeoman's service as noun, verb and adjective. Some had taken the same cruise before, several times, revealing either a deep affection for the region or a limited imagination. We were made cautiously welcome, our outsider status reinforced by the fact that, unlike our fellow passengers, we were not camera-toting amateur photographers. Coexistence required avoiding drawing attention to ourselves.

The way it worked was quickly and unhappily clear. Routing avoided subjecting the ancient mariners to ocean motion. Water conservation on small vessels requires two-minute sailor showers – wet the body (30 seconds), lather with the shower turned off (30 seconds), then rinse off (60 seconds). Our plutocratic companions required frequent and long ablutions. As freshwater storage was limited, the ship was forced to make frequent unscheduled stops to top up its tanks. A crew member joked about expedition rules: 'Avoid rough water; request the leviathan to be directly ahead of the boat and not during meal times.'

On the last afternoon, alone on deck, I saw a Bryde's whale blow, but the ship did not change direction to follow it. Everyone else was below deck, sharing or comparing their photographs. The two-dimensional, manipulated images cannot compare to the real thing.

The sales pitch of modern ecotourism is about getting close to wild animals. It is about doing something unique, and bringing back stories, memories and photos. You are a pioneer who has a privileged, personal view of the world's natural wonders, along with a few like-minded others.

The marketing typically features gorgeous photos of wildlife. The copy overuses certain adjectives – *exceptional*, *extraordinary*, *breathtaking*, *inspiring* and, perhaps most frequently, *priceless.* Suitably rugged-looking guides dedicated to ensuring that you miss nothing will add to your understanding and appreciation, it says. Everything will coalesce into a cohesive narrative.

Most operators' websites prominently display reports on past trips prepared by tour leaders or guides to market their itineraries. These trip reports, which usually show that everything was seen well and most things went brilliantly, are deceptive. Their accuracy cannot be verified unless you were on the particular trip. It may be of an especially successful expedition. Like the health warning on most financial investments, past performance is not a guide to future outcomes, at least yours. Our Antarctica cruise had calm seas, favourable weather and unusually good wildlife sightings. Years later, one of the guides told us that our voyage is still talked about.

There are subtle reasons for the differences between the advertised version and the reality. Unless you are dealing with local on-the-ground firms and guides, the marketing spiel is likely from an outbound operator, based on a reconnaissance or an early trip. The local firm will try to guarantee good outcomes, to ensure the foreign operator sends more clients their way.

Even after thirty years of journeys, trips are still a challenge for us to arrange. We try to deal directly with locals, believing that this will best meet our needs and benefit the destination's economy and communities. We regularly encounter difficulties. Recommended agencies do not reply. The inbound operator turns out not to be what he or she claims. Tourist guides are passed off as wildlife specialists. What is promised is not delivered. The requirements of two independent travellers unlikely to return are secondary to the demands of large tour operators, repeat customers. That said, some firms relish leading individuals or couples, allowing them to go to places that they only visit infrequently.

Ultimately, nature is unpredictable; animals do not show on demand. Even with the best plans you may not see what you came for. Luck is the crucial differentiator. Like Napoleon Bonaparte, who favoured lucky generals over good ones, we hope for fortunate as well as good operators and especially guides, who are vital to wildlife viewing.

When published in 1869, Alfred Russel Wallace's *Malaya Archipelago* revealed South-East Asia's rich flora and fauna to Western audiences for the first time. But Wallace's romantic representation as a solitary explorer is deceptive. Hundreds of unacknowledged indigenous guides and hunters guided him, collecting and preserving specimens.

Wallace's best assistant was Ali, a young Malay boy. He was crucial to the naturalist's achievements, remaining with him throughout his time in South-East Asia. Ali's contribution is barely recognised, especially in the occidental canon. Wallace, like other nineteenth-century naturalists, shared prevailing colonial attitudes on race, gender and class relations.

Wallace is not an outlier. Upon reaching a peak in the Snow Mountains, part of the New Guinea's central cordillera, a recent Western explorer celebrated being the first person to ever visit the area. He had travelled along trails created by indigenous tribes who had lived there for millennia and was being guided by their descendants.

Our guide in the far south of Madagascar worked briefly as a field assistant for an Australian biologist who had visited the small private reserve to research a bird. The guide was promised feedback on the findings, which he never received. Learning we live in Australia, the guide asked if I could follow up with the scientist. I tracked down the biologist, who refused to take calls or answer emails. In the end, I found and sent our guide his paper, which had no acknowledgement of local assistance.

Without a skilled guide, you will see little. In Australia's Cape York Peninsula, we searched for night birds. On several occasions, we saw

Papuan frogmouths, eyes bright in the spotlight beam. Our guide, Klaus, led us in search of a greater prize – a marbled frogmouth. In the pitch-dark rainforest, something flew soundlessly into a nearby tree, responding to a recorded call. Klaus unerringly found the bird with his flashlight. The marbled frogmouth called in response to the playback: a high *coo-lew* followed by a lower one, then a loud tocking, then a laugh, finished off by a repeated gobbling noise. It is one of the strangest calls in the avian world. Without Klaus, we would never have found the bird or even known where to look.

Wildlife guiding is challenging work. Animals are difficult to find or identify. The environment is frustratingly changeable – even if you saw the animal or bird in a location a few hours ago, finding it again is not assured. It is all about understanding the habitat and knowing the quarry's behaviours. Elusive creatures must be coaxed into view. Guides follow tracks and markings, listen for calls signalling presence. They need sharp eyes and acute hearing. One birder complained that his guide wasn't looking, as he seemed to walk the trails with his eyes fixed on the ground. The guide retorted, 'I see with my ears.'

Many are autodidacts, having educated themselves about the animals. Despite a lack of formal credentials, some are more knowledgeable than scientists. Biologists and ecologists sometimes become guides, but scientific training alone does not guarantee the necessary skills. In Ethiopia, we asked for a different guide because the qualified ornithologist was clueless. In the end, our driver, Tade, proved far more informed about locations and adept at finding birds.

Local people, familiar with the environment, can make excellent guides. Hunters can too, using their preternatural senses and understanding of prey. You have to accept a difference in beliefs. Most traditional Inuit would find the concept of vegetarianism incomprehensible, for example. They have to kill wildlife to survive, as nothing grows in their Arctic homeland.

In countries with well-developed wildlife tourism industries, such as South Africa, guides must undergo a demanding formal accreditation program. The examination requires identification of hundreds of bird calls, some which are difficult to differentiate. In a room in an office building, without natural cues, this is not easy. But in most places, you can brand yourself a wildlife guide with little other than chutzpah. In India, guiding is almost a government employment scheme. Guides are allocated by rotation. Many lack the requisite skills or basic equipment. We have had to hire our own guides in addition to the compulsory local, who, if enterprising, has used this opportunity to acquire some useful tips.

There is a hierarchy in guiding. Local or in-country guides work on the ground. In Africa, they are sometimes segregated into guides and trackers, the latter usually skilled at tracking wild animals by their spoor, scat or vocalisations. If you are foreign and travelling in a group, you may also have a tour leader, usually Western and white, who may or may not be knowledgeable about the destination. They are the group's chaperone, the interface between the travelling party and the local guides. Sometimes the local guide is discouraged from talking directly to customers and asked to channel communications through the tour leader.

Unlike foreign tour leaders, local guides must often stay in more affordable accommodation than their charges. This may be guide's quarters, usually a basic dormitory, or cheaper hotels that cater for locals. In some lodges, they are excluded from common areas reserved for guests. On polar ships, where space is at a premium, living conditions for crew are cramped. The meal allowance for staff is a fraction of that for paying guests. It is ecotourism apartheid.

Relations within the hierarchy can be testy. Some underhand operators undertake scouting trips using local guides who they ultimately want to bypass. We have watched foreign guides surreptitiously note GPS coordinates and make detailed reference notes. The incentive is financial: better profit margins. In the Colombian Amazon, we are guests at a small ecotourism project organised by the local community, who operate lodges and provide guides. In the forest, we come across another group that has chosen not to work with the locals. Our indigenous guide tells us not to tell them, if they ask (which they did), where we have just seen the Guinean cock-of-the-rock, the bird they are seeking.

Local guides face multiple barriers. Becoming a guide requires investment in binoculars, telescopes, playback, pointers, spotlights and wildlife books. Increasingly, guides even carry thermal imaging devices to track elusive skulking mammals and birds using their heat signature. This is beyond the financial means of aspirants in poorer countries.

The best guides must undertake enormous amounts of unpaid reconnaissance to allow demanding ecotourists a small chance of seeing secretive species. One we met in north-east Brazil told us about his work with the rarely seen Bahia tapaculo. He had spent months searching for the birds, estimating there were less than ten in an area around 300 square kilometres (80 square miles). When he found one, he spent several weeks living in the forest to understand its behaviours. He then habituated the bird by feeding it mealworms, necessitating a 16-kilometre (10-mile) daily walk from his house over months. Sometimes, after a few months, habituated birds disappear or cease to come to feeding stations, so the whole process must be repeated.

As with all tapaculos, which are typically heard but not seen, any view is brief – if you manage one at all. The guide told us that most birders barely glanced at the bird, anxious only to tick it on their lists. Photographers complained that it wasn't still for long enough or that the light was too poor for a good picture.

Guides and tour leaders are mainly contractors. They are, generally, poorly paid and heavily reliant on tips, which they must degradingly solicit. Operators tempt young guides by promising travel and the pursuit of their passion. The work is seasonal. Some manage to combine specialties, like Arctic and Antarctic guiding, to fill out the year. Otherwise, they must find alternative employment or earn enough to cover the low periods. Many are away from home for long periods. Relationship breakdowns are not uncommon. Our divorced Ugandan guide, Martin, had been unable to attend the birth of his daughter. He sought to earn enough to educate her so she would have better options in life.

Guides we have gotten to know also speak of their poor treatment by bigoted tourists, who see them as incidental and instrumental – merely a means to their ends. Having paid good money, travellers place enormous pressure on guides to find sought-after animals. The ecotourist's schedule and wish lists take precedence over everything, including, at times, the health and welfare of those guiding them in their searches. Meeting expectations constantly is stressful, especially when nature is capricious. In his nightmares, one guide was known to scream about some creature that he had just spotted and needed to show clients.

There is joy in seeing one of the planet's perfect creations in a natural setting, sometimes unexpectedly, especially if this is something you have sought all your life. If you turn to the guide in that moment, their expression will likely be a mixture of happiness and relief.

Specialist clothing is big business. An ecotourist in a popular wildlife location is often kitted out each day in apparel with a dollar cost in the hundreds or thousands. The footwear – waterproof, with high-grip soles and cushioned support – might cost hundreds alone. In extreme climates, weatherproof insulated items are needed, and garments made from high-tech materials are often preferred. There is specially designed ergonomic luggage and other accoutrements. Demand for the best gear benefits branded outdoor clothing and footwear companies.

The benefits to tourists are unclear. On our first trip to see gorillas, Jade and I wore sneakers. One of our party sneered at my footwear, wishing me luck. It was not always easy to negotiate the slippery and muddy trails, but we managed. For the most part, travellers do nothing more strenuous than walking or climbing short distances. Sturdy walking shoes, warm or cool clothing and a good raincoat are generally all that is needed.

The contrast between what kitted-out ecotourists and locals wear is striking. In poorer countries, guides are clad in guest cast-offs or promotional clothing given to them by foreign tour operators. They might be barefoot or in flipflops. In wet or colder places, they wear simple rubber boots.

In the central highlands of Papua New Guinea, I climb to the top of a ridge with our guide at dawn, in search of birds. It takes us about two hours to negotiate the steep, muddy path. As we wait for first light, a staff member from the lodge below arrives with our breakfast. He is barefoot and has shimmied up the same route in half an hour. We are dressed in fleece and rain jackets against the misty rain and early morning chill. He is wearing shorts and a worn t-shirt.

Travellers are advised to be vaccinated against multiple diseases. They are encouraged to take prophylactics against malaria, although simple acts such as covering up at dawn and dusk, using mosquito nets and avoiding high-risk conditions may be just as effective. Our travel medical kit is better equipped than a typical rural clinic in a developing country. Most of the medicines will expire unused. The beneficiaries of this overcaution are pharmaceutical companies.

Wild animals sometimes share the ecotourist's health concerns. A BBC crew member filming in Madagascar told us a rodent visited her hut each night, eating everything, including her anti-malaria tablets.

As ecotourism is about seeing and capturing, it is unsurprising that excess reaches its peak with optics. The global markets for binoculars and cameras in 2023 was around $16 billion. Ecotourists are major consumers of these items, especially high-end gear. While a reasonable pair of wildlife-watching binoculars can be purchased for a few hundred dollars, top-of-the-range brands like Swarovski, Leica and Zeiss cost thousands. Telescopes run into the tens of thousands. The differences are only noticeable in low light and if you have especially acute vision. The price of the equipment is sometimes inversely related to the individual's knowledge of or interest in the animal or bird being watched.

Ecotourism has increasingly oriented itself around photography. Like binoculars, expensive cameras are mandatory accessories for many modern ecotourists. Photographs can play a pivotal role in education, promoting interest in and conservation of wildlife. In practice, they are more likely examples of consumption, sanitised hunting where the lens replaces the gun.

On our trips, we have come across professional photographers who seek out arresting images. Even such commercial photos are not always what they seem to be. London's Natural History Museum runs the prestigious annual Wildlife Photographer of the Year competition. When it started in 1964, it attracted 600 entries. Today it attracts tens of thousands, with famous artists competing with aspirants. In 2009, the winner was controversially stripped of his prize: his picture of an Iberian wolf leaping a cattle pen in Ávila was allegedly staged using a captive animal. In 2018, a prize-winning photo of a giant anteater near a termite mound against a starlit night sky was disqualified: the animal in the photo was suspected of being a taxidermy specimen.

But the bulk of photographers are hobbyists with varied skills and intentions who can be even more problematic. Some look to share their journeys with family and friends. But with the advent of social media, more and more ecotourists are now content generators, searching for the right viral photo or video to impress their followers and increase subscribers. Jade and I have watched, horrified, as camera-toting ecotourists ignore ethical standards and animal welfare in their quest for a defining photograph. Some think nothing of disturbing a feeding or nesting animal. Indiscriminate use of drones, previously only available to specialists, is now depressingly routine. Many online photos and videos use abused captive animals. Most are oblivious to damage to wilderness.

On the Baja photographic expedition, the aggregate cost of the passengers' cameras, lens and paraphernalia would have easily run into the millions. Several *National Geographic* photojournalists were onboard, running workshops and providing personal tutelage. Curiously, most tourists seemed absorbed by technical details – brands, bodies, lens, doublers, image stabilisers, tripods and editing software. Baja California's natural history, scenery and wildlife at times seemed irrelevant, except as an image in their viewfinders.

Patience and skill are no longer mandatory. Overuse of playback allows bird photographers to get the subject into a well-lit spot and exhaust it to be still enough for a shot. In a point-and-hope numbers game, technology focuses the camera automatically, and rapid multiple shutter releases increase the chance of taking at least one random good picture. In Iceland, a visitor tells us that he had taken 6000 photos of one minke whale that day. In Australia, a photographer fires off a thousand shots of a flying black-chested buzzard in seconds. Evenings are spent staring at a computer screen deleting blurry or truncated images. A deficit of even basic technical expertise is not a handicap, as it is not unknown for the guide to actually take the photo for the clients – a kind of intermediated art.

Wildlife photography also encourages reliance on hides and feeding stations. Some are even equipped with special chairs fitted with a discrete pot for the photographers to relieve themselves to avoid missing any photo opportunity that might present itself.

All photographers fantasise about the perfect picture, which creates a tangible and lasting memento of the moment that can be physically or digitally possessed. In the case of the amateurs, this frequently entails mimicry rather than imagination.

Professional photographer Thomas Mangelsen's best-known picture is 'Catch of the Day'. It captures the moment a spawning sockeye salmon leaps over rapids and flies dramatically towards the waiting jaws of a grizzly bear. Shot in 1988 on film before Photoshop became popular, the photograph took Mangelsen months of perseverance.

Fellow professional Tom Walker's best-known photograph is a study of a nesting red-throated loon. The bird is a soft grey-brown. The throat and eyes are subtly different shades of red. The grass stems in the background are gold. The loon sits on the nest, its head slightly raised, perfectly reflected on the still surface of the pond. Walker, ill with a flu-like sickness, waited for days in terrible weather amid clouds of mosquitoes for this shot. It was taken at around 2.00 am. The wind had died down briefly. The sun shone for an instant. The photo captures the fleeting moment the bird raised its head to look at a nearby Arctic fox. It is magic incarnate.

In 2009, Toshiji Fukuda, a Japanese wildlife photographer, managed to photograph a wild Amur or Siberian tiger, one of only a few images of the species taken without a camera trap. There are perhaps 300 of these animals left, and less than twelve in Russia's Lazovsky Nature Reserve on the shore of the Sea of Japan, where the photograph was taken. Fukuda spent months in a hide overlooking a beach where sika deer feed on seaweed on the shore. On day fifty, he was woken by the alarm calls of ravens. There was a tigress less than 150 metres (500 feet) away. In the soft light of a clear morning, the orange and black of the animal contrasts with the white snow. The tigress has her head slightly raised, looking at the camera. It was the only time he saw the animal.

A casual ecotourist is unlikely to capture such original images. At Brooks Falls, where Mangelsen's shot was taken, people are rotated through for short stays on a viewing platform with limited space overlooking the waterfall. They push and shove one another in their determination to reproduce 'Catch of the Day'.

Individuals have the right to spend their money and time pursuing the perfect experience, but it cannot be at the cost of the subject. Who looks at the endless photos of the same popular animals, mostly lacking redeeming aesthetic or other values, that chew up energy in data centres and digital storage?

A key purpose of wildlife photographs appears to be to sell binoculars, telescopes and cameras. Makers sponsor feted photographers to promote their equipment. In this circular economy, wildlife photos feed interest in photographing animals, which, in turn, creates new images, restarting the cycle. The winners are the brands who sell the equipment. But expensive technology is a deception. As French photographer Henri Cartier-Bresson noted, photos are not made with the camera, but with the eye, heart and head. And no matter how ravishing, the pictures are now little more than memento mori, each an elegy speaking to disappearing or threatened wild places and creatures. What if the vast amount of money spent by the average ecotourist on photography, gear and accessories was instead directed towards conservation?

In 2003, the BG Wildlife Photographer of the Year award went to German photographer Gerhard Schulz. The winning photo is of a gorilla and a child in Miami's Metro Zoo. The gorilla is seated in his enclosure behind glass. A reflection shows the child admiring the primate closely related to him in the chain of evolution. The gorilla has a resigned expression. He is a prisoner far from his home. His species, once abundant, is near extinction. There is no place in this world for him and his kind. The only existence that is afforded this magnificent giant is as an object of curiosity. Photographs testify to the natural world's transience and human abuse at every level.

From modest beginnings in 1989, the annual British Bird Fair has grown into a global event that *The Guardian* called the birder's Glastonbury. It is part industry networking conference, part jamboree.

In a normal year, more than 20,000 people attend to visit stands taken out by tour businesses, optics and clothing makers, booksellers and wildlife artists. Over three days, operators from around the world meet one another. Potential customers examine offerings, collect show-bags of free goods and, hopefully, make purchases. There are lectures, celebrity appearances and even visits to the nearby nature reserve. The event is ticketed but sponsored by tour and equipment companies.

Advocates argue that it has democratised birding. The fair supports conservation, generating hundreds of thousands of dollars for worthy charities. Critics argue that it has over-commercialised wildlife. Promoters have used it to further their profile and pocketbooks. Similar events have been launched in South America, Asia, India and Australia.

Wherever you sit in this debate, in gloomier moments, it seems that the almost total commoditisation means it is impossible to see wildlife without entanglement in the insidious dynamics of commerce. The wild animals themselves are like feedstock for the business of ecotourism, which has taken on a life of its own. Somehow, our civilisation's priorities don't seem right.

8

THE ATTENBOROUGH EFFECT

How Wildlife Documentaries Misrepresent Nature

Plato's cave is among Western philosophy's most repeated allegories. Chained inside a cave, a group of people spend their entire lives facing a blank wall, seeing the shadows of objects passing in front of a fire behind them. Not knowing otherwise, the prisoners take the images to be an accurate presentation of the world outside.

It is an apt metaphor of how we perceive reality and why those perceptions are incomplete. Nature documentaries and images of animals and wild places in films, books and advertising deceive us into thinking that we know wilderness. In truth, this knowledge is shaped by highly selective media representations. The version depicted, as in Plato's cave analogy, can be misleading.

Natural history programming draws large audiences. Hundreds of millions tune into blockbuster series such as the BBC's *Our Planet*. Luc Jacquet's 2005 Oscar-winning documentary feature *March of the Penguins* grossed over $127 million. Pay-for-view cable television wildlife channels such as Discovery, National Geographic, Animal Planet and BBC Earth have substantial subscriber bases.

Documentaries, definitionally, speak to verisimilitude. Wildlife filmmakers originally sought to accurately portray the natural world. But technical considerations, audience demands and business necessities forced them to balance fact with entertainment. As a result, what the audience sees is, to a greater or lesser degree, contrived. Skilfully edited footage fits a preconceived script to provide drama and excitement. Sometimes, wild animals are harassed to elicit certain behaviours. Tame, drugged or captured beasts are passed off as wild. Genuine shots are spliced with library footage or portions filmed in a zoo, cage or studio.

The programs mispresent nature, and have become vehicles for the promotion of travel in search of wildlife.

Animals have been a popular subject since Eadweard Muybridge's locomotion series. Early wildlife films showed animals on screen for the first time. Technical limitations meant that early efforts, including the Lumière Brothers 1895 film *Lion*, were filmed in zoos. *The Monkey's Feast*, showing two monkeys eating bananas, made no mention of the fact that the animals were tame. Lacking other frames of reference, people assumed that animal behaviour in captivity was the same as in the wild.

Hunting films were popular. The 1910 feature *Theodore Roosevelt's Return from Africa* documented the former US President's year-long expedition netting over 40,000 taxidermy specimens. Paul J. Rainey's 1912 *African Hunt*, and the French films *Hunting a Polar Bear* (1909), *Hunting Sea Lions in Tasmania* (1910) and *Hunting the Hippopotamus* (1917) were hits at home and abroad. The 1920s and 1930s films of adventurers Osa and Martin Johnson, such as *Trailing African Wild Animals* (1923), attracted large audiences and gave many Western viewers their first look at unknown, faraway places. The travelogue-expedition tradition continued in productions such as Frank Buck's

Bring 'Em Back Alive (1932), a jungle adventure documentary filmed in Malaya.

These films were often presented as fact, but scenes of charging lions, elephants and rhinos were frequently staged. Producer William Selig even established a dedicated facility in Los Angeles to film such sequences. Naturalists objected to the fakery, crass commercialism and conformity to Hollywood norms.

Audiences liked the blood lust and the drama of stalking, capturing or killing animals. A common storyline was humanity's struggle to dominate nature. There were gender and racial stereotypes aplenty. The armed great white hunter led, his wife followed dutifully in tow and unnamed black or brown savages carrying equipment brought up the rear. Animal behaviours were described in human, familial or comic terms.

Despite the falsehoods, the films were backed by museums and natural history bodies. Roosevelt's expedition was financed by the Smithsonian. The Johnsons were able to secure financial support from wealthy patrons. The works were defended as creating a lasting record of the natural world.

Scientific wildlife films were made. After World War I, the German film and television company UFA's Kulturfilm-Abteilung (documentary unit) became leaders in such productions, mainly featuring small animals and shot in a studio due to a lack of money. During the Weimar Republic, they focused on the combat for survival. Under the National Socialists, they conveyed ideological and racist propaganda. Ants and bees were popular subjects, emphasising social efficiency, discipline and sacrifice for the collective good.

After World War II, entertainment values moulded wildlife filmmaking. European filmmakers such as Armand Denis and director of the Frankfurt Zoo Bernhard Grzimek pioneered the use of films to garner public support for conservation efforts. Between 1948 and 1960, Walt Disney produced the *True-Life Adventures* series, a collection of fourteen films including *The Living Desert* (1953), which showed the lives of desert animals in southwestern United States, and *The Vanishing Prairie* (1954), which explored America's disappearing grasslands. Profitable wildlife documentaries helped to finance Disney's expensive animated features, such as *Bambi* (1942), which initially performed poorly at the box office. They addressed distribution problems in an era of double-bill showings, meaning that Disney films did not have to be paired with works from other studios.

Disneyfication meant pretty images of landscapes and animals, edited around a narrative in which animals are anthropomorphised. Cringeworthy voiceovers spouted clichés about natural harmony and the arc of life and death. Cute music underscored the action. Violent and gruesome truths were taboo. Several modern films follow in this tradition: *Born Free* (1966), which is based on the true story of Elsa the lioness, an orphaned lion cub raised by a couple in Kenya and released to the wild; *Le peuple migrateur* (*Winged Migration*, 2001), which shows the immense migratory journeys of birds; and *March of the Penguins* (2005), which follows Antarctica's emperor penguins.

Wildlife documentaries were well suited to the new medium of television and its regime of weekly shows. Beginning in 1950, *Zoo Parade*, hosted by Chicago's Lincoln Park Zoo director Marlin Perkins, showcased animals from the institution's collection. Competing networks launched similar shows – *Wild Kingdom*, *The Natural World* and *Survival*. In 1954, the BBC started airing *Zoo Quest*, introducing a young TV presenter: David Attenborough.

The BBC broadcaster had earlier produced and presented *The Pattern of Animals*, a three-part program on nature. In the course of that series, he met Jack Lester, the curator of the reptile house at London Zoo. Attenborough and a young Czech photographer, Charles Lagus, were invited to accompany Lester to Sierra Leone to capture snakes and a white-necked rockfowl for the zoo's collection.

Originally slated to produce *Zoo Quest*, Attenborough took over as presenter when Lester fell ill after only one instalment, dying in 1956 at the age of forty-seven following several recurrences of an unknown tropical disease. The show enjoyed a successful ten-year run.

The formula was simple. Attenborough joined London Zoo staff on expeditions. While the focus was on collecting specific animals, the format allowed for coverage of other wildlife, local peoples and their customs. The show made technical advances, including the use of 16mm instead of standard 35mm film, allowing the use of colour film stock, which provided better picture quality.

Another important figure to emerge in the 1950s was Jacques Cousteau, a former French naval officer and co-developer of the Aqua-Lung, the first underwater breathing device to achieve global success. In partnership with French film director Louis Malle, Cousteau released *Le Monde du Silence* (*The Silent World*, 1956), featuring pioneering underwater cinematography. Subsequently, Cousteau created two television series: *The Undersea World of Jacques Cousteau* and *The Cousteau Odyssey*.

The blockbuster series expanded the market for wildlife films. Following the success of Kenneth Clark's *Civilisation* and Jacob Bronowski's *The Ascent of Man*, David Attenborough, who designed and produced both, gave the natural world the same treatment, creating the pathbreaking *Life on Earth: A Natural History*. The thirteen fifty-five-minute episodes featured Attenborough travelling the globe to explain the evolution of life on the planet. It inspired many journeys, including ours.

The programs featured rarely seen animals and never-before-recorded events. It revolutionised the presentation of wildlife. In each episode, Attenborough outlined an overarching thesis about a species or behaviour that the footage illustrated. *Life on Earth* paved the way for subsequent series based around particular groups of animals (*The Life of Mammals* or *Birds)* or habitats (*The Blue Planet*, about oceans, and *Life in the Freezer*, on the polar regions). Attenborough became a globally recognisable figure.

These successes produced imitators. Many public broadcasters set up natural history units. Networks commissioned work from independent film production units. While some of these programs showcased previously unseen animals or behaviours and focused on less explored areas, many recycled the same themes and footage.

Where not publicly funded, wildlife series typically rely on prepaid licence fees from broadcasters and distributors with rights to sell the show into other territories. Alternative financing sources include foundations, wealthy philanthropists or corporations. Smaller, low-cost productions are self-financed, including by borrowing from the filmmaker's family and associates.

Natural history documentaries have broad appeal. The programs enjoy large international markets, with around 80 per cent uptake outside the home country. The reasons are obvious. They are generally uncontroversial. There is little about nature and animals, especially in their sanitised presentation, not to like. They are wholesome beacons of hope in a world of rising material comfort but increasing anxiety. Disney's *True-Life Adventures*, *Zoo Parade* or *Zoo Quest* were considered educational. Today, the climate emergency is boosting interest.

Civic and religious support for natural history documentaries was based on their potential to bring households together around television screens. They were consistent with traditional Christian doctrine, espousing humanity's pre-eminence and the exclusion of animals from divine grace. The emphasis on family and parenting was ideal. Religious conservatives praised *March of the Penguins*' portrait of monogamous emperors as upholders of traditional family values. The stoic and hardy birds were hailed as proof of intelligent design, the belief system that rejects Darwin's theory of evolution.

Advertisers found that natural history documentaries could reliably deliver large audiences. The initial focus was on selling pet products, tourism packages, travel equipment and cameras. It expanded to building public awareness and soliciting funds for environmental causes and animal charities. While aspiring politicians are counselled to avoid babies and animals, the power of cute and cuddly creatures to sell goods and services should not be underestimated. Advertising and sponsorship was cheap, as wildlife shows cost less to produce than a typical sitcom, in part because the stars were unpaid.

Private funding meant some wildlife shows were suffused with explicit advertising, the dramaturgy fitting around obligatory commercials. In deference to sponsor Mutual of Omaha, *Wild Kingdom* presenter Marlin Perkins would draw parallels between conservation and insurance, assuring viewers that the firm sought to protect future generations just as the show helped protect the environment.

Advertising and sponsorship dictated content. The story should have a happy ending with the forces of good prevailing. Filmmaker Alan Root's film on the Mzima Springs was rejected by sponsor Kraft. The company's food products, such as cheese and crackers, were incompatible with shots of hippos defecating and hornbills smearing mud and excrement to seal their nests. Today, many advertisers and sponsors are reluctant to explicitly reference climate change.

As cable subscriber numbers peaked and then fell, audience demands, broadcast economics and the exigencies of filmmaking had to be juggled. Power shifted away from wildlife documentary-makers focused on animals to studio executives interested in profitable content.

The well-traversed subject matter made it difficult to find radically different content that appealed to audiences. There are only so many documentaries you can make about lions or Africa. Programs about birds, fish, obscure species or little-known places proved unpopular. Wildlife films became repetitive, as if baked from a standard recipe with stock ingredients.

One solution was technological. Improved cameras, lenses and lighting were deployed to show nature better. Night vision and infrared equipment captured nocturnal footage for the first time. IMAX or 3D formats provided originality. Miniaturisation allowed the use of crittercams, video and audio devices that could be attached to animals or concealed to look like part of the landscape. Self-propelled or manipulated at a distance by an operator, they provided close-ups and different perspectives. The intrusion was justified as allowing observation of rarely seen or recorded behaviours. It was really a marketing gimmick to create new interest in old themes.

Major nature documentary programs take years to make. The technology is expensive, the logistics complex. The original 2001 *Blue Planet* series cost $10 million for a seven-year shoot, at the time the most expensive natural history series created. The 2016 *Planet Earth II* allegedly cost $25 million over five years. These figures became part of the marketing of the programs, another way to renew interest in the genre.

To balance costs, the blockbusters had to be supplemented with smaller, quick and cheap productions. This drove the growth of animal reality shows featuring dangerous animals – crocodiles, snakes and sharks. Heroic presenters who pursued and handled animals attracted large audiences. *The Jeff Corwin Experience*, *Dangerous Encounters with Brady Barr*, *The Crocodile Hunter* and *River Monsters* played to the bold self-image of people living otherwise risk-averse lives.

Unfortunately, the viewer sometimes feels the need to be an active participant. In Costa Rica, we came across a 2-metre (7-foot) boa constrictor curled up in the middle of the road. Manuel, our guide, stopped the car. We wanted to get the reptile off the tarmac, where it risked death or injury. A crowd gathered to see what was happening. One tourist strode confidently towards the reptile and tried to grab it by the head, his snake-handling skills seemingly acquired from watching gung-ho television presenters. The snake rose up, opened its hinged jaws and lunged. Boas are not poisonous but can deliver a nasty bite. The man, now terrified, fell backwards. Manuel eventually managed to coax the snake to the safety of the jungle.

Nature tends to stillness. Animals spend much of their time feeding or resting. True wildlife watching is long periods of inactivity with occasional bursts of action. Documentaries require constant movement and drama to satisfy the audience's short attention span. This forces the use of literary and dramatic archetypes familiar to viewers. Documentaries are made to a predetermined storyline, not driven by the animal behaviours observed or the actual footage shot. The content is directed by budgets, available filming time, audience tastes and sponsor preferences.

Scripts use standard tropes. There is the quest – a difficult journey in pursuit of a goal, with the character overcoming obstacles. The filmmaker may be searching for an animal. A young animal's growth into adulthood, or an adult's migratory journey or mission to find a mate, is another option. Quests lend themselves to symbolism and moral questions about survival, life and death. Another standard formula follows the seasons, allowing the filmmaker to explore wildlife in a particular place. The enduring popularity of Antonio Vivaldi's *Four Seasons* violin concerti demonstrates the perennial potential of natural cycles.

The story must engage audiences, emotionally and intellectually. David Attenborough's first *Zoo Quest* trip was to West Africa in search of a bird that few had ever seen alive – *Picathartes gemnocephalus*, or the white-necked rockfowl, a crow-like bird with a yellow bald head and a skull cap like a black patch. In his autobiography, Attenborough describes being accosted on the street: ''Ere, Dave, are you going to catch that *Picafartees gymno-bloody-cephalus* or aren't you?' The audience had embraced the show.

Animals in wildlife films are sometimes humanised with Kipling-esque names: Sinbad the Gorilla, Heinie the Chimpanzee, Nero the Lion, Judy the Elephant, Faud the Fennec Fox, Sweet William the Skunk. They conform to stereotypes – primates are human-like, lions regal, elephants funny, jackals sneaky, orcas vicious and Beluga whales friendly. Snakes have never recovered from their bad press over the whole Garden of Eden thing. Animals must display human emotions – playfulness, fear, sadness, anger, heroism. The result can be soporific melodrama.

Available footage may not fit the storyline. In Yellowstone, we visited a photographer, in search of the pine martens that frequent his bird feeder. He was monitoring a nearby winter den for some filmmakers engaged in a project about bears bringing up their young. I asked how he could be certain that there was a female with cubs inside. He confessed that he wasn't. When I asked what would happen if time proved him wrong, he drawled: 'Guess they'll make some'in up.' We were unsure if he was serious or being funny.

A surprising number of the sequences in wildlife documentaries are created largely through editing. This requires high shooting ratios – that is, the total footage shot relative to what appears in the final cut. *Blue Planet II* necessitated 125 visits to thirty-nine countries over four years to capture over 6000 hours of footage for seven sixty-minute episodes. *Planet Earth II* is thought to have required 2000 days of filming by forty camera operators in around 200 locations. Huge amounts of time are spent in the studio compiling the feature from the material shot.

Wildlife documentaries can bear little spatial or temporal relationship to reality. Finding and following the same individual over long periods is nearly impossible, especially in difficult terrain such as the polar regions or oceans. Where the viewer is told there is one animal, it may actually be composite footage of several animals filmed separately in different locations. One film purporting to follow a female leopard has her descending a tree. Close inspection reveals she is a he, a la Lou Reed's lyrics, sporting prominent testicles.

Documentary filmmakers cannot always get the footage they want. During our stay at Madagascar's Kirindy Reserve, a film crew were shooting a series on the island's wildlife. They had closed off part of the reserve to film mating fossas, mammalian carnivores unique to the island that look a bit like miniature pumas. Typically, a receptive female occupies a suitable tree and males visit, bringing food. Sexual congress takes place in the tree, which may be used year after year. The filmmakers had identified such a tree. A camera hide was built high off the ground, at great expense, the scaffolding transported in by helicopter. In the finished documentary, we could not find footage of fossas at the mating tree. Perhaps the animals did not use the tree, or the filmmakers were unable to get suitable shots.

One workaround is to use stock footage, if it can be found. In Yellowstone's Lamar Valley, on several occasions we saw an award-winning cinematographer and documentary filmmaker videoing animal behaviours or landscapes for use in future projects as needed. Another is to provoke the required behaviour. For the 1958 Disney documentary *White Wilderness*, crew members hurled lemmings over a cliff to capture the famous footage of them plunging to their deaths. Shots of running animals usually entails chasing them in cars. The famous pink clouds of flamingos taking to the air over Kenya's Rift Valley lakes can be provoked by a low-flying plane or a drone. Night hunting scenes are staged with bright lights to blind prey. Chum, an oily mixture of blood and fish, is used to attract sharks when filming. Calls are used to attract birds.

In *Gorillas in the Mist*, there is a memorable scene in which a silverback charges at Dian Fossey. In his biography, filmmaker Alan Root recalls that the Rwandan gorillas, accustomed to humans, ignored provocations and refused to charge. He jokes that they sat around reminiscing about meeting David Attenborough instead. The actual footage was of Mushamuka, the gorilla Jade and I would later see, in the Kahuzi-Biega Park in the Democratic Republic of Congo. Our guide told us that he had incited the silverback in order to stage the scene.

A documentary on Borneo records tarsiers' reactions to an approaching python. Our local guide had been hired by the filmmakers to catch the snake and place it near the primates to elicit the response.

Footage of wild animals mating, giving birth or interacting with other animals can similarly be faked. A well-known sequence of a polar bear giving birth was shot in a Belgian zoo. Footage of a wolf suckling newborn pups used captive animals in a specially constructed set. Trained bears, lions or tigers conditioned to snarl on command provide close-ups. A bear feeding on a carcass may be a captive animal searching for hidden jellybeans in the entrails of a deliberately slaughtered deer.

Filmmakers wanting to capture snakes hunting their prey routinely use captive specimens placed in close proximity on a set. Ramon, our guide in the Venezuelan Llanos, told us that in order to create an anaconda mating ball, one filmmaker placed an assortment of males with one female in a large oil drum overnight. He then dumped the snakes at a suitable spot to film what appeared to be a writhing mass of bodies trying to mate.

Some of the animals used in wildlife films come from game farms. Most have been caught in the wild. Others are raised from captive breeding stock. Many facilities keep the animals under appalling conditions. Desired responses are elicited using electric cattle prods or piano wire tied around their necks. Most animals are killed when they reach the end of their usefulness.

Sometimes wild animals are temporarily captured. High-speed cameras and bright light is required to film nocturnal fishing bats. It means trapping individuals and habituating them to hunt in a specially created and lit set. In his autobiography, Alan Root details how he filmed captured rare animals such as okapi, tree pangolins and aquatic genets in specially constructed sets. These animals were typically released back into the wild.

At Kirindy, we observed a crew filming a captured paddle-nosed Labord's chameleon. The species spends the majority of its existence (up to nine months) within an egg and lives for only a few months outside it. The captured specimen was being kept in a glass enclosure and hand-fed to allow its entire life cycle to be filmed. It presumably lived out its whole short life in captivity for a few seconds of airtime.

The justification is the scientific merit in recording behaviours that cannot be filmed easily in the wild. David Attenborough admitted to arranging scorpions to mate in a studio, with a painted sunset and Styrofoam clouds. It would take months in the Mojave desert to try to record this event naturally, with no guarantee of success.

Soundtracks of wildlife films require ingenuity. Capturing sound contemporaneously with the action is impractical. For close-ups of a bear or tiger walking in a stream, the noise may be from a sound library or created in the studio, for example by the engineer splashing his hand in a basin of water. Opening and closing an umbrella mimics the sound of a large bird's beating wings. Biting a celery stick approximates a predator tearing into flesh.

In India, we see a sound engineer working on a wildlife series. He has a few days to record various jungle sounds, which will later be synchronised with the footage in post-production. Here, too, there can be errors. The call may not match the bird in shot. Sometimes, the vocalisation is from a bird not even found in the place depicted.

Wildlife documentaries claim realism but the final product is manufactured. Filmmakers say they are after the true story. At least the story part is accurate.

Early wildlife films eschewed graphic content due to the values of studios and sponsors. *Flipper* avoided dolphin's sexual lives, which involve coercive copulation, rampant sex play among males and masturbation.

That did not mean an absence of titillation. Some films featured bare-breasted young indigenous women. In the 1950s, filmmaker Bernhard Grzimek wanted scenes of naked native women dancing to increase the appeal of his *Serengeti Shall Not Die* (1959). The scene was faked using buxom sex workers. Jacques Cousteau's biographer noticed the Frenchman's preference for lingering shots of striking, well-proportioned female divers and marine biologists brushing their long hair. Supposed anthropological context allowed censorship rules to be circumvented.

Over time, sex and violence have become more prominent in wildlife documentaries. Today, close-ups of genitals and slow-motion mating sequences are routine. Violence is pervasive. Crocodiles, snakes and sharks, especially great whites, are demonised. The Discovery Channel has been making high-octane shark programs for more than two decades. Sophisticated cameras capture every detail of attacks on seals or people. The scenarios portray nature as violent, unpredictable and a threat to humans. *Feeding Frenzy* or *Predators at War* depict animals battling one another. *Untamed and Uncut* shows animal attacks on humans, conveniently avoiding the true cause – the victim's own actions or ignorance.

To promote the BBC's *The Trials of Life*, Time Life Video used a collage of attack sequences set to dramatic music. The voiceover proclaimed that the law of the jungle is kill or be killed. David Attenborough objected to the sensationalism, although he has included lurid sequences in his television programs. In one documentary, he controversially used graphic footage of chimpanzees hunting colobus monkeys. Jane Goodall complained about the overemphasis on the blood thirst of chimpanzees when meat makes up about 2 per cent of their diet. Attenborough defended the inclusion, arguing that footage shown was far less explicit than that left on the cutting-room floor.

The fact is that sex and violence sell. Television executives admit that audiences want more extreme, strange or shocking programs. Tabloid films about dangerous poisonous snakes rate better than programs emphasising science or conservation. There is a perverted pleasure in seeing the slaughter of animals. In *The Full Monty*, one character admits that he gets aroused watching nature programs. In an episode of *Friends* titled 'The One with the Sharks', Monica mistakenly believes that her husband, Chandler, is sexually excited by shark documentaries. It may be a simple appeal to our primal instincts; we are still animals, after all.

A cutaway shot interrupts or introduces action in a film without contributing dramatic content. In his documentaries, David Attenborough uses the technique to introduce and narrate each sequence, but primarily to establish his presence on location. In India's Ranthambore Reserve, Jade and I listen to a BBC crew and Valmik Thapar, an Indian naturalist and writer, animatedly discuss camera placements and shooting lines to have him and the tiger in the same frame.

A presenter is not crucial. Alternatives include voiceovers matched to the pictorial images. But following cinema verité custom, the industry favours narrators who are part of the action. Real nature must be seen through the presenter's eyes. During the chimpanzee hunt sequence, the camera switches between the chase and a breathless Attenborough struggling to keep up with the hunting party to convey immediacy.

David Attenborough is one of the most trusted figures on the planet. Jacques Cousteau became one of the most recognised men in the world. Neither were scientific experts; nor did they claim to be. The self-deprecating Attenborough thinks of himself as a filmmaker but admits that he is a convincing image of what people assume a naturalist should be. Cousteau mined a new form of luminary, the television explorer. Both are good storytellers, using a visual formula combining mystery, drama, technology and adventure.

With advancing age, Attenborough mostly does voice-of-god narrations rather than going out on location. The scripts are written by production teams and he edits them. Cousteau was rarely aboard his famous boat, the *Càlypso*. He helicoptered in for film shoots, and archive footage was also sometimes used. Both men's primary contribution has been not to science but to entertainment.

Now there is a new breed of presenter. Documentaries are increasingly drawing on famous actors, musicians and sporting personalities. Filmmakers seek to leverage their popularity to secure funding and promote the film. Some stars are looking for opportunities to further their careers by burnishing green credentials. Others are driven by genuine concern about species extinction and climate change.

The hands-on-hips passive documentary presenter has also increasingly been replaced by action men and women. In a throwback to early wildlife-hunting documentaries, animal wranglers are back in fashion. In *The Jeff Corwin Experience*, the star seeks out exotic animals. Seemingly shot off the cuff but in reality loosely scripted, Corwin hunts out dangerous creatures, especially poisonous snakes, ostensibly for research. The title of herpetologist Brady Barr's show – *Dangerous Encounters* – signals his sensational approach, where he wrestles with crocodiles and snakes. Australian Steve Irwin's *Crocodile Hunter Diaries* specialised in getting close to hazardous wildlife and manhandling animals for little discernible purpose.

The common denominator is danger. The theme is excitement. Ebullience is combined with a brazen disregard for personal safety and wild creatures. In 2006, Irwin was killed by a stingray while filming his new program *Ocean's Deadliest*. The video footage of the incident was never released. Some suspected it might confirm that Irwin had harassed the animal. The crocodile hunter had previously been accused of getting too close to penguins, seals and humpback whales while filming. It would make for an undignified end.

Some wildlife filmmakers regard Irwin and his ilk as narcissistic clowns whose sensationalism does little for animals and nothing for science or conservation. For them, Irwin's death was an inevitable finale. His supporters allegedly mutilated stingrays to avenge their idol. The real crocodile hunter, an African who had killed thousands of the reptiles, was surprised to learn that Irwin, for all his heroics, had met his end at the hands of a fish.

Following Plutarch's *Lives*, George Monbiot blames the herald for presenting a false portrait of nature in documentaries: 'The first messenger, that gave notice of Lucullus' coming was so far from pleasing Tigranes that, he had his head cut off for his pains; and no man dared to bring further information.' The *Guardian* columnist argues that David Attenborough has betrayed the natural world by downplaying the pressures on wildlife. In continuing to pretend that vast tracts of pristine wilderness and abundant wildlife exist, he fosters an impression that cultivates complacency and inaction.

The accusation is not entirely fair. Some filming practices are questionable, yes. But documentary filmmakers such as Attenborough are not responsible for destroying or saving the natural world. For the most part, their work has helped people gain a better appreciation of wildlife, seeing things they would not generally have seen in real life. In a small village in Sulawesi, we watch a program with the locals showing tarsiers hunting insects. Although shot in a nearby reserve, the villagers have never seen the process directly.

Nature documentaries today increasingly cover the effects of climate change and species loss. But documentaries cannot inspire ecological concern in unreceptive audiences. They cannot engage those seeking an escape from reality into superficial optimism. Some recent BBC environmental series have drawn criticism for being depressing, not entertaining. Audiences do not want to be confronted by the true state of nature and endure the fear and guilt that it may provoke.

The internet and social media may be changing the ways we see wild animals, and, as with wildlife documentaries, the representation does not conform to the reality.

In the last decades, there has been a proliferation of online animal influencers. One chimpanzee, Limbani, has 650,000 Instagram followers. Viral photos and videos of the ape show him playing the guitar, bouncing on a trampoline and dressed up in a giant banana costume. It taps into bored and unhappy people's need for diversion and laughter. The likes, happy emojis and 'so cute!' comments pile up.

Human influencers, many with hundreds of thousands of followers, also target the large market for animal videos and posts. Some pose with dangerous predators, attempting to communicate fearlessness, while other influencers film themselves with exotic cute animals. They direct their followers to advertisers offering staged close encounters, primarily photo opportunities, with tigers, bears, elephants and monkeys, some of which are drugged, defanged or cruelly restrained.

Biologists have raised concerns about the abuse of intelligent and social wild animals. Many of these animals are captured in the wild, some taken from their mothers as infants. Kept in squalid conditions without proper nutrition, exercise or veterinary care, they are trained through the infliction of physical pain or the withholding of food. Performances are elicited by the same means. Separation from their species and exposure to humans stresses them. They suffer trauma when forced to perform. Smiling primates are distressed – the expression does not typically signify happiness but fear or submission.

Once they have ceased to be revenue-generating, these animals are killed, used for breeding or sold off to tawdry sideshows. The chimpanzee in *The Wolf of Wall Street* has allegedly since been kept in a roadside zoo, forced to perform circus tricks.

Social media platforms profit from advertisements selling body parts of threatened animals, including elephant ivory, rhino horn and tiger teeth, facilitating anonymous trafficking. The International Fund for Animal Welfare counted more than 11,000 protected wildlife, including big cats, primates, otters, tortoises, owls and parrots, for sale on social media and online marketplaces in one six-week period in 2017 in France, Germany, Russia and the United Kingdom alone. In 2021, following Myanmar's military coup, which resulted in political and economic upheaval, illegal trade in wild animals and their body parts via social media and digital platforms increased dramatically, with buyers offered endangered species, including elephants, bears, gibbons, hornbills and pangolins.

In Australia, as wildfires ravaged wilderness areas, social media was awash with photos of koalas, distressed by the fires, drinking from firefighter's water bottles, water cans or swimming pools. There was a flood of comments along the lines of 'OMG, so adorable.' Informed commentators pointed out that in normal circumstances koalas drink limited water, obtaining moisture from the gum leaves that are their primary diet. These were desperate animals near death and, in many cases, destined to die agonisingly due to their injuries and loss of habitat.

In 2021, netizens were transfixed by fifteen Asian elephants who trekked more than 500 kilometres (310 miles) across China after escaping from a nature reserve. Drones provided live footage of the animals around the clock. Human internet stars tried to trade on the elephants' celebrity, posting constantly about the journey and linking to their own online feeds to promote themselves. The real causes – habitat loss, lack of food and probably the loss of herd memory, essential in elephant communities – were ignored.

Media depictions create insidious expectations of what ecotourists can see in the wild and encourage them to seek unrealistically personal, close experiences. Manipulated images mislead in other ways, lulling us into a false sense of security. While clever filmmaking provides an impression of abundance and untouched ecosystems, the natural world faces a series of ecological calamities, with habitats and animals disappearing rapidly, making even brief encounters increasingly unlikely.

Wildlife documentaries that seek to inspire appreciation of the natural world may perversely distract us from a true assessment and from taking action to ensure their continued survival.

In Chile's Torres del Paine National Park, we watch a female puma and her cubs. A National Geographic cameraman is filming nearby. Suddenly, the film crew's minder approaches, asking us to leave. The cameraman wants a panning shot showing the animals against the vast empty spaces of Patagonia. Having us in the footage would detract from the notion of pristine wilderness the filmmaker wants to capture.

9

GREENWASH

The Saving-Nature Corporation

In the 1970s, as Greenpeace began in Canada, an astute observer asked how the group would mobilise the public sentiment they had tapped into. The answer, it turned out, was to create the multi-billion-dollar conservation industry.

Failures of and loss of faith in existing institutions has meant that NGOs are now key agents in shaping attitudes and policies towards nature. Over 6000 NGOs attended the latest UN Climate Change Conference. They constituted a broad church: business and industry NGOs (BINGOs), environmental NGOs (ENGOs), farmers (F), indigenous peoples organisations (IPOs), local government and municipal authorities (LGMAs), research and independent NGOs (RINGOs), trade union NGOs (TUNGOs), the women and gender constituency (WGC) and youth NGOs (YOUNGOs).

Saving nature is now the orderly grifting of activists, lawyers, lobbyists and financiers.

The idea of conservation is not new. America's Audubon Society and Britain's Royal Society for the Protection of Birds were founded in the nineteenth century. John Muir established the Sierra Club in 1892. But in the 1960s, a young, radical and combative generation modernised the movement.

They were against the Vietnam War, nuclear weapons, pesticides, pollution, loss of wilderness, industrial capitalism and patriarchal society. They were for civil, gender and indigenous rights, wild animals and freedoms. Organisations such as Greenpeace, Friends of the Earth and others would emerge from the tumult. The latest is Extinction Rebellion. Founded around 2018, it uses civil disobedience to compel government action to stem climate change, biodiversity loss and the risk of social and ecological collapse.

Despite an ostensible commitment to the same ends, individual environmental NGOs reflect their specific origins, support base, location, ideology, size and funding. The formula remains constant. A few dedicated and messianic individuals find a galvanising cause. They garner grassroots support, money, media attention and celebrity support, perhaps from the likes of Brigitte Bardot or Leonardo di Caprio. Once the ingredients are assembled, they stir.

Tactics dominate. For Greenpeace's founder, the *I Ching*–consulting Robert Hunter, the key was the mind bomb, an exploit to shake the public from complacency and spur them into action. Hunter and his fellow Rainbow Warriors shocked the world by attempting to sail into an atomic blast area. They put themselves between a harpoon and a whale and stood in the path of an approaching ship in pack ice to save baby harp seals. They understood, right from the start, that the best headlines and images win.

Traditional environmental activism involved writing to politicians or newspapers, petitions, street marches, protests or pickets. Increasingly, the battles are legal.

In 2008, the Natural Resources Defence Council sued the US Navy over the effects of sonar on whales. In a 6–3 decision, the US Supreme Court supported the admirals on national security grounds. The late Justice Ruth Bader Ginsburg was a dissenter, arguing that the likely harm, which the Navy's own environmental assessments confirmed, could not be dismissed.

In 2010, campaigners brought an action before the UN International Criminal Court seeking formal recognition of ecocide. Ten years later, lawyers agreed on a definition: unlawful or wanton acts committed with the knowledge that there is a substantial likelihood of severe and either widespread or long-term damage to the environment due to those acts. If ratified by signatory states, ecocide would be a crime that could be investigated and prosecuted by the ICC.

In 2011, People for the Ethical Treatment of Animals brought a legal action, asserting that a Celebes crested macaque should be granted the copyright to a selfie taken when it had triggered the shutter release on British nature photographer David Slater's camera. The court ruled against the monkey.

Such actions have helped to create laws to stop hunting and safeguard threatened wildlife. Legislation in many countries requires proposals for development to be balanced against the interests of vulnerable animals. To preserve biodiversity, governments must assess individual species and implement recovery plans for those at risk. Global initiatives such as CITES (Convention on International Trade in Endangered Species of Wild Fauna and Flora) and the International Union for Conservation of Nature (IUCN) Red List of Threatened Species encourage international cooperation. The UNESCO (United Nations Educational Scientific and Cultural Organization) World Heritage

List contains around 1200 sites of significance to date, of which more than 260 are natural or both cultural and natural.

But laws offer limited protection. Despite short-term benefits, bans on trade in elephant ivory, rhino horns or tiger body parts have proved ineffective. While restricting international trade of more than 35,000 species, CITES does not stop the killing or address the demand for banned products. The prospect of listing perversely accelerates the slaughter before restrictions are implemented.

Many developing countries do not support or enforce the bans. Critics argue that they reduce potential sources of income from controlled hunting or farming of animal parts, which could finance conservation. Stockpiles of prohibited animal products, confiscated from poachers, cannot be sold because this risks supporting demand.

The IUCN Red List aims to establish conservation priorities by assessing the extinction risk of species. Detractors argue that the process is opaque and poorly documented. In its effort at greater scientific rigour and transparency, IUCN's analyses are now long, technical and rarely read. Critics joke that the main operative body, the Species Survival Commission, stands for 'secret science commission'.

This makes for arcane disputes of what qualifies as critically endangered – that is, at an extremely high risk of extinction in the wild, defined as the species having suffered an 80 per cent decline in numbers over the past ten years or three generations, whichever is longer. Scientific dishonesty is common. Biologists have told me that some animals have been elevated to full species status because the case for legal protection for variants or sub-species is weaker. But the IUCN lacks enforcement powers, making protection pyrrhic.

Legislative solutions, whether national or global, are inherently political. Opponents argue that restrictions favourable to wildlife slow or prevent economic activity and impose unacceptable costs on businesses. In 2018, US President Donald Trump explicitly reduced protection for threatened species to allow more resource extraction and development. Environmental safeguards can be diluted by strangulation. In the early 1980s, US President Ronald Reagan all but halted species listing by restricting funding, requiring economic analysis of all federal government actions and limiting enforcement.

Possessing great natural beauty and numerous endemic species, Australia considers itself at the forefront of conservation. In fact, the country leads the world in mammal extinctions. A 2019 review found that its legislation was ineffective. Environmental standards were vague, unenforceable and not policed. Loss of habitat was widespread. Recovery plans were regularly not implemented. Penalties were weak. Instead of remedying identified failures, national and state governments bickered about accountability.

None of this legal wrangling helps endangered wildlife. In Malaysia, a pair of critically endangered helmeted hornbills flew low above Jade and me. The huge bird is black with a white belly. The tail is white, with a black band near the tip of the two central tail feathers. It has a bare, wrinkled throat patch, pale blue to greenish in females and red in males. The unforgettable call is a succession of hoots, quickening to a final witch's cackle.

Helmeted hornbills are hunted for red ivory – their solid red and yellow casque is worth more by weight than elephant tusks. In recent years, demand for jewellery and ornaments made from the material has decimated numbers. Since 1975, helmeted hornbills have had the highest level of protection under CITES, making all trade illegal. Yet criminal networks in South-East Asia operate with impunity, protected by politicians and local officials. Law enforcement is lax. Judicial systems do not treat wildlife trafficking seriously.

Indigenous people believe that helmeted hornbills guard the river between life and death. Within a few years, the last individual will have crossed that boundary, leaving the world without one of its most astonishing birds.

One focus of conservation is setting aside tracts of land or water as national parks. Today, protected areas total about 15 per cent of land and 3 per cent of the oceans. But many protected areas are paper parks, existing only in theory.

The Great Limpopo Transfrontier Park, totalling approximately 35,000 square kilometres (13,500 square miles), links Mozambique's Limpopo, South Africa's Kruger and Zimbabwe's Gonarezhou national parks. First proposed in 1938, the park was finally created in 2002. However, anti-personnel mines from decades-long wars posed a threat to wildlife movement and access to water. Against all odds, these were eventually removed at great cost.

In 1997, Michael Fay, an ecologist and a National Geographic Society explorer-in-residence, walked 3200 kilometres (2000 miles) over fifteen months to draw attention to the deteriorating condition of Central African forests. Welcome media coverage came from an unexpected source. Where Gabon's rainforests meet the ocean, hippopotamuses, elephants, forest buffaloes, leopards and gorillas are sometimes seen wandering the foreshores. Footage of hippos body-surfing the waves became an online sensation.

Gabon created thirteen national parks spanning 28,500 square kilometres (11,000 square miles). Under Fay's tutelage, the country sought to turn itself into West Africa's Costa Rica. A lack of money, resources and skills means the vision remains unrealised. The national parks, declared with fanfare, are poorly managed. Inadequate infrastructure, political instability and corruption discourages tourism. The protected areas could revert to logging and mining interests.

UNESCO can anoint a location with World Heritage status but responsibility for its protection remains with national governments. Unlike archaeological or cultural places, nature reserves are part of interconnected ecosystems. Protecting a site, of itself, cannot ensure its survival. The Galápagos Island and the Great Barrier Reef are World Heritage sites. Overfishing around Ecuadorian territorial waters affects the protected area of the islands. The reef is being damaged by dredging for shipping access to service mines and industry, algal blooms from agricultural fertiliser run-off and invasive species. Both sites are seeing an impact from global factors such as warmer seas temperatures, ocean acidification and altered weather patterns. They are exposed to damage from human activity, including rising tourist numbers. Neither is likely to survive the century unless something changes.

Designation is politicised. A World Heritage status lures visitors. In 2016, the Australian government allegedly lobbied for the reef's problems to be deleted from a UNESCO report because of the potentially negative impact on tourism. In 2021, the government was outraged when it emerged that the reef's status was listed as 'in jeopardy'. Last-minute lobbying deferred the classification of the reef as endangered. There was no meaningful action to address the underlying problems and reverse the decline. The World Heritage emblem is mainly a marketing tool for things to see before you or it dies.

Protection is rarely permanent. Created by President Dwight Eisenhower, Alaska's Arctic National Wildlife Refuge is regarded by the indigenous Gwich'in people as the sacred place where life begins. The area is home to caribou, polar bears and migratory birds from six continents. In the last days of the Trump administration, the US federal government opened more than 400,000 hectares (1 million acres) of the refuge to oil exploration and extraction. Its future remains uncertain.

Under President Hugo Chávez's Bolivarist agenda, the properties we visited in Venezuela were confiscated for redistribution to poor landless farmers. The new owners did not have the skills and capital to manage the livestock or the ecotourism operations. After Chávez's death, the country slipped into economic and social chaos. Foreign tourism largely ceased. Today, little information is available about the state of the properties. The rich animal life we saw a quarter of a century ago has probably been lost.

Saving wild animals is an arena for ideological wars. The New Conservation movement seeks to replace a nature-only viewpoint with a people-too perspective. This approach promotes economic development and quality of life by reducing elements such as air and water pollution. The idea is that higher aspirations will be possible only when the material needs of populations are met. The economically disadvantaged, once they achieve better living standards, will be more inclined to preserve nature.

Modernists believe that traditionalists are out of touch with economic realities. Henry David Thoreau, John Muir and Edward Abbey were hypocrites and misanthropes. National parks and reserves only serve the elite (despite independent polling showing overwhelming support for preservation and expansion of protected areas).

The approach creates false dichotomies between helping the underprivileged and saving the environment. It ignores the connection between species diversity and the stability of ecosystems. It originates in a fear that anthropogenic changes to the climate, resource scarcity, rising inequality and social instability will overwhelm an overpopulated Earth, unhinge human civilisation and plunge millions, maybe billions, into misery.

The vitriol has been diluted over time due to exhaustion of the combatants. New conservationists now back away from claims that preservation of habitat is not important. They acknowledge the importance of biodiversity. Traditionalists have incorporated new but really old ideas, such as emphasising local involvement and economic empowerment. There is a renewed emphasis on ecotourism. The uneasy truce claims that the differences are about means, not ends.

The philosophical differences originate from fundraising pressures. Public money from governments and multinational bodies such as various UN agencies makes up around a quarter of conservation funding. The rising claims on budgets has meant government cash follows people and the electoral calculus. Animals do not vote. Attracting private contributions is now crucial.

When Jade and I first took an interest in conservation, NGOs relied on donations or annual membership fees. This was supplemented with income from commercial activities, such as selling t-shirts and other paraphernalia. Today, these revenues make up between 10 and 30 per cent of funding. Other sources must make up the shortfall.

This has increased conservation groups' reliance on foundations, philanthropists and corporations. The problem is that environmental causes attract less than 10 per cent of all charitable donations. Humanitarian and religious causes do much better. Even large environmental groups rarely make the higher echelons of charity rankings. The change in emphasis within conservation was a simple recognition that projects related to development attract greater support. Humans do not need to be convinced of the importance of humans.

The need to appeal to private donors creates complications. In 2012, the Bill and Melinda Gates Foundation gave $10 million to Conservation International. The contribution was emblematic of a shift – the rise of the penitent rich. Today, practically everyone above a certain net worth has a project to save the environment. In his 2009 book, Edward Humes called them eco barons.

For Humes, the wealthy are conservation's saviours. The book provides flattering portraits of individuals such as founder of The North Face and Esprit clothing companies Doug Tompkins, co-founder of lip-balm empire Burt's Bees Roxanne Quimby and media magnate Ted Turner. Several billionaire financiers have also embarked on similar do-it-myself quixotic crusades, purchasing large tracts of land and lodges in Africa and the Americas. These purchases privatise the environment. The eco barons crave exclusivity.

Faith in the wealthy, who may be indifferent to general welfare, may be misplaced. The idea that money and passion alone can save the environment is risible. Donors channel funds to their pet projects, which often do not stand up to rigorous analysis. The money is placed in trusts or foundations, with the donor retaining substantial authority. Contributions are tax deductible or protect wealth from the ravages of death, inheritance or estate duties.

Payments to erase sins, like papal indulgences, have durable appeal. The source of the money is often neglected. Profits from commercial exploitation of the environment and local communities might be being given back in part, pennies thrown onto a collection plate. The nineteenth-century industrial barons amassed fortunes in steel, oil, railroads, real estate and finance and then endowed many cultural and civic institutions. Similarly, the eco barons want to create an honourable legacy.

In the Colombian Amazon, Jade and I came across a group of visiting American philanthropists, major donors to a jaguar protection initiative. The owner of the cattle ranch and its employed scientists genuflected before their benefactors. They had access to parts of the ranch closed to us to see what their money had purchased. We overheard complaints that no jaguar had been forthcoming.

Conservation groups do not always disclose their funding sources. In Malaysia, we met the head of a foundation running a rehabilitation centre for rescued sun bears. It relied on money from palm-oil plantation owners, who presided over the destruction of the animal's native habitat. Others partner with mining companies, paper manufacturers, loggers and the banks that finance these businesses. In the practice of cause marketing, conservation groups are increasingly paid to certify a firm's products as sustainable or environmentally friendly.

Engagement with businesses is justified on the basis that it increases awareness of conservation and how it could bring higher long-term profits, reduce financial risks and secure access to scarce resources. The companies use it to polish their green credentials and appearance of good citizenship as well as meet their ESG (Environment Social Governance) performance indicators.

The conservation movement is increasingly conflicted by these associations. NGOs find it difficult to criticise major donors that provide important funding for environmental damage from oil spills, habitat loss or emissions resulting from their business operations. There are disingenuous arguments about seats-at-tables and behind-the-scenes discussions leading to change. In her book *Green Inc.*, Christine MacDonald argues that the arrangements favour companies. It entrenches compromise, ensuring minimal, marginal and only incremental change.

Improvements in the environmental impact of business activity have been slight compared to the overall damage. The most disturbing element is the undemocratic logic of collective action, identified by American economist Mancur Olson in 1965. Concentrated benefits and diffuse costs mean that focused minority interests are overrepresented, and disorganised majority interests defeated.

The structure of the environmental movement is now part of the problem. Large corporatised NGOs are headed by businesspeople, bankers, lawyers and lobbyists. Many are juggernauts, with nine- or even ten-figure dollar revenues and thousands of staff. Big Conservation has convinced itself that size, monetary resources and collaboration with donors grants the power to shape policies. It also fits the career ambitions of now-besuited conservationists who have taken over from their rag-tag, khaki-clad predecessors.

Once uncompromising defenders of nature have become lethargic institutions run by marketing and public relations staff. It is PowerPoint presentations, glossy brochures and anodyne missions and strategies. The key metrics are membership numbers, fundraising and media minutes.

Size makes organisations inefficient and ineffective. The growing cost of fundraising, publicity and administration absorbs a large proportion of resources supposedly intended for conservation. Internal governance is variable. Many NGOs, including the UN-backed climate fund, have been accused of corrupt practices and misconduct. Employees and volunteers complain of internal politics and toxic cultures. Environmental NGOs are now frequently mired in infighting.

Conservation arguments must increasingly be phrased in terms of economic value. The Davos World Economic Forum estimated that around half of global output, $50 trillion, depends on nature. More than

75 per cent of global food crops, including coffee, cocoa and almonds, are pollinated by birds or insects. The value of this service alone is more than $500 billion per annum.

Economists now puzzle over the monetary value of individual species. Each mountain gorilla generates $3 to $5 million in tourism revenue over its lifetime. A lion in East Africa or a grizzly bear may be worth $1 million or more; one macaw in Peru several hundred thousand dollars. A single great whale is worth more than $2 million, based on its contribution to carbon capture and tourism. The International Monetary Fund valued whale populations at more than $1 trillion. The idea is that the worth of an animal will translate to its preservation, perhaps because it is a financial asset and store of human wealth.

Think tanks talk about the biodiversity funding gap, a $700 billion shortfall in money needed to finance conservation work. Financiers practised in trading securities have now turned to the monetary value of the natural world and how to design investment strategies to profit from it.

Even international relations infuse conservation. After the Cold War, China sent giant pandas to other countries as a goodwill gesture, following the precedent of Empress Wu Zetian, who sent a pair to Emperor Tenmu of Japan during the Tang period. One indication of rising political tensions between America and China is the recall of leased pandas from US zoos. Pakistan allows wealthy Arabs to hunt the vulnerable houbara bustard, despite the bird being protected under international and local wildlife laws. Soft diplomacy exchanges the killing of an endangered species for oil and short-term financing.

There is little recognition of nature for its own sake or of the animals themselves. That is not the currency of humans, who measure wealth and power by different standards.

The work of conservation has changed. Larger NGOs operate as venture capitalists, raising and allocating funds to smaller organisations. They advise on fundraising, publicity and training, taking credit for the work of smaller groups to maintain their global brands.

There is pressure to push money out the door, but the types of programs funded are different. Donors' penchant for immediate results and returns on their investment mean big, glamorous programs are favoured – headline-grabbing new parks, for instance. Officials at state and private wildlife reserves have told us that it is difficult to secure long-term donor funding for unsexy work, such as adequately managing existing protected areas or vulnerable species. There is limited money for employing and training rangers, removing thousands of snares from forests or enforcing anti-poaching regulations. There is scant interest in stopping the global illegal wildlife trade.

Even in initiatives directed to protecting wilderness and key wild animals, little translates into desperately needed action. 'More research needed' is a frequent conclusion designed to offend nobody and attract funds.

Many NGOs have shrunk their teams of scientists. Expensive technical gimmickry rules instead. The presence of endangered species is determined by satellite or drone imaging, sound monitoring and sampling faeces or the blood from leeches. Techno-heavy approaches, which attract favourable media coverage, come at the expense of laborious fieldwork.

At the same time, there is insistence that diagnosis, solutions and evaluation of interventions must be evidence-based. The mantra of best practice and key performance indicators is a response to costly failures or poor outcomes. Sponsors demand it as a sign of good governance. The process relies on published, peer-reviewed publications as well as independent expert advice. Valuable local or indigenous knowledge is rarely sought.

In practice, it is a minefield. Data is scant if available, and rarely objective, reliable or decisive. Conclusions and predictions may depend on context or geography. Expert egos can disagree. Theories are unrefuted conjectures. There are inevitable political subtexts to the science.

Population estimates are central to many conservation decisions. Wildlife surveys use a variety of methods. A common technique is a transect, a path along which the occurrence and populations of individual species are documented. There are strip, line, belt, point and curved line transects, dictated by geography. They are not equally effective and may not be comparable. The observer moves along the plotted route and counts occurrences. They must estimate the distance of the animal from the path to allow calculation of the area covered and numbers detected. Population density is determined using the raw count adjusted for probability (low far from the path; high near the path). Where sight observation is used, estimates of numbers can diverge wildly. Where based on sound, it is even more variable. Having participated in bird counts, Jade and I have encountered significant differences in estimates even among people when standing next to one another.

Another option to determine animal populations is trail cameras. Automatically triggered by activity, they record wild animals without the need for a human presence. Despite their widespread use in population surveys, the effectiveness of this method is uncertain. The placement of the camera, which requires detailed knowledge of the area and wildlife behaviours, is crucial. The use of attractants, such as food, with camera traps affects results. Weather or technical glitches can bias results. Data from different locations is not strictly equivalent.

In addition, individual animals must be distinguished to avoid double counting. While most animals have distinctive identification marks, the process is inexact. Each tiger has, in theory, an individual paw print, or pugmark, recognisable by an expert. In an experiment, Dr Ullas Karanth presented tiger census operators with thirty-three pugmarks taken from four captive tigers. The census operators estimated between six and thirty-three separate individuals.

In 2018, Indian Prime Minister Narendra Modi announced that the wild tiger population had increased to around 3000, a 33 per cent rise in four years. Biologists pointed out that the counts were done by poorly trained staff lacking the necessary skills and using suspect methodologies. One scientist diplomatically told newspapers that the estimates had higher uncertainties than being reported. The population was inconsistent with known territorial requirements and availability of prey species.

There is an obsession with invasive technology. One long-standing technique is banding wild birds. A small, numbered metal or plastic tag is attached to the leg to allow monitoring of movements. This requires capture, usually using a mist net (a thin net), to fit the leg ring and take measurements (sex, weight, condition). One banded bird – a Laysan albatross – has provided information on avian longevity. Based on when she was first banded, she is at least sixty-nine years old and has raised more than thirty-five chicks.

Increasingly, radio or satellite tracking is used to monitor movements and behaviour. This involves attaching a transmitter to an animal. Birds must be netted to do this, whereas large animals must be tranquillised to fix and sometimes also remove the device. The stress of capture, anaesthesia and handling may harm the individual and alter their behaviours, biasing the data gathered. Investigations into the effects of tracking devices show short- and long-term effects, some fatal. Animals become snagged in vegetation or suffer injury from overtight collars. Birds have been electrocuted where whip antennas came into contact with electricity lines. The devices affect swimming, lifting and flying ability. Tagged animals show increased preening to remove the transmitter, weight loss, decreased feeding, greater susceptibility to predation, reduced reproductive success and lower survival rates. Studies of radio-tagged deer found higher death rates. The collars, brightly coloured for ease of aerial spotting, allowed predators to track the animals more easily.

Satellite tracking is now the primary method of studying large predators, such as polar bears and tigers. The method, which is stressful to the animal, inevitably involves a chase from a helicopter or vehicles, darting and other painful procedures. The death of several tigers during seizure have been documented. There have also been cases of polar bears taking extraordinarily long swims. These were cited as evidence of endurance, but it was more likely that the animal was desperate to avoid capture.

Nikita Ovsyanikov argues that satellite tracking by collaring individuals adds little to knowledge of polar bear biology, once distribution, population structure and spatial patterns are known. There are alternative non-invasive methodologies. On Wrangel Island, Nikita and his colleagues studied polar bears through observation. I asked Nikita why Russian scientists placed great emphasis on ground-based field work. He laughed: 'We never had money!'

Macho scientists eager to manhandle dangerous animals are less patient. They overlook the torture, pain and suffering of the objects of their projects. The irony is that this invasive science, costing millions, merely provides information for scientific recommendations on how many polar bears can be killed by native peoples or by other hunters to whom their quotas are sold.

For several years, Jade and I volunteered for a citizen science project studying the powerful owl, a large Australian species that has adapted to urban environments. After years of gathering data from nightly fieldwork, the organisers of the project received a substantial grant to radio-tag several birds to track their hunting patterns. The invasive research merely confirmed the birds' movements, established through observations by volunteers over time. Entreaties for funding to preserve old tree hollows and protect nesting birds to promote breeding success were disregarded.

In her later years, Dian Fossey was joined by students eager to collect data for their PhDs and learned papers. Few seemed interested in her anti-poaching efforts, despite the fact that this, and her habituation of the gorillas, made the academic work possible.

Conservationists take credit for saving grizzly bears, whales, rhinos, tigers, gorillas, giant pandas, European bison, bald eagles and Californian condors. In reality, the victories are equivocal. While outright extinction of some species has been avoided, several remain endangered. Conservation NGOs often cite the unprovable contrafactual case: without their efforts, many more species would have disappeared.

Even successes are ambiguous. The beauty and languid grace of tigers belies a superb forest predator. The memory of seeing them over two decades ago still inspires awe. At the start of the twentieth century, shortly after Rudyard Kipling published *The Jungle Book*, there were around 100,000 tigers across Asia. Populations have fallen to 3000 to 4000. Even that number is questionable. It reflects the politics of funding because too little or too much improvement would jeopardise the flow of foreign cash. The 10,000 captive tigers, kept as exhibits, entertainment, pets and livestock, outnumber the wild population.

The Royal Bengal tiger is the species' last hope. In 1973, Indian Prime Minister Indira Gandhi established Project Tiger, with the aid of foreign donors, to preserve the species in their natural habitat. The program created special reserves in which all human activity was banned and anti-poaching measures initiated. The idea was that inviolable reserves would form a breeding nuclei, with the expanding population migrating to adjacent forests. Except it didn't happen. It proved difficult to relocate villagers, who were incensed at the loss of rights to graze livestock or gather wood in these areas. Regulations were rarely enforced.

Male tigers need a home range of about 60 to 150 square kilometres (20 to 60 square miles). Females use about a third of that. The tiger reserves average less than 1500 square kilometres (600 square miles), creating small, isolated, genetically impoverished populations. Tigers are highly territorial. When a male cub is about one and a half years old, it must find territory in which to live and hunt by taking over the space of an old or weak tiger or moving outside the reserve, which is impractical.

In 2017, a radio-collared individual, T3, left India's Panna tiger reserve, a 540-square-kilometre (208-square-mile) patch of dry tropical forest. The five-year-old male had been relocated from Pench reserve, 650 kilometres (400 miles) to the south, to improve Panna's gene pool. T3 did not like it there and started walking home. Eventually, after a lengthy chase over 450 kilometres (280 miles), the tiger was tranquillised and trucked back to Panna.

The tigers that remain in the wild are highly managed. Some of the reserves are fenced, dotted with watchtowers and cameras. Individuals, especially breeding females, are collared and constantly monitored. Tanks have been installed to overcome water shortages. The animals are wild in name only.

Conservation efforts sometimes become an extravagant farce. In the Russian Far East, weather stopped us visiting Meinoypil'gyno, a 40-kilometre-long (25-mile-long) shingle spit that is an important breeding site for critically endangered spoon-billed sandpipers, small wading birds with unusual spatulate bills. The migratory species summers and breeds on the Chukchi and Kamchatka peninsulas and winters in south and South-East Asia. In 2011, collected eggs were artificially incubated and hatched in a Moscow facility and then flown 8000 kilometres (5000 miles) back to the north-east Russian tundra for release. A parallel English program took eight years for the first two birds to be raised. With only a few hundred remaining, the spoon-billed sandpiper is unlikely to survive in the wild.

In Australia, twenty-eight Tasmanian devils were translocated, a risky procedure, to isolate them from the risk of facial tumour disease. They were placed on an island, decimating breeding seabird colonies unused to terrestrial predators.

Wildlife must now survive in protected areas that are really pseudo zoos. Seeing these magnificent animals in untouched wilderness is now a far-fetched dream.

As with all dissident political movements, the mainstream has absorbed conservation and watered down the message while continuing to use its language. Extinction Rebellion co-founder Roger Hallam argues that letters, emails, marches, litigation and laws are ineffective. He favours the strategies of the suffragettes, Gandhi's Satyagraha and the civil rights movement. It revolves around mass arrests, jailing and court appearances to get media attention and overwhelm the court system. In 2022, activists began gluing themselves to artworks or streets to gain publicity. Rather than support, it drew angry reactions from the general public, who were unhappy at the disruption.

Others advocate more radical actions. In his 1975 novel *The Monkey Wrench Gang*, Edward Abbey endorsed the use of sabotage to protest environmental damage. The novel's hero, George Washington Hayduke – pro-conservation, pro-guns, pro-alcohol, anti-mining, anti-tourism, anti-dam – is the self-appointed saviour of 'the f*****g wilderness'. He pioneers monkey wrenching, or ecotage: using industrial weapons to demolish or damage the infrastructure of industry to protect the biosphere.

Dian Fossey came to hate the poachers who killed gorillas and whose wire snares sometimes crippled them. She distrusted the unhelpful authorities who secretly profited from illegal capture and sales of babies. For Fossey, the last straw was when Digit, a silverback she had watched grow up, was found speared to death, with his head and hands cut off. She ordered her men to capture the poachers, beat them or kill them. Fossey was eventually murdered.

Paul Watson of the Sea Shepherd Conservation Society, an animal-welfare group that broke away from Greenpeace, favours forceful tactics. His ships seek to challenge whalers, sealers and illegal fishers on the open seas, flying a piratic skull-and-crossbones flag. Watson once used the bow of his vessel, strengthened with concrete, to disable an illegal whaling ship in the Bay of Biscay, France.

Rejecting accusations of law-breaking, ecowarriors argue that their targets are acting illegally or immorally. Vandalism and ecologically motivated mayhem may be more successful in bringing about change than any number of press releases, reports, meetings, consultations and laws. Watson's guerrilla tactics in the Southern Ocean and the Antarctic whale sanctuary, documented in the weekly reality television series *Whale Wars*, may have done more to discourage Japanese whaling than more-genteel efforts.

Protection of the environment is always a fine balancing act. Ecological imperatives clash with economic priorities. Even desirable initiatives, such as renewable energy, are not always compatible with ecological needs. Large-scale solar arrays change habitats. Biofuel production leads to more land clearing. Environmental protection agencies write out long-term permits for wind energy farms to lawfully kill bald and golden eagles with their turbines in order to reduce carbon emissions.

The conservation movement must accommodate different demands – deep ecology, scientific ecology, social ecology, animal rights, anti-nuclearism, feminism, militant veganism, social justice and Edward Abbey's radical anti-industrialisation. Pure dark greens promote equal rights for human and non-humans, urging drastic social, cultural, economic, political and personal transformation. They want people excluded from protected areas, population limits and the relinquishing of technology. Light greens seeks to protect natural areas but not to exclude sustainable human use. They subscribe to proper management of natural resources, balancing continued extraction with human well-being. They are concerned with environmental justice, linking social and ecological concerns – for example, combating exposure to pollution in low-income and minority communities.

Bright greens embrace technology, sustainable and ethical consumerism, believing that it will ensure the continuation of their standards of living. They argue that it is possible to enable people to live prosperous lives responsibly and sustainably. For this group, environmentalism is a lifestyle choice.

Cornucopian optimists dismiss environmental concerns on the basis that the Earth's bounty is infinite. A subset go further, arguing that technology and free markets are capable of solving all ecological problems. Transhumanists believe that humankind could even avoid extinction by abandoning Earth for another home. The disillusioned espouse self-reliance: small-scale, environmentally sustainable off-the-grid living.

There is an unavoidable internal contradiction. Bad news for the environment is good news for conservation causes and NGOs. Habitat loss, climate change and extinctions provide them with power as social actors. They work within a system that contributes to environmental damage. Perversely, they cannot finish the job because it would mean putting themselves out of one. Unable to reconcile these inconsistencies, conservation NGOs limp on, mixing romantic naivety and self-serving commerce. Greenpeace founder Robert Hunter feared that the conservation movement would simply become *another* NGO, hawking statistics and courting special interests. Where there is money, influence and fame to be had, even well-meaning individuals can easily lose sight of the objective. Albert Camus thought that good intent could harm in the same way as malevolence.

But the failure of environmental NGOs does not detract from the efforts of passionate individuals. Thousands devote energy and time to the frustrating, trying, financially unrewarding, Sisyphean work of conservation. Most are unknown and survive on small grants, if they receive any funding at all.

In South-east Brazil, we met Jonas and the unlikely named Elvis. Both have retired and purchased small patches of forest, which they are restoring. The areas are rich in birdlife because of the lack of suitable habitat elsewhere. Jonas' hummingbird feeders attract several rare species. As Jonas does not accept money from visitors, Fred, our guide, takes him two large bags of sugar for his feeders, which consume several kilos each day. We stay at Elvis' guesthouse, seeing a number of special birds on and near his property.

Others volunteer their spare time to improving habitat or to work on projects to assist wildlife. They do it for their love of nature and animals, often fighting a losing battle.

The hardest thing is people's indifference. Few care. Those who do are focused on a handful of charismatic mammals or birds. Only a small percentage of endangered species receive any targeted conservation attention. Threatened species with non-existent public profiles are abandoned to their fate.

Greenwashing may not be the problem, but it is also not the solution. We have learnt that conservation is less about wild animals than about humans. It is about writing epitaphs for the wild.

10

BIOTIC ATTRITION

The Destruction of Wilderness

Life on Earth prospered in the Holocene – the last 12,000 years, when the relatively stable climate fostered great biological richness. The Anthropocene is the name given to the most recent period, when human activity began having a significant impact on the planet's climate and ecosystems. It is ushering in the sixth mass extinction, defined as the loss of at least 60 per cent of extant species within a short geological time period (a few hundred thousand years). The last, the fifth, was the end of dinosaurs 65 million years ago, at the end of the Cretaceous Period. The sixth extinction is unique in that it is caused by the actions of one species – homo sapiens.

Today, the long-term survival of more than 500,000 land species is in the balance. Almost all critically endangered and two-thirds of other endangered species may be lost within the next century. Six factors underlie the current rate of extinction. First, destruction of animal habitats. Second, overexploitation, such as hunting and fishing, reducing numbers below levels required for viable populations. Third, introduced foreign species gaining ascendancy over endemic life forms. Fourth, islandisation (fragmented habitats), isolating populations and damaging genetic diversity. Fifth, the climatic impact of human activity. And sixth, the damaging effects of ecotourism.

Over the last thirty years, Jade and I have watched this biotic attrition, a euphemism for extinction. Common species are now hard to find. Uncommon ones are rarely seen. Many are lost. Even if you find a rare species, chances are it is alone in a small patch of isolated habitat – the last of its kind. Without animals, watching wildlife or ecotourism is an oxymoron.

Space for wild animals is now scarce: only 20 per cent of the land and 13 per cent of the ocean can be still classified as wilderness. Expanding human activity means that more than 40 per cent of the world's land is now agricultural or urban. Accessible and hospitable areas in Europe, North America and Asia are almost totally modified for human use. Growing populations increasingly encroach on more remote and less productive areas.

Tropical forests or islands hold over half of the world's species. Only 40 per cent of remaining forests are in good condition. Since 1990, forests, not managed for timber or agricultural extraction, have halved, with 420 million hectares (over 1 billion acres) lost. The best remaining, located in Canada, Russia, South America, Africa and Papua New Guinea, are under threat.

Deforestation continues at alarming rates. Over the last twenty years, huge areas of the Amazon basin have been cut down for cattle and soya bean cultivation to meet rising demand, especially from China. Brazil's former president, Jair Bolsonaro, prioritised agriculture, logging and mining. He saw the rainforests as a national possession, ignoring their importance as a global store of carbon and a source of oxygen. When challenged on this, the relevant minister, nicknamed the anti-environment minister by opponents, asked foreign governments to pay

Brazil at least $10 billion per year to conserve forests. He subsequently resigned after allegations of collusion with illegal loggers. The re-election of President Luiz Inácio Lula da Silva (Lula) offered hope. But resistance from the Brazilian Congress, the state oil company and agribusiness, as well as Lula's desire to boost the economy and living standards, means policies to stop deforestation have been difficult to implement.

Where not destroyed, pollution and damaging agricultural, logging, mining and fishing practices degrade the ecosystem, resulting in extinction or forced migration of species. Even superficially intact wilderness has been transformed by human activity. Altering the spacing of trees, changing the understorey or the distribution of plants, threatens wild animals.

Habitat degradation is not localised. Pollutants, such as heavy metals, have reached once pristine Svalbard in Norway, north of the Arctic Circle. Nitrogen and sulphur oxides released from fossil fuels fall to the ground as acid rain, sometimes long distances from the source. Waste, fertiliser run-off and industrial pollutants affect marine ecosystems. Plastic pollution clogs inland waterways, shorelines and oceans. A submersible found plastic at the bottom of the Mariana Trench, the deepest point of the ocean.

Approximately half the live coral cover on reefs, one of the most species-rich habitats on Earth, is gone. Losses are growing by around 4 to 5 per cent per decade. Deterioration in freshwater areas is even greater, with 90 per cent of all global wetlands lost and the hydrology of major river systems altered. Freshwater biodiversity has declined by an average of 84 per cent. More than 40 per cent of amphibians, key indicators of water quality, are threatened.

Oil spills, such the 1989 *Exxon Valdez* and 2010 *Deepwater Horizon*, damage oceans, shorelines, animals, fish and seabirds. When Jade and I visit the site of the Exxon Valdez spill more than a decade after the event, there is no immediate evidence of the accident. But weathered oil, dangerous in even small concentrations, remains trapped beneath rocks and on the deep ocean bed, where it enters the food chain.

Waste and contaminants affect the mortality, immune response and reproduction of marine life. Fish and turtles may ingest plastics, mistaking them for jellyfish and fish eggs, resulting in death. By the middle of the twenty-first century, the sea could contain more plastic than fish by weight.

Disturbance of habitat can be subtle. Artificial light and sound pose a threat to wildlife, killing millions, perhaps billions, of birds and bats annually. Each year on 9/11 the city of New York stages Tribute in Light, an art installation in memory of the victims of the 2001 World Trade Center attack. Two intense blue light beams rise dramatically into the night sky. The event coincides with the annual autumn bird migration, when billions of small songbirds travel south. The lights, visible from up to 100 kilometres (60 miles) away, draw passing birds, disrupting their passage. Even if they are not killed or injured from colliding with buildings, a short detour wastes the bird's energy reserves, to disastrous effect.

Shipping near marine feeding and breeding areas is another form of disturbance. Collisions can be lethal. Underwater noise, such as sonar and seismic testing, interferes with whales' ability to navigate and communicate and may contribute to strandings. Outside of water, size and the blubber designed to allow the animals to survive cold water become a death sentence. A stranded whale's mass crushes its internal organs and boils its alive. Death is slow and excruciating.

Even attempts to preserve habitat can create disturbance. The United Kingdom's new Environmental Improvement Plan pledges that everyone will live within a fifteen-minute walk of water or green space. Right to Roam campaigners demand access to these areas, asserting their right not only to walk but also to exercise their dogs off-lead, camp, kayak, swim, ride and climb. They have encouraged several mass trespasses into these remaining reserves, ignoring the effects on wildlife.

The effects of loss of habitat are amplified by highly localised populations. Lithium for batteries, used in electronics and electric vehicles, is found in the Andes Mountains, one of the world's driest areas. Mining requires large volumes of water taken from high-altitude lakes, home to half the Earth's flamingo species – the Andean, Chilean and James. They are the mythological flame-pink firebirds, the immortal phoenix that dies in a burst of fire only to be reborn from the ashes. On a cold, sunny day, we see all three species in a single lake. They stand on one leg or feed with their heads upside-down, sieving crustaceans from the brine. Locals talk of flocks that once numbered in the hundreds. Today, populations are declining because of the loss of the lakes.

Many primates have small ranges, which are being rapidly reduced by agriculture and development. The golden snub-nose monkey, with its bright blue face, upturned nose and orange fur, is confined to the high mountains of central and western China. The douc langur is found

only in Indochina. It is an explosion of colour, with a human-like face, white whiskers and a beard, a grey pot-belly, red legs and black hands and feet. Only a few hundred remain in patches of shrinking forests.

Evolutionary forces have concentrated mountain gorillas and chimpanzees in politically unstable central Africa. The Rift Valley mountains are the frontline in constant civil wars and ethnic rivalry. Poaching and deforestation is rampant. Alongside the human threat, the shrinking area available for gorillas means that further population increases are difficult. Young males seeking to create new territories and form new families clash with one another and with silverbacks.

Key biodiversity hotspots, such as Australia, Madagascar, the Philippines, Indonesia and Latin America, are deteriorating faster than anywhere else on Earth. Much of the planet is now incapable of supporting the native species coveted by ecotourists.

Overharvesting reduces animal populations. Many large predators have been extirpated to protect humans and livestock. Australia's thylacine, known as the Tasmanian tiger because of its striped lower back, was the largest-known carnivorous marsupial. Intensive hunting motivated by bounties led to its extinction. The only Tasmanian tiger you can see is grainy footage of the last-known animal restlessly pacing its tiny cage.

Animals are viewed as a resource. An Australian indigenous guide we encountered on a boat tour described the animals and birds in purely culinary terms, highlighting their taste and the right season to take them. Crowned pigeons, large, bluish-grey terrestrial birds with a deep maroon breast, dark red eyes and elaborate lacy crests, are found only in the lowland forests of Papua New Guinea. Our local guide casually remarked that the birds are 'delicious'. Once abundant, they are now rare due to hunting for meat and plumes.

By the late nineteenth century, only around 500 of the eight million North American bison or buffalo that are thought to have existed were left. The near extinction was the result of indiscriminate slaughter by hunters and cattle-borne disease. Alongside the destruction of the species, it was an economic cataclysm for indigenous peoples heavily reliant on the animals as a food source.

In a museum in Russia's Commander Islands, we saw a skeleton of a Steller's sea cow. Related to dugongs and manatees, adult animals were up to 9 metres (30 feet) long and weighed around 10 tonnes (22,000 pounds). Within twenty-seven years of discovery by Europeans, the slow-moving and easily caught mammal, one of the largest creatures outside of whales, was hunted to extinction for its meat, fat and hide.

An estimated 500 million birds are killed annually for food in north African and Middle Eastern countries bordering the Mediterranean. In Asia, large numbers of internationally protected shorebirds are slaughtered at just three sites – Pattani Bay in Thailand, West Java in Indonesia and the Yangtze River Delta in China. Even when animals are not directly hunted, incidental effects are significant. In Yellowstone, we saw a bloody trail from the injured leg of a wolf caught in a trap.

In Africa and Asia, dead primates are sold as bushmeat. Roadside stalls sell gorilla-hand ashtrays. Wildlife photographer Karl Ammann's graphic photographs portray severed heads and orphaned infant gorillas and chimpanzees. Given their close relationship to humans, the killing and eating of these animals feels like murder and cannibalism.

Fishing and aquaculture provide around half the world's population with almost a fifth of their protein, as well as livelihoods for one in ten. Industrial fishing using advanced technologies for locating and catching prey has left almost 90 per cent of all fish species either fully or overfished.

A doubling of consumption in the last half-century has decimated many fishing grounds. Advanced nations now import more than half their fish. Heavily subsidised fleets fish waters off poorer, developing countries, reducing available protein sources for locals. Fisheries in international waters or in disputed exclusive economic zones are treated as a common resource – no fishing fleet exercises restraint in harvesting from a specific area because it is not owned by that harvester. The outcome is to denude the supply, often beyond repair.

Illegal fishing constitutes 30 per cent of all fish caught. Around 40 per cent of fish are bycatch, marine species unintentionally captured and thrown back into the sea, many dead or dying. The vaquita, the world's smallest porpoise species, found in the Gulf of California, is nearly extinct. The animals drown when caught in gillnets used in illegal fishing for totoaba, whose swim bladder is a prized delicacy in China. Similar factors, combined with dams and pollution, doom many species of river dolphins.

Populations of large fish, including tuna and cod, are endangered. Salmon runs are in sharp decline. Even tiny krill – the main source of food for many large animals, including baleen whales – are increasingly overfished. Ever smaller and younger specimens are harvested, preventing populations from regenerating, especially among slow-reproducing species. Reduction in predatory fish including sail fish and sharks (the latter killed for their fins) favours smaller fish species, altering the ecosystem.

A growing problem is entanglement in fishing equipment, including ghost gear – abandoned, lost or discarded fishing nets, ropes and lines. They constrict body parts or cut into flesh and bone, causing abrasions, infections and sometimes severance. Affected animals struggle to eat, swim, dive and breathe, often taking years to die.

Aquaculture, dubbed the blue revolution, is designed to increase supply and offset the falling global wild catch. But fish farms damage coastal habitats, mangroves and seagrass beds. Effluent promotes algal blooms. Tightly packed fish maximises yield but results in disease, requiring antibiotics and disinfectant, which leak into the sea. Escaped farmed and non-native species damage wild populations. Aquaculture also accelerates overfishing because farmed fish are typically fed the wild variety, usually smaller bait species. Each farmed salmon requires one and a half to three times its body weight in fishmeal.

Oceanic food chains are particularly delicate. Temperature and chemical composition – especially the amounts of nitrogen and phosphorus – acidity, salinity, interaction of currents, upwellings and density stratification determine ocean productivity.

Phytoplankton is the backbone of these food chains and produces more than half of the oxygen we breathe on Earth. The one-celled microscopic algae uses photosynthesis to convert the sun's energy, nutrients and carbon dioxide into organic compounds. On the coast, seaweed and seagrasses perform a similar function. Near-invisible zooplankton, fish larvae, barnacles, molluscs, jellyfish, herbivorous fish species, turtles and manatees feed on the phytoplankton and sea plants. In turn, they become food for carnivorous marine animals. Overfishing disturbs the chain of nutrients, killing oceans.

The population of North Atlantic puffins, small, clown-faced seabirds, has fallen by nearly 80 per cent because of changes in oceanic ecosystems. Cold-water zooplankton numbers have decreased due to higher water temperatures, reducing the number of once superabundant lesser sand eels, which eat them. In turn, this has reduced numbers of puffins, marine mammals and seabirds, and those that prey on them.

It has proven difficult to reach agreement on control of fishing. In 2022, the Commission for the Conservation of Antarctic Marine Living Resources, which can only act by agreement between all members, failed to arrive at a consensus on creating three new Marine Protected Areas and fishing regulations in the overfished Southern Ocean.

Trophy hunting of some species endures. Trade in body parts continues to drive poaching. Buyers prefer medicinal products obtained from wild rather than captive animals, believing them to be more potent.

During the early twentieth century, hats decorated with bird feathers were fashionable in Europe and the Americas. Up to 80,000 birds-of-paradise were killed annually for their brilliant plumes. Teddy bear–like slow lorises, found in Borneo and Malaysia, are hunted for their large eyes, used in Asian medicine and for love charms.

The global exotic pet business harms wild animals. Primates are prized as pets. Mothers, fiercely protective of their offspring, are killed before the young is captured and sold. Monkeys, chimpanzees or orangutans are not suitable as domesticated animals. As they grow, their size and strength means many are abandoned or killed when their owners tire of or cannot manage them.

Parrots and songbirds are popular. There are perhaps 80 million captive birds on the Indonesian island of Java alone, a doubling over the last decade. According to recent surveys, nearly a third of households on the island keep them. Regarded as a cultural and social marker, the songbirds compete in avian idol contests. Indonesia's president, Joko Widodo, once entered his white-rumped shama in a competition.

As wild specimens are believed to have superior singing ability, millions of birds are trapped annually. In northern Australia, our guide, Laurie, took us to a waterhole to see Gouldian finches, resplendent in their blacks, greens, yellows, reds and purples. A retired wildlife ranger had learned of the location from bird trappers, who would trap thousands of the now threatened species for the aviculture trade in the dry season. For birds that are difficult to breed in captivity, the aviary trade ensures extinction. This was the case for the highly prized paradise parrot, considered superlatively beautiful.

Falconry requires captured peregrines, sakers, lanners and gyrfalcons. The practice affects birds of prey and also prey populations. The houbara bustard has been effectively wiped out across the Arabian Peninsula by the sport.

The best view of a great bill parrot we have had was on the Indonesian island of Halmahera. It was chained to its perch. The large bird pecked futilely at the steel clasp with its huge beak in an effort to regain its freedom.

Medical use affects the wild populations of several species. Each year, hundreds of thousands of horseshoe crabs are caught by pharmaceutical companies to extract their blood for developing safe vaccines and injectable drugs. They are returned to the ocean, but many die. The practice, combined with loss of habitat, means that the animal, which has existed for more than 440 million years, is in severe decline.

More than 150,000 monkeys are used in medical experiments globally, nearly half of them in the United States. Under American legislation, around 95 per cent of animals used in laboratory research, such as mice, rats and birds, are excluded from protection under laws designed to ensure animal welfare.

Scientists justify the practice on the basis of necessity, placing a greater value on human life. Ethicists debate animals' inability to consent. Philosopher Jeremy Bentham thought the question was whether they can suffer.

Introduced animal, plant, fungus or bacteria can displace native wild animals that ecotourists prize. Our best view of a California quail, originally only found on the west coast of the United States, was in Chile, where it was introduced in 1864.

Deliberate introduction is primarily for economic reasons. Non-native crops and livestock today account for the bulk of food production. Fish such as carp and tilapia were introduced, especially into poorer countries, as a source of protein. The timber industry globally favours pine and eucalypts, displacing native vegetation essential to local animals. Some species were intended as biological regulation agents. Australia imported dung beetles to reduce the effects of livestock manure. Introduced poisonous cane toads, while failing to eradicate pests damaging sugarcane plantations, have spread across the continent, killing indigenous wildlife.

Nostalgia played a part, with settlers transporting alien species that reminded them of home. Ornamental plants to beautify properties, such as water hyacinth, have slipped out of horticultural control, clogging waterways.

Animals were introduced for fishing and hunting. Non-native Nile Perch have eliminated several species of cichlid fish found only in

Africa's Lake Victoria. Thomas Austin, a British landowner, imported European rabbits into Australia to shoot them. The fecund animals expanded, requiring expensive and unsuccessful remedies, including the construction of a 3200-kilometre (2000-mile) rabbit-proof fence and viruses toxic to endemic life. Another popular introduced species is the fox. While transported for the fur trade, it was mainly used for hunts by English gentleman – Oscar Wilde's 'the unspeakable in full pursuit of the uneatable'.

Non-native pets damage local wild animals. Foxes, rats and feral cats and dogs have ravaged whole continents, like Australia, and especially islands, where local animals lack defences against introduced predators. Many of New Zealand's native animals, including the moa, a large flightless bird, disappeared after the arrival of humans. Birds such as the distinctive kiwi, takahē and kākāpō hover on the brink of extinction.

Long-living pet goldfish released into ponds and waterways, when their owners tire of them, are voracious eaters that outcompete local fish, damaging ecosystems, leading to calls to phase them out of the pet trade. In the late 1980s, drug baron Pablo Escobar imported hippos illegally into Columbia. After his death in 1993, the government took over his estate, including his personal zoo near Medellín. Most of the animals were shipped away, but four hippos were left in a pond. Now there are an estimated eighty to 100 individuals polluting local waterways with their toxic waste and dangerous bacteria, harmful to native species.

Alien species can enter surreptitiously. Rats spread globally on ships. Marine organisms, such as zebra mussels, travel in bilge or ballast water of ships. Insects enter countries in shipments of grains, fruit and vegetables. Some non-native species become established, damaging habitat, predating on or forcing out local animals.

Bird malaria contributed to the extinction of Hawaiian honeycreepers, nectivorous birds with a variety of slender, down-curved bills for probing flowers. Before the arrival of humans, there were probably more than eighty-five species of honeycreepers. The original settlers exterminated around thirty-five, mainly for their colourful feathers, which were made into cloaks – each requiring thousands of birds. In 1827, mosquitoes entered Hawaii from a whaling ship. The insects acted as a vector, allowing bird malaria to be transmitted from North American avian migrants to local species. Today, as a result of over-harvesting, damage to its habitat and alien diseases and parasites, only twenty-one species of honeycreeper survive, with fourteen classified as endangered.

Chemicals for vermin control or livestock, such as rodenticides, can poison wild animals. During the 2021 mouse plague in Australia, the use of bromadiolone, an anti-coagulant banned in many countries, killed large numbers of native birds of prey and owls.

In India, the number of vultures has declined by over 99 per cent, from 80 million to a few thousand. Vultures eating a dead cow treated with the anti-inflammatory drug diclofenac can die from kidney failure. Essential in recycling carrion, the fall in numbers has left rotting carcasses, resulting in increases in feral dogs, rodents and diseases such as rabies. Zoroastrian burial rites require the cleaned corpse to be placed atop the Tower of Silence for vultures to devour. Indian Zoroastrians must now import vultures to continue the tradition.

In its 2023 study, the Intergovernmental Science-Policy Platform on Biodiversity and Ecosystem Services estimated that humans had transferred 37,000 species of animals, plants and microbes to new habitats around the world. Almost 3500 of these were classified as invasive aliens because of the extensive damage they caused.

Introduced species were a major factor in 60 per cent of global animal and plant extinctions and the sole factor in 16 per cent of such events. The journal *Nature* estimates the negative economic impact of invasive species at around $1.3 trillion since 1970. The annual cost of damage to nature, human health and economic activities, such as farming and fishing from alien species, is conservatively set at $423 billion. This amount is quadrupling every decade.

In Patagonia, we searched for the critically endangered hooded grebe. The bird is mainly white and has a black head, a dark grey back and a red, peaked forecrown. Hooded grebes have been displaced by introduced trout and salmon. Imported American mink, escapees from fur farms, have wiped out entire breeding colonies. Now rarely seen, the species will probably die out soon.

Habitat loss, overharvesting and invasive species alter the physical environment. Remaining or protected wilderness areas become spatially separated.

Even a road or water diversion can split a forest, limiting movement, isolating populations. In 2021, a radio-collared young grizzly bear repeatedly attempted and failed to cross an interstate highway traversed by around 11,000 cars per day. Animals trying to negotiate a road are susceptible to death or injury from traffic.

The remaining wildlife islands are vulnerable to disruption. A small population may lack suitable breeding partners. Reduced gene pools and inbreeding affects fertility. In territorial species, competition for space creates conflict and impoverishes food supplies. Spillover from protected areas leads to tensions between animals and humans.

The giant panda, once found in many areas of Sichuan, now only exists in fragmented and isolated regions in the southwest of China. Malaysia's nomadic Asian elephants need more space than afforded by national parks. They damage adjoining farmlands, resulting in death at the hand of farmers. In Colombia, the Andes creates pockets of endemism. We glimpse an Antioquia wren briefly near the Cauca River. Only described in 2012, the endangered bird's tiny localised dry forest habitat is threatened by the spread of coffee plantations and the Ituango Dam.

Habitats do not recognise political boundaries. America's border wall with Mexico is disastrous for ocelots, jaguarundi and many birds.

In 2021, a prize-winning photo of a nomadic roadrunner, a primarily terrestrial bird that usually only flies for short distances, shows it stopped, its path blocked, by the barrier in Southern Arizona.

Smaller fragmented populations create other issues. Deprived of company in customary large flocks, Australia's critically endangered regent honeyeaters, which usually learn their songs from adults, are losing their language. They have less success in attracting mates, reducing breeding and accelerating their demise. The lack of large groups also make them vulnerable to losing territory to larger birds seeking to monopolise food resources. Regent honeyeaters are almost extinct in the wild.

Islandisation forces adaptation or, more often, results in loss. Animals disappear slowly, long after the destruction or fragmentation of their habitat, a phenomenon known as extinction debt.

Anthropogenic climate change is an existential threat for both humans and wildlife. Since the eighteenth century, fossil fuels have driven economic development. Ecologist Jeff Dukes calculated that each gallon (3.8 litres) of gasoline required about 89,000 kilograms (196,000 pounds) of plant matter converted by pressure, heat and time into oil over millennia. Fossil fuels burned in a single year total around 400 times the annual growth of all plant matter, including vast amounts of microscopic plant life in the oceans. The human race is on track to exhaust hundreds of millions of years' worth of sunlight stored as coal, oil and natural gas in a few hundred years.

The release of the carbon over a very short geological time is altering the Earth's atmosphere and chemistry. The concentration of carbon dioxide in Earth's atmosphere is currently over 420 parts per million (ppm) and rising, a 50 per cent increase from 280 ppm at the beginning of the Industrial Age. Carbon dioxide concentrations have increased around 15 per cent since 2000, when it was near 370 ppm. This has set in train damaging alterations of the biosphere.

Global temperatures have already risen more than 1 degree Celsius (2 degrees Fahrenheit) since 1880. The 2010s was the warmest decade on record, with more frequent and pronounced extremes. The year 2023 was the hottest ever on record. Heat stress will be a factor in coming extinctions.

In Australia, which is particularly vulnerable to climate change, most of the thirty-nine known extreme heat waves have taken place since 1994. Studies of the 2011 heat event in Australia found severe damage and losses. There was large-scale coral bleaching and loss of seagrass and kelp. Populations of endangered terrestrial bird species, such as Carnaby's black cockatoos, crashed. Breeding success in marine penguins collapsed. There were outbreaks of terrestrial wood-boring insects. In November 2018, when the temperature in northern Australia soared to 42 Celsius (107 degrees Fahrenheit), 23,000 endangered spectacled flying foxes died.

Physiology and habits determine impact. Birds are exposed to higher temperatures as they are more active during the day. Even desert avian species are vulnerable. Birds reliant on water from insects or animal prey may need 30 per cent more food, which, if available, has a high calorific cost to catch. Increased temperatures cause populations of native bumblebees to plummet. It boosts some insect numbers, such as locusts, which damage food supplies.

The oceans are warming faster than forecast. Marine phytoplankton, which account for roughly half of Earth's total photosynthetic biomass, have declined by up to 40 per cent due to warming. Higher temperatures and acidification of the water are destroying coral reefs, coastal mangroves and the marine ecosystems they support, contributing to falling fish stocks.

Warmer seas show greater stratification. Nutrients cannot rise from deep waters to where needed by fish and plankton. The change in ocean chemistry affects reef systems and shelled creatures such as crabs, oysters and larvae.

Since the 1950s, higher Antarctic air temperatures (up 3 degrees Celsius, or around 5.5 degrees Fahrenheit) combined with warmer oceans have reduced sea ice levels by 20 per cent. The loss leads to massive declines in krill, because the underside provides habitat for algae on which they feed which, in turn, reduces food stocks for many species.

High temperatures affect inland aquatic habitats. In 2023, the water in the region around Tefe Lake in the Brazilian Amazon rainforest reached 38 degrees Celsius (over 100 degrees Fahrenheit), some 20 per cent above normal. More than one hundred boto or pink river dolphins, perhaps 10 per cent of the local population of this exemplary Amazon species, died.

Shrinking glaciers and melting Arctic and Antarctic ice is driving sea-level rises. In the United States alone, this threatens more than 200 protected animal and plant species, 17 per cent of America's threatened and endangered species. Sea turtle and seabird nesting beaches are vulnerable to more high-tide inundation. Rising sea levels have indirect effects on wild animals. In the next few decades, hundreds of millions of people will be below the waterline at high tide or will live in zones with annual flooding, resulting in further habitat loss as wilderness areas are taken over to house displaced communities.

Increased severity of weather events such as La Niña, El Niño or the Indian Ocean Dipole also places stress on animal and plant life, which need time to recover and rebuild populations between occurrences. The effects are likely to be widespread, especially in unforgiving environments such as polar regions, where even the smallest change can push life beyond biological thresholds.

Brown bears are dependent on salmon runs to build up fat reserves for hibernation. The combination of changing conditions and excessive fishing means that fish stocks are increasingly variable, affecting the health and size of the animals. With the Arctic increasingly ice-free in summer, polar bears must travel greater distances for food. Over nine days, one female was forced to swim 675 kilometres (420 miles) nonstop. More and more are dying of starvation.

Walruses use sea ice as a base to look for bivalve molluscs on the seabed. As the sea ice platform shrinks, they must swim long distances to their feeding grounds. Needing to rest, the animals haul out onto whatever is available. In 2014, more than 35,000 walruses crammed onto a tiny spit of land in Alaska, forcing flight paths to be rerouted to avoid the risk of creating a stampede. Scientists have recorded mass deaths due to crowding, with smaller calves especially vulnerable to being crushed. Geographically concentrated around the Bering Sea, the species is now vulnerable to extinction.

Each year, more starving sea lions wash ashore in the northern hemisphere. Warming waters are driving fish from the coastal islands where the sea lions breed and wean their young. As mothers are forced to travel further away from the islands for food, the abandoned pups die.

Seabird populations are affected by changing marine ecosystems. High metabolic rates mean they must consume a large proportion of their body weight every day. Warmer, more acidic oceans mean fish stocks and zooplankton densities are lower or further away from traditional feeding grounds. As cold-water fish are fattier and nutrient-rich, even if the birds find warm-water fish to eat, this will not meet their needs. Their ability to fly, moult, weatherproof, thermally regulate and reproduce is adversely affected. Mass die-offs are now a yearly occurrence.

Emperor penguins are at risk of extinction due to climate change. Delays in the sea freezing and earlier melting means that emperors cannot complete their reproductive cycle. At Halley Bay in the Weddell Sea, the second-largest emperor penguin colony, all the chicks died in each of the last three years. In 2023, there was a disastrous die-off of up to 10,000 chicks – they drowned or froze to death when the sea ice underneath them melted and broke apart before they could develop the waterproof feathers needed to swim in the ocean. The likely cause was abnormally elevated temperatures in the Antarctic. Scientists fear that more than 90 per cent of emperor penguin colonies will be destroyed by the end of the century, as the continent's seasonal sea ice diminishes in a warming world.

Life finely honed to conditions over millions of years cannot adapt to such rapid changes in conditions. Some animals and plants may be able to relocate, climbing to higher latitudes or migrating towards the poles. Hundreds, then thousands and finally millions will become marooned and go extinct.

Few ecotourists acknowledge how their activities affect the ecosystem. Travel and accommodation consumes fossil fuels. Tourism contributes around 8 per cent of the world's carbon emissions, the majority from visitors from high-income countries.

Jade and I have seen firsthand how even low-impact ecotourism places pressure on the local environment. Infrastructure built for tourists – airports, roads and accommodation – contribute to deforestation and habitat damage. Lodges, water treatment plants and sanitation facilities normally use non-renewable energy. In many cases, untreated sewage and refuse affects existing water courses used by local people, livestock and wildlife. The lack of toilets in the Pantanal combined with a growing number of ecotourists wanting to see jaguars means that some riverbanks are now heavily contaminated by human waste and sanitary products.

Presence of humans inevitably represents an intrusion. Noise and vibrations affect animals who rely on these signals. Boats and underwater sounds, which can travel long distances, can disorient marine life. Artificial light can confuse migrating birds and animals, such as turtles, who rely on stars to navigate. Where the disturbance cannot be easily escaped, it creates stress. The animals respond by fleeing, hiding or defending territory, or become habituated to the stressor.

The ecotraveller's desire to see wild animals can put the animals at risk. Habituated gorilla groups spend hundreds of hours each year close to tourists, trackers, guides, guards and rangers. Close proximity between humans and gorillas during tourist encounters increases the risk of potentially fatal transmission of infections, especially diseases that can spread without prolonged or direct physical contact, such as measles, tuberculosis, pneumonia, influenza and other respiratory ailments. It does not help that many tourists violate the visitation rules, especially the maintenance of specified distances or staying away if they are ill.

Overzealous birders invade territories, tramping through habitat and breeding areas. In one incident, a group of birders trying to see a rare species of skulking bird crowded around an individual, trampling it to death. One South American birding guide we know stopped dealing with a foreign ecotourism operator because of their clients' behaviour, which included disturbing nest sites in the quest for photographs.

Increasing tourist numbers threaten polar regions. Regulation is limited to voluntary compliance, with conditions agreed by the fifty-three nations who are party to the 1959 Antarctic Treaty, or by the International Association of Antarctica Tour Operators. The code specifies rules designed to control environmental impact, restricting the size of ships, type of fuel used and numbers of visitors at sites.

There is always the risk of accidents due to poor maps and rapidly changing ice conditions. In 2007, the tourist ship *Explorer* sank after hitting an iceberg near the South Shetland Islands. Favourable weather and nearby ships allowed more than 150 people to be rescued. The vessel was carrying more than 208,000 litres (55,000 gallons) of oil, lubricant and petrol, which was still visible more than a year later. In 2023, *Ocean Explorer*, an Arctic cruise ship with 206 people on board, became stuck in Alpefjord off Greenland's remote east coast, requiring rescue. The vessel was carrying tourists paying up to $27,000 each to see the fragile, icy landscape and its wildlife before it disappears. The damage to the environment is not known.

In Antarctica, landings were originally restricted to a few sites to minimise damage. Increasing numbers of tourists mean more and more rookeries are visited. Penguins and seabirds unused to humans are abandoning nests because of the disturbance. Scientists now sacrifice some sites to tourists in order to preserve others from intrusion.

Polar systems are particularly ecologically delicate. In temperate zones, the ecosystem – long growing seasons, mild temperatures, moderate rainfall and great variety of creatures – is more accommodating to disturbance. In the Arctic and Antarctic, marks left by visitors are indelible. Even footfall damages plants and soils that need many years to grow back. Visitors' foot holes when they crash through snow crust are deadly traps for penguins.

At about 1 metre (3 feet) in length from the top of its head to the tip of its pointed tail, the hyacinth macaw is the world's largest parrot. Its striking cobalt blue feathers are set off by a vibrant yellow ring around the eyes and underneath the beak. We saw a single older bird that had probably lost its mate on the Transpanteneira Highway. Perched on an electrical pole, the large bird overbalanced and desperately grabbed the live wires, electrocuting itself. It did not die instantly, shrieking in agony before falling to the ground. A group of passing tourists got out of a car, walked to the body to take photos and collected the colourful feathers as souvenirs.

Ecotourists like Jade and me believe that we are furthering conservation efforts. But commercial ecotourism frequently damages rather than preserves. The Inuit fear Westerners, specifically their ability to alter the land. They call us people who change nature. Our personal part in this ecological catastrophe brings profound shame, and does not do us credit.

In 2017, wildlife photographer Paul Nicklin published harrowing footage of an emaciated polar bear on Canada's Baffin Island. The exhausted animal desperately searches for food. It drags a leg. A painful death is imminent. It is not clear how the bear lost the capacity to hunt; it could have been illness or injury. Critics saw the video as a calculated public relations exercise to raise money for Nicklin's Sea Legacy NGO. Some criticised him for not helping the bear or euthanising it.

In 2020, Australia saw an apocalyptic fire season, the result of record heat and dry conditions. There was darkness at noon as the conflagrations acted as a solar eclipse. Horrific pictures recorded birds on fire, and burnt koalas and kangaroos trying vainly to outrun fires. An estimated three billion animals were killed or displaced. Losses will ultimately be higher due to the damage to the habitat, with some species becoming extinct.

In the northern autumn the same year, hundreds of thousands of migrating flycatchers, swallows and warblers died in the United States.

The birds fly south from Alaska and Canada over America's southwest to reach wintering grounds in Central and South America. The journey pushes the small birds to their physical limits. Many carcasses had little remaining fat reserves or muscle mass. They need to rest and feed at waypoints of their migration. Climate change probably reduced food supplies at their usual stopping sites.

At the same time, Brazil's Pantanal was on fire due to drought. The wetland, which is not generally combustible, has over 1200 vertebrate animal species, including thirty-six threatened with extinction. Along the Transpanteneira Highway, starving jaguars walked in a blackened landscape. Their paws were burnt. The animals could not breathe, their lungs damaged from inhaling smoke. Immolated caimans and monkeys in grotesque poses were everywhere.

In central California, webcam footage showed a four-month-old Californian condor chick, part of the breeding and reintroduction program, looking at advancing flames. Then, the live stream went dead as the fire engulfed the nest and the bird.

Wild places are increasingly empty. Extinctions unbalance ecosystems, affecting those animals that a species preys on, those that prey on it or those that rely on it in other ways. Insects are food sources for many bird, fish and mammal species, some of which are in turn relied on by other animals and humans for food or as pollinators or agents for the regulation of insect populations. Living creatures embody billions of years of biological information and events. Losing one species means the loss of something irreplaceable.

One of the most melancholy and haunting sounds on Earth we know of is a recording of Hawaii's last Kaua'i 'ō'ō, which died around 1987. The bird, a male, calls repeatedly to attract a female. There is no answer. If animals become extinct, how can homo sapiens, just another species, survive?

11

CLICK HERE TO SAVE THE PLANET

The Challenge of Preserving Biodiversity

In April 2018, civil rights attorney and environmentalist David Buckel doused himself in gasoline and set himself ablaze near his home in Brooklyn. In 2022, activist Wynn Bruce died by suicide by self-immolation outside the US Supreme Court. Their pleas were for meaningful action to halt the slide into an ecological apocalypse. They hoped that their final act might give voice to the voiceless natural world. The calls barely registered outside their immediate circles.

Needless to say, this level of commitment is not the norm. In the main, words are batted back and forth among policymakers, scientists, intellectuals and thought leaders. The dialectics of preserving biodiversity are straight from the British political satire *Yes Minister*. In the beginning, you say nothing is going to happen. Then, you admit something may be happening, but nothing should be done. Then, you acknowledge that perhaps something should be done but there is nothing that can be done. Finally, you admit that something should have been done but it is now too late.

Bjorn Lomborg, a former Danish public servant and head of his own think tank, has written two books with telling titles: *The Skeptical Environmentalist* and *False Alarms*. According to Lomborg, global warming is real and human-made but unimportant. Action would be costly, lower economic growth and living standards and have no meaningful effect. Resources should be focused instead on addressing malnutrition and preventable diseases.

At the other end of the spectrum, US writer Jonathan Franzen argues that it is now impossible to save the planet. He favours adaptation and easing the suffering of affected animals. Academic, author and former Australian of the Year Tim Flannery rejects negative thinking, placing his faith in science, our highly developed intelligence and advanced social structures, and nations ceding sovereignty to secure a common good. In a nod to the 1960s, he urges people to love one another and the planet as much as they love themselves.

Lomborg was originally a lecturer in statistics in the political science department. In 2003, the Danish committee that investigates scientific fraud and misconduct ruled that the *The Skeptical Environmentalist* was deceitful but found Lomborg himself not guilty because he lacked expertise. The ruling was overturned principally on procedural grounds. The examiners refused to reconsider the case, arguing that the original conclusion would stand.

Lomborg's selective use of statistics remains controversial. Contrary to specialist biologists, he finds no evidence of declines in polar bear numbers, instead citing anecdotal evidence of increased sightings by locals. The truth is that they now venture closer to towns in search of food. Lomborg claims that the major threat comes from hunting, ignoring the reduction of their habitat, changed ice conditions affecting the ability to hunt, lower prey numbers, drops in body condition, lower cub survival rates, loss of denning areas, rising incidents of drowning and increased incidents of cannibalism. In December 2020, a *Siberian Times* video emerged of polar bears trying to move from Wrangel

Island onto the fast ice to hunt. Even in winter, the ice is not solid as it should be. The bears could neither swim in nor walk on this sludgy substance. They just made it to shore, exhausted.

Lomborg discounted climate change as a cause of Australia's 2020 fires on the logic that the continent is naturally fire-prone and 5 per cent of the country burns every year. He claims that in 1900, 11 per cent of Australia burned annually. Given the spread of human habitation, the remaining wilderness areas are now smaller, making the statistics uncertain. Averages are deceptive, as the areas burnt have different biodiversity. Following Lomborg's reasoning, concreting over all of Australia would eliminate any fire risk.

Opponents dispatched Franzen as a crass publicity-seeking novelist. Critics thought that Flannery, a mammologist and a palaeontologist, commented on things outside his expertise. They questioned the certainty of his views and the lack of supporting data.

The scientific dishonesty hearings attracted global attention, making Lomborg a media celebrity. Franzen's views reinforced his reputation for controversy. Flannery's frequent lament that his years of climate activism were a colossal failure was simply anxiety about his fading popularity or fear of global waning, unkind detractors snidely carped.

Conservation is not immune from culture wars. Semioticians and deconstructivists analyse debates about the environment in terms of power relations. Supporters of climate action tend to be white, affluent people from developed countries. Although climate protest is seen as the preserve of the young, around a quarter of climate protestors are baby boomers.

There are ideological matters. Some conservation groups are seen as extremist, seeking the breakdown of liberal democracy and capitalism in addition to action on climate. Traditional leftist forces worry about the exclusion of the working classes, who favour jobs over conservation. A narrow focus on the environment attracts criticism for leaving aside concerns about political identity, social justice, gender and sex.

Others criticise the lack of clarity and concrete demands when it comes to the environmental movement. Some question Extinction Rebellion's rhetoric, arguing that the timelines they propose are unrealistic and cannot be met technically, economically or politically. Bitter, scarring exchanges between conservationists of different stripes distract from the commonalities of their demands.

While the intellectual sophistry continues, Jade and I have watched entire ecosystems and species suffer irreparable damage, while the clock on the available time to act runs down.

Our priority should be halting damage to the environment and, where possible, reversing it. This would entail stopping habitat loss, eliminating overharvesting, removing introduced species, avoiding fragmentation and addressing climate change. But agreement on how to do these things is elusive.

Opposition to reducing land clearing, hunting and fishing remains strong. In developed countries, obstruction comes not just from recreational hunters and fishers but also from agriculturalists and current and aspiring homeowners. In impoverished countries, survival often depends on utilising natural resources. Addressing the health of local habitats would require displacement of communities, which is difficult and expensive, especially with suitable land availability limited. And it overlooks the fact that many local communities have long and enduring links to the land where they are based.

Yet the risk of inaction is great. John W. Reid and Thomas E. Lovejoy in *Ever Green: Saving Big Forests to Save the Planet* urge preservation of the world's five remaining mega forests – in New Guinea, the Congo, the Amazon, the North American boreal zone and the Russian Taiga – to avoid releasing carbon locked in trees and soil. The boreal forests alone hold 1.8 trillion metric tonnes, equivalent to 190 years of worldwide emissions at 2019 levels. Glamorous initiatives such as renewables, carbon capture and electric vehicles to limit emissions will not matter if these forests are lost.

The fashion is for less effective proposals that offend no one. The latest, especially in developed countries, is rewilding – the re-creation of wilderness by combining state land and purchased farms or properties and reintroducing keystone species. There is even an underground network of wildlife enthusiasts in Europe introducing rare species without permission.

Rewilding makes a virtue of necessity. It often involves poor-quality land, unsuitable for food production. In Europe and post-Brexit Britain, declining agricultural subsidies mean that up to 30 million hectares (over 70 million acres) may become unviable for farming by 2030. But priorities are changeable. The 2022 Ukraine war meant land slated for rewilding was reallocated for agriculture to ease potential food shortages.

In any case, rewilded areas are generally small and difficult to connect due to topography and property ownership. Restoring natural diversity is not easy. Regeneration of native plant species takes time and what was destroyed cannot be replicated precisely. One hectare (2.5 acres) of rainforest can contain over 750 types of trees and 1500 species of plants.

Rewilding can involve reintroduction of species into existing protected areas, such as wolves in America's Yellowstone National Park, lions in Rwanda's Akagera and some forty different species, including bears and lynx, into various European reserves. In 2022, twelve African cheetahs were released into one park in India. The last Asiatic specimens in India were shot in 1948 by Maharajah Ramanuj Pratap Singh Deo of Madhya Pradesh. The reintroduction was ironic given India's poor record of protecting endangered wild animals. After three of the animals died in mid-2023, concerns were raised about the program, including the suitability of the habitat.

Reintroduced carnivores may pose a threat to domestic animals as numbers grow naturally and spill out of rewilded areas. In 2023, Ursula von der Leyen, President of the European Commission, supported a review of the protected status of wolves, arguing that were a real danger to livestock and people. A pack had killed her pony, Dolly, in September 2022. Even the reintroduction of beavers is mired in controversy because they reshape water courses and landscapes.

Introduced wild animals can carry diseases detrimental to domestic animals. In Scotland, released wild boar may carry antibiotic-resistant superbugs. Conversely, introduction of expensive wild animals susceptible to livestock diseases is self-defeating. Rewilding has exposed societal divisions. Rural populations resent wealthy urbanites purchasing farmland and allowing it to revert to wilderness.

Efforts by Singapore, among the most densely populated places on Earth, to clean up its waterways and create green areas has allowed the return of some mammals and birds. The program is not universally popular. Residents complain that smooth-coated otters have invaded homes and eaten prized koi carp from pools. In 2023, a rare, endangered Malayan tapir, which can weigh up to 560 kilograms (1200 pounds), swam over to Singapore, alarming locals.

Ultimately, self-regulating and sustainable stable ecosystems, with anything approaching pre-human levels of biodiversity, are immensely difficult to recreate. Rewilding alone cannot address global threats such as climate change.

Attempts to deal with emissions highlight different challenges. The 2018 United Nations Intergovernmental Panel on Climate Change (IPCC) report concluded that it is critical to keep global temperature rises to 1.5 degrees Celsius (2.7 degrees Fahrenheit) or less, 25 per cent below the previously agreed safe level of 2 degrees Celsius (3.6 degrees

Fahrenheit). Even at 1.5 degrees Celsius, many ecosystems will undergo major transformation – 6 per cent of insect species, 8 per cent of plants and 4 per cent of vertebrates would lose more than half their habitat. The figures for 2 degrees Celsius are 18 per cent, 16 per cent and 8 per cent respectively. The IPCC found that a rise of 2 degrees Celsius would wipe out more than 99 per cent of corals. Even a rise of 1.5 degrees Celsius would leave only 10 to 30 per cent alive.

Climate agreements seek to hold increases to within 2 degrees Celsius above pre-industrial levels and to pursue efforts to limit them to the lower level. However, specific measures adopted are insufficient to achieve the target. That would require eliminating emissions immediately and removing existing greenhouse gases already in the atmosphere. It is probable that temperature rises will be in the range of 2.7 to 3.5 degrees Celsius (4.9 to 6.3 degrees Fahrenheit).

The agreements are a potent mixture of geopolitical blackmail and financial carrots, the work of creative lawyers skilled at hiding the thornier details in the contours of clever drafting. The treaties rely on voluntary compliance. The rules for accounting, reporting and reviewing emission reductions are unclear. They lack effective sanctions or enforcement mechanisms.

Many countries have announced distant hypothetical emission-reduction targets. Several of these vague commitments rely on unproven or unfunded technologies. Well-intentioned policies have unintended side-effects. The need for critical raw materials to undertake the transition to renewables creates environmental damage, for instance. Large areas of land have been cleared to meet demand for lithium, copper, nickel and other substances needed for batteries and new power sources to transition away from fossil fuels.

The overwhelming rhetoric of stopping the mass extinction of life on Earth is not being matched by appropriate resourcing. Rich countries have consistently failed to provide already agreed climate finance to the developing world or worst-affected poorer nations, let alone meet the yawning gap in nature funding. Advanced economies seem oblivious to disparities in global living standards. Fighting climate change is an option when your lives are comfortable and material needs have been met. It is not for poorer people struggling to ensure the essentials of life, who go hungry and watch their children die.

The necessary watchmaker's care to actionable detail is absent. Most countries are willing to sign largely meaningless documents because of the political imperative of announcing headline-grabbing progress. They are less engaged in the grinding work of solving the complex underlying issues. Leaders, unlikely to be in power when the problems become unmanageable, prefer to defer real choices into the never-never.

The path of climatic change is difficult to predict. Feedback loops in atmospheric chemistry and physics are poorly understood. The Amazon basin, one of the planet's largest stores of carbon, is beginning to release more carbon dioxide into the atmosphere than it absorbs as deforestation and fires spread, potentially exacerbating global warming. In some scenarios, the glaciers that hold back Antarctica's and Greenland's ice sheets collapse, sending massive quantities of ice into the oceans, accelerating sea-level rises. Extreme weather sequences could accelerate deforestation, releasing more carbon into the atmosphere. Thawing permafrost may release large amounts of methane, a potent greenhouse gas, into the atmosphere.

It is difficult to reverse the trajectory that has been set in motion. Carbon dioxide lasts in the atmosphere for a century. Outcomes may already be baked in.

Alongside other concerned individuals, Jade and I want to help overcome the dysfunction and preserve wilderness and wild animals. We try to lower our ecological footprint, following recommendations on sustainable housing, food and beverage choices, energy use, transport options, purchases, packaging, recycling and repair rather than replacement of household items. The hope is our deeds will help usher in the circular economy, decoupling economic activity from the consumption of finite resources to create a more environmentally sustainable world.

Travel planning could follow similar precepts. But in a setting that prioritises personal freedoms, especially in wealthier societies, this is dangerous territory. Any attempt to restrict choice is branded moralistic or elitist. What right do I have to place restrictions on others? Our journeys compromise our standing.

But that does not mean that nothing can be done. When planning, commence with the frequent governmental safety advice – reconsider your need for travel.

Motivation is important. What will your trip achieve beyond impressing your peers or ticking off a vague item on your bucket list? Will documentaries or virtual reality in the metaverse allow the experience you seek at lower economic or environmental cost? But, of course, this might entail sacrifices. Will we fairly evaluate our need to travel to fragile ecosystems? After all, a hunter or poacher can claim a passionate interest in wild animals.

The destination is significant. Looking closer to home can theoretically reduce the environmental impact. Ideally, travellers would seek out less 'touristy' destinations, and prioritise community-driven initiatives. However, this is not as easy as it sounds.

Before the pandemic, the UK's Lake District, where poet William Wordsworth 'wander'd lonely as a cloud' amid 'golden daffodils', attracted millions of national and international tourists annually. During the pandemic, the area was locked down to protect vulnerable older local residents and avoid pressure on health services. After restrictions eased, visitors, mainly British, returned in large numbers, with unexpected results. The influx damaged the landscape and wildlife. Residents complained about rubbish left behind. Visitors going off track on 4x4 vehicles in search of new, less frequented spots promoted on social media caused soil damage. Sediment washed off hillsides collected in lakes and rivers, reducing fish breeding habitat. It also damaged plant and insect life, meaning the area will attract fewer birds.

When travelling further afield, carbon emissions from transportation and accommodation can be ameliorated through carbon offsets, though there are questions about their efficacy and some programs are poorly verified. Look to choose more sustainable travel options, sacrificing creature comforts and accepting less luxurious accommodation, food and travel. We have found a certain pleasure in rustic living, even if it is for a short time.

Ecotourists can also reduce consumption by avoiding expensive one-off purchases of unnecessary special clothing and equipment. Avoiding storing too many digital photographs and promulgating needless images via social media will reduce energy use – while these acts are small, individually it adds up. Jade and I often choose to purchase a professional photographer's book of photos of the area as a memento of the visit.

If you are genuinely interested in wildlife, then ensure your journey contributes to the conservation of animals and wilderness. In addition to researching locations and travelling to less visited places to avoid overcrowding, ensure more of your spending stays in the place visited by using, wherever possible, local operators, despite complications of communication, cultural differences and distance. Always follow ethical standards of observation to safeguard animals and avoid stressing them. Ecotourism businesses that adopt good wildlife watching and guiding practices should be promoted. Naming and shaming is effective in separating good from bad outfits.

Alongside supporting conservation NGOs, we must also hold them to account. Given that most are tax-exempt charities, governments can readily force disclosure of their sources of funding, how money is used and how their programs help the environment or wild animals.

Oversight of individual philanthropy must warrant that wilderness cannot be de facto privatised.

Given its reach, the media has the potential to inform the public about environmental questions. Instead, producers and publishers worry about gloomy facts, even if they are the reality. They prefer to focus on optimism and hope, perhaps mixed with the occasional judicious mention of the truth. Discussion of environmental destruction and extinction are seen as incompatible with escapist entertainment. The money people – sponsors, advertisers, distributors and networks – argue that any message that preaches or is overtly depressing alienates audiences. Some creators, such as wildlife filmmakers and writers, are reluctant to take sides in the conversation on climate, defending their position as admirably apolitical. They argue that the beauty and wonders of nature will shift public opinion. We can insist that artists and the media honour their responsibility to present the facts about the true state of the planet.

The income from ecotourism must be better shared. Instead of appropriation into general state revenue, money raised should be set aside in a dedicated fund to be used for preserving and maintaining wilderness areas and investing in animal welfare. This requires legislation, which governments might resist as setting an unwelcome precedent. Pressure from environmentalists, tour operators and travellers might nudge authorities to act.

Nature is a public asset, which should be treated with respect to best ensure its long-term preservation. Many destinations are driven by the economic imperative to accommodate as many tourists as possible. This creates oversupply of low-quality operators and large numbers of visitors, who place higher stresses on and sometime vandalise wilderness areas. Restricting access, through quotas and visitor permits, is one response. Alaska allocates visitor permits by ballot, ensuring that access does not become a preserve of the rich. Another response is cordoning off some remaining wilderness areas permanently or for a protracted period to alleviate the pressure on them. Such rotation might better balance tourism with the health of ecosystems.

Ultimately, ecotourists must be willing to pay a fair price, consistent with the preservation of the destination and its wild animals. Botswana, location of the wildlife-rich Okavango Delta, operates a high-cost, low-numbers approach to manage environmental pressures. Rwanda uses a similar model in regard to its gorillas. In 2022, reopening to international travellers after the pandemic, Bhutan introduced a sustainable development fee of $200 per person per day to maximise economic benefits while limiting the ecological and cultural impact on the small Himalayan kingdom. A year after its introduction, the fee was halved to $100 as tourists proved unwilling to pay the asking amount and visitor numbers declined sharply. Travellers, it seems, know the cost of things but are unwilling to pay for their true value.

Jade and I are engaged in a continuous and not always successful attempt to balance the impact of our presence on natural environments with our interest in these places. If we do not ensure their continuation, wouldn't it just amount to destructive voyeurism?

Filtering travel choices using these criteria may help redirect ecotourism towards its true purpose and promise. But these initiatives will prove mere palliatives and virtue signalling unless societies directly address the deeper issues – population, economic growth, living standards, intensity of resource use and inequality.

James Lovelock, author of the Gaia hypothesis, thought the Earth was suffering from disseminated primatemaia – a plague of people. Currently, demand from the world's population, most of it from developed nations, requires 1.7 Earths. If developing countries attain the living standards of advanced nations, then three or more planets' worth of resources will be needed. Conservationists are reluctant to raise the population issue, fearing being branded as eugenicists. Some hide behind the argument that declining global fertility rates will solve the problem. Technophiles argue the unproven and unlikely case that human ingenuity can stretch the carrying capacity of the Earth. Unanchored optimism and fuzzy timeframes masquerade as a plan.

Speaking in 2010 to *Cosmos* magazine, Sir Peter Scott, founder of the World Wildlife Fund, lamented that the organisation had failed in its objective of saving endangered species from extinction. All the money should have been spent on condoms to lower population growth, something that might actually have done some good.

Over the last three hundred years, expectations of constant improvements in living standards have become entrenched. Betterment is intrinsically linked to perpetual economic advances based around consumption. For Edward Abbey, never-ending growth was the ideology of a cancer cell. David Attenborough thought that the idea of infinite expansion in a finite environment could only be that of a mad person or an economist.

A 2020 report on biodiversity produced by the University of Cambridge's Partha Dasgupta for the British government documented how human activity takes resources from nature and dumps waste back into it. Where extraction and disposal exceeds nature's capacity to repair itself, the stock of natural capital shrinks and, with it, the flow of valuable environmental services. Subsequent analyses confirm that the planet is being depleted at an unsustainable rate. Reversing this trend requires a reduction in population, reigning in living standards and decreasing resource use.

The problem is compounded by inequality, both within and between countries. The richest 10 per cent of households are responsible for 40 per cent of global emissions. Resource-intensive lifestyles among the more affluent consigns the rest to scramble for what is left over, leaving little room for environmental concerns. For Mahatma Gandhi, the planet had enough for humankind's need but not for its greed.

Current arrangements are deeply flawed. Failures need to be addressed. Radical changes in behaviours and attitudes are required. But in a world built around consumption using borrowed money to impress people who don't know us and don't care, the identified measures are unlikely to be popular. Any proposal that seeks restraining living standards is painted as non-egalitarian, regressive and anti-progress. At the launch of the Redefining Prosperity Project exploring limits on economic growth, Tony Jackson, professor of sustainable development at the University of Surrey, reported that a UK Treasury official accused the authors of wanting to 'go back and live in caves'.

Yet inaction is consequential for humans as well as wild animals. Critical functions performed by the natural world, especially climate regulation, are now compromised. Human activity alters the water, carbon and other chemical cycles, increasing the frequency and severity of acid rain, algal blooms and fish kills. It disturbs the Earth's chemistry, affecting oxygen production, pollination, nitrogen fixation, recycling of nutrients and waste treatment. Deforestation and warmer oceans diminish the planet's oxygen production and sequestration of carbon dioxide. Reduction in tree cover and mangroves reduces natural barriers against storms, floods and wave damage.

Environmental degradation increases vulnerability to shortages of food and water, as well as natural disasters. Erosion, rising salinity, compaction, nutrient depletion, pollution and urbanisation have degraded 40 per cent of agricultural land over the past fifty years. Damage to marine and freshwater ecosystems has reduced fish catches dramatically, affecting diets and livelihoods. Recreational activities such as hunting, fishing and tourism rely on habitat protection. Australia's Great Barrier Reef makes an economic contribution of over $4 billion annually and supports more than 60,000 jobs that will soon vanish.

In March 2020, the world shut down. In a few short weeks, countries progressively closed to combat the fast-spreading Covid-19 outbreak. The enigmatic pathogen was contagious and could unpredictably turn deadly. With populations that had no natural immunity, governments sought to limit infections with mandated isolation, quarantine and restrictions on movement, strategies originally devised by medieval Italian city-states.

Covid-19 provided a window into the interconnections between humans and nature. The virus, like SARS and ebola, was a product of zoonosis, where viral mutations crossover from animals to infect humans.

Deforestation to accommodate ever-growing populations or to access resources brings humans into contact with wild animals. When biodiversity decreases, animals that thrive around human populations proliferate. Many, such as bats and rats, can transmit diseases to humans. Overfishing in African waters by foreign fleets forced Africans to turn to bushmeat for protein, which is behind the spread of ebola. In some places, rising living standards created demand for exotic wild animals, considered delicacies.

Economics dictates the concentration of people in large, densely populated cities. The appetite for leisure travel helps contagious pathogens spread rapidly. Natural barriers, such as bodies of water, mountain ranges or deserts, no longer prevent the spread of many diseases.

Industrial agriculture and livestock husbandry to feed growing populations promotes zoonotic diseases. Poor food safety, inadequate hygiene and the mixing of livestock and wild animals is common. Animal faecal matter can enter groundwater, allowing viruses and bacteria to cross species boundaries. The pandemic should not have been unexpected.

Covid-19 was a stark warning. A complex silicon chip–based civilisation was brought to a halt by the simplest life form. Humans, despite their overweening conceit, are passengers along for the ride.

Some seventy years ago, economic historian Karl Polanyi described how industrial civilisation flourished at the expense of nature. He prophesised how, if left unchecked, it would destroy the very things it depended upon.

Despite the obvious and immediate danger, there is little urgency. Policy-makers offer bromides to milquetoast masses eager to receive them. Cognitive dissonance is the rule. The tense of choice is the present continuous: a future unlike the present is unthinkable. This is prognostic myopia, the disconnect between the human ability to think about the distant future and the lack of interest in the consequences of our actions that are altering it. Climate change is global, long-term, slow-acting, irreversible and uncertain. Its precise nature and timetable is unknown. Conditioned by evolution to focus on immediate survival needs, we live in the present, ignoring long-term contingencies that will affect us, collectively if not individually.

Kari Marie Norgaard's 2011 book *Living in Denial* studied the disavowal of climate change in a rural community in western Norway. Despite it being common knowledge, citizens separated this information from political, social and private life. In his 2014 book *Reason in a Dark Time*, Dale Jamieson, a professor of environmental studies and philosophy, argues that humans are poorly equipped to deal with such problems. We find it difficult to balance short-term losses of personal wealth and lifestyle against long-term vague benefits. We do not equate personal choices now with invisible benefits for other humans or animals thousands of miles away.

Evolution has conditioned humans to react defensively to serious threats. Despite claims of rationality, we innately shut out such anxieties as a form of self-preservation. Comfort is found in denial or accepting simplistic schemes that do not solve unwelcome situations. The response is compounded by declining trust in authorities and institutions. It traps people in the prisoner's dilemma: lacking confidence in societal processes, each person believes that their interests can only be safeguarded by caring about individual, not collective, fates.

In May 2022, at a *Financial Times* Moral Money conference, Stuart Kirk, global head of responsible investing at HSBC Asset Management, questioned the risks of climate change. The presentation, entitled 'Why investors need not worry about climate risk', included one slide stating 'unsubstantiated, shrill, partisan, self-serving, apocalyptic warnings are ALWAYS wrong'. Like Y2K, climate change, he argued, was some nutjob repeating that the end of the world is nigh. While he did not disagree with the science, any risk was too far away from the present to be financially relevant. He asked provocatively, 'Who cares if Miami is six metres underwater in 100 years?' because 'Amsterdam has been six metres underwater for ages and ... is a really nice place.' Kirk's message was that humans are good at adapting to and managing change.

The gloomy 2022 IPCC report admitted that emissions and global temperatures will continue to rise, bringing about extreme environmental changes, and emphasised adaptation. Natural systems – coral reefs, rainforests, coastal wetlands and polar and mountainous ecosystems – are reaching their biological limits of survival, and the pace of climatic change is too quick to allow them to adapt. In Australia's northern wet tropics, home to over 45 per cent of the continent's bird species, the fate of golden bowerbirds and fernwren, found nowhere else, is dismal. Forced to ever-higher altitudes, they will soon have nowhere to go as temperatures increase to unsuitable levels even at mountain peaks.

Adaptation may be detrimental. Efforts to deal with the impacts of climate change may do more harm than good. Building ever higher sea walls to protect against rising sea levels and storm surges can alter currents, worsening erosion elsewhere. Dams and levees change water flows and create a false sense of security, encouraging human populations to live in areas prone to flooding. Solutions to one hazard simply alter the risk. Adaptation also means a massive loss of biodiversity, with unknown consequences for human life on Earth.

Kirk might parlay his views into a new career supported by those confident in their belief that climate problems are merely a temporary concern and that humans will adjust. But can we be sure that the risks are as small as claimed? Homo sapiens may not have the luxury of running an experiment to see what the outcomes look like. The consequences of being even slightly wrong are grave, as each successive year demonstrates.

In the aftermath of the modest trial of the pandemic, where safety nets protected the population, especially in advanced countries, tired populations retreated into fantasy. Confronted with the forbidding scale of environmental challenges, people withdrew and looked for the off-ramps they felt was their due. Gatekeepers and opinion shapers too sought to shield audiences from unpleasant truths.

With attention spans short and receptivity to unpleasant news limited, it is unlikely that the human race will suddenly be moved to act. Elaborately constructed arguments and entire belief systems justify an unwillingness to change – because countenancing restrictions on common activities and a reduction in living standards is uncomfortable. Instead, we rely on specious excuses and a quasi-religious belief in innovation to vanquish scarcity and sidestep scientific laws. The debate around energy sources ignores the need to rein in consumption because our lifestyles are intrinsically dependent on increasing amounts of cheap power. Most people are hoping for a killer app to save the world with a single click. The magical thinking is consistent with Arthur C. Clarke's Third Law: any advanced technology becomes indistinguishable from alchemy.

Today, everyone believes that something should be done as long as it is by someone else. Like anything that should be everybody's business, it becomes nobody's business. Hard-wired to prioritise individual goals and prone to inaction when confronted with species-level threats, humans seek escape in hope, rejecting uncomfortable facts. A large part of the population believes in endless economic gains and consumerism, favouring selfishness at the expense of social decay. Real and enduring change is impossible under those circumstances.

Homo sapiens invert subject and predicate: animals are not human but humans are animals. For Ernst Haeckel, the Earth was a mere speck in the universe and humanity a tiny grain of perishable protoplasm. Portuguese poet Fernando Pessoa, writing as his alter-ego Bernard Soares, found nothing that distinguishes human life from that of any other animal. Both moved through life following similar organic itineraries. Both thought nothing beyond what they thought. Neither could escape the bounds of what they were, their environment or mortality.

All life forms exist within boundaries set by the planet and laws of physics, chemistry and biology. The stability of ecosystems relies on a few simple rules. Finite resources place limits on the growth of all living systems. If one species expands beyond the available resources, then it must monopolise what is there or prey on other species, reducing biodiversity. Overpopulation and damage to the ecosystem is corrected by the decline or extinction of the offending group.

Resource-poor Patagonia illustrates these principles. It is a world of miniatures to accommodate scarcity, such as the pudú, the world's smallest deer. Humans have chosen a different path, growing steadily more populous, requiring additional resources, which multiplies environmental stresses. As with an invasion of a pathogen, there are four possible outcomes: destruction of the host, the eradication of the invading organism, chronic infection or development of a symbiotic relationship between host and invader. The last is the least likely.

In *Socio-biology*, the late biologist E.O. Wilson analysed the adaptability of different animal groups. He found that colonial invertebrates –mould, coral, sponges and jellyfish-like creatures – were best at working together in the face of challenges. Slimes, microscopic fungi that live on plant or animal matter, start as free-ranging predators consuming bacteria and multiplying rapidly. When food becomes scarce, they merge into tight-knit groups that form sausage-like bodies to seek out new sources of sustenance. More developed species emphasise individuality over group solidarity, a tendency that increases sharply in mammals, especially humans.

We want to believe that we stand outside nature. Religion, science, dogma and now technology underlie our belief in unparalleled human control over the planet. This hubristic exceptionalism assumes superior rights to the Earth, ignoring other creatures' prior prerogatives to its air, oceans and lands. We seek to monopolise resources, dismantle processes and practice violent tyranny over other animals for short-term economic wealth. Yet our existence depends on the health of those very elements.

Nature is impassive and indifferent, unconcerned with the wellbeing of individuals or of entire species. Its relentless logic only favours those fitted for and able to live within ecological constraints. Darwin argued that responsiveness to change, not strength or intelligence, is the key to survival. Species appear and thrive based on advantages over competitors and sustainable use of the available setting. Failure results ultimately in extinction.

In *If Nietzsche Were a Narwhal: What Animal Intelligence Reveals About Human Stupidity*, psychologist and animal behaviouralist Justin Gregg recognises the remarkable feats of human intelligence. But he warns that these very same qualities are currently on track to produce the extinction of homo sapiens, which is how evolution rids the Earth of failed adaptations. There is nothing permanent about us.

A world without humans is already observable. On 26 April 1986, the Chernobyl nuclear power plant failed, releasing 400 times more radiation than that of the 1945 atomic bomb dropped on Hiroshima. The accident resulted in many human and wildlife casualties. Severe restrictions on permanent settlement in the area remain.

In 2019, scientists found that the Chernobyl exclusion zone, which now straddles Ukraine and Belarus, had regenerated with surprising levels of biodiversity. The contaminated zone contained stable and viable populations of brown bears, bison, wolves, lynxes, introduced Przewalski's horses, and more than 200 bird species.

The studies confirmed that the animal and plant populations were more resistant to high radiation levels than predicted. Some organisms may have adapted to the radioactivity. The absence of humans was positive for larger species. It seems that humanity's activities were more damaging to wildlife than a nuclear event.

A demilitarized zone (DMZ) divides North and South Korea. A large military presence oversees the thin verdant strip of land between the two nations. Yet this dangerous place teems with life, including thousands of species that are extinct or endangered elsewhere on the peninsula. Here, too, the absence of humans has allowed other animals to thrive undisturbed. The DMZ's land and marine ecosystems hold amur goral, Asiatic black bear, musk deer, spotted seal, red-crowned and white-naped cranes. There are reports of tigers, believed extinct in the region for over half a century. The small area has immense biodiversity – 100 species of fish, up to 45 types of amphibians and reptiles, over 1000 different insect species, 1600 types of vascular plants and more than 300 species of mushrooms, fungi and lichen. The relative health of the DMZ contrasts with the failing ecosystems in the Korean Peninsula.

Paleobiologist Thomas Halliday, writing in *Otherlands*, describes the extinct ecosystems of a disappeared Earth, decoded from bones and fossils. His is an urgent message for the present – our world risks becoming another defunct ecosystem. Alone in deep forests, the tundra or polar regions, it is not difficult to imagine a future without us.

In 1897, sick, unable to afford treatment, in debt and unhappy with his failed tropical paradise, Paul Gauguin planned to take his own life. Before his unsuccessful attempted suicide, he directed his remaining energy to creating an allegorical painting that now hangs in Boston's Museum of Fine Arts. Awakening and seeing it, Gauguin found himself asking: 'Where do we come from? What are we? Where are we going?' The signature questions became the title of the picture. For Jade and me, every encounter with nature poses those same questions.

Boundaries do not exist between humans and nature. We are a species of primate, one example of evolution, no different to other life forms on Earth, certainly not eternal. We cannot manipulate the planet for our own purposes without consequence. Humans cannot avoid current pressing and existential problems, many of our own making, for much longer. Without acknowledgement of the interests of the planet and that other living things are no less a creation of evolution than humans, no solution is possible.

There was a world before humans and there will be one after us. The planet would need millions of years to regain the biodiversity that existed before modern humans. That is not long in deep time. Our species' history is irrelevant in such time scales.

In 1947, unveiling a monument to the once abundant but now extinct passenger pigeon, Aldo Leopold grieved the loss. He thought it novel for one species to mourn the death of another, adding that it was the only evidence of humanity's superiority over animals. After we are gone, the animals may return. They will not mourn our passing.

EPILOGUE

A MOST TRAFFICKED ANIMAL

The journeys I took with Jade spanning three decades have involved quixotic searches, but none more than that for a pangolin, the only scaly mammal in the world. The body, the size of a large domestic cat, is covered in large yellowish-brown plates of keratin. Crocodilian tail at one end and pointy, toothless head at the other, the prehistoric creature looks like a walking artichoke or a pinecone.

Pangolins eat ants, termites and other insects. Small eyes with thick lids protect against bites. A protruding snout and a long tongue are used to hunt. Insects are trapped in the sticky mucus produced by its salivary glands and then eaten. A single pangolin eats around 70 million ants and termites a year, playing an important role in regulating insect populations.

The animal walks on its hind legs, front claws held up out of harm's way, the tail extended as a counterbalance. Young are carried on the mother's tail. When threatened, pangolins curl up into an armoured ball, which gives the animal its Malay-derived name, which means 'roller'. It scythes the tail back and forth, its blade-like scales threatening paws or fingers. It can spray a pungent, skunk-style liquid from the anal glands to deter predators. Its ecology and population are poorly understood.

There are eight known species, four each in Africa and Asia. All are on the IUCN Red List, with three critically endangered.

Pangolins are among the most trafficked animals on Earth. Despite defences that can ward off lions, tigers and leopards, it has no protection against humans. Over the last two decades, it is estimated that between one and two million pangolins have been killed. No one is certain of the number because the only evidence is seized body parts. In China and Vietnam, the flesh is an expensive delicacy. Pangolin scales are used in traditional Chinese medicine. Despite no proven medical value, they are widely used for treating rheumatism, asthma, cancer, infertility and promoting lactation.

In 2020, there was speculation that Covid-19 may have passed from bats to humans through an intermediary animal: the pangolin. The attention led to further persecution, this time to prevent the spread of the virus.

In recent years, actions to conserve pangolins – combating poaching and trafficking with community education – have increased. There is a worldwide ban on trade in the animal. The pangolin was removed from the official 2020 listing of ingredients approved for use in traditional Chinese medicine. The third Saturday in February is promoted as World Pangolin Day. None of these measures will ensure the continuation of the species. Even before the new initiatives, pangolins were already protected. The rate of killing is unsustainable.

Our search for a pangolin started more than two decades ago. The distinctiveness of the animal was one factor. Ecotourism snobbery, the desire to see exotic species that rarely feature on most travellers' to-see wish lists, was another.

Pangolins are elusive. Their habitat varies from jungles or forests (where they are difficult to see) to scrublands (where they are easier to see). They tend to be nocturnal and shy. Some species spend much of their time in deep inaccessible burrows. Even some wildlife biologists and rangers with years in the field have never seen a wild specimen. It dawned on us that we probably would never see one.

Our South African friend Asher is a hunter. At his Joburg home, I once opened his refrigerator to be confronted by an entire dismembered wildebeest, including the head, neatly sectioned and vacuum-packed for consumption. Like many hunters, he is a conservationist. The two seemingly opposing concepts coexist in people like Asher, who kill selectively but use everything from the animal.

In 2013, a laconic email from Asher arrives: 'Just returned from a week in the bush – and guess what – we saw a pangolin – my very first in 38 years of regular bush going.' It was the ranger's third specimen in over 5000 game drives. The park ecologist estimated that you see one pangolin for every 50,000 kilometres (about 30,000 miles) driven in the reserve. The email ended: 'So don't feel too bad!'

The good news is that it is possible to see pangolins in the wild. The bad news is that it might take thirty-eight years, which we don't have. A line in Asher's email offers hope: 'That being said … the best place in Africa to see them is Tswalu.'

That is how we came to be at the Oppenheimer-owned property.

On arrival at Tswalu, our guide conveys unwanted news. He has just spent ten days with an older woman who was also searching for a pangolin. They tried everything, including staking out a burrow for days. They saw nothing.

Other attractions are plentiful – lions, cheetahs, rhinos, buffalo, foxes, antelope, meerkats and an abundance of birds. On a night drive, we see our first-ever aardvark, a medium-sized, burrowing nocturnal mammal native to Africa. It looks like a hastily assembled collage of body parts borrowed from other animals. The stout body is covered in hair. The prominent arched back and hind legs, which are longer than the forelegs, give the animal an unbalanced appearance. The elongated head at the end of short, thick neck, resembles a pig (aardvark means 'earth pig' in Afrikaans).

The individual is burrowing for ants and termites, its primary diet. We watch it create a trench with its front feet, adapted for digging, halting periodically, sniffing for the scent of prey. Aardvark feeding habits require a special anatomy. At the end of the snout, the nostrils are in a disc and thick with hair to filter out dirt. It only has peg-like molars that lack roots. The teeth have no enamel coating and are worn away and regrow continuously. Aardvarks have a keen sense of smell, with nine olfactory bulbs, more than any other mammal. The tubular mouth and thin, 30-centimetre (12-inch) long tongue are used to take as many as 50,000 insects in a night.

One evening, our guide rings – a pangolin has been seen. Within minutes we are hurtling along corrugated tracks to where the animal was located, about an hour away. Descending from the open vehicle, we rush to where the other guides are standing. There it is – a Temminck's or Cape pangolin.

The pangolin is relaxed and allows us to approach. It curls up characteristically when anyone gets too close. There are low growls from the resident group of lions only metres behind us. But we are not moving. It has taken us over twenty years to find our pangolin.

A few days later, near the same place, our tracker picks up footprints, tiny nearly invisible lines in the dirt. We trace the pangolin's erratic path through the scrub. The trail sometimes disappears, then the tracker finds it again. We try over several hours but cannot locate the animal.

A Zimbabwean woman told me about her encounter with a pangolin. She and her family were camping. Sitting around the nightly campfire, she saw something small moving behind her father's chair. Her father and the workers began shouting the Shona word for pangolin: 'Haka, Haka!' The tribesman began touching the animal, which had curled itself up in a ball. Some put coins on the scales. In local culture, pangolins are believed to bring good luck.

Makoza, a tracker friend of her father's, explained that the haka chooses who it is seen by. If you are the one to spot it, your life is blessed with good luck, happiness and prosperity. The haka's magic is particularly strong if it chooses to show himself to a young person. The animal would reveal in some way that it had chosen her.

The pangolin eventually unravelled itself and spent time foraging around the camp. Then it headed purposefully for the circle of tents and walked directly into the one where she usually slept, settling himself in a ball under her camp bed. Sometime later it got up and headed out of the tent and disappeared into the night.

Her father still lives on the same farm in Zimbabwe. To this day, there are many there who talk about the child blessed by the haka.

The sad part of the Shona belief is that it became fashionable to bring hakas to the late President Robert Mugabe as gifts, resulting in their relentless hunting. Given Mugabe's supposed personal wealth, the hakas apparently bestowed much fortune on the President. Unfortunately, there are not enough pangolins left to bring any magic or prosperity to indigent Zimbabwe.

We arranged to meet Asher in Joburg in March 2020 on our way to Ghana, but the pandemic meant our trip was cancelled.

In July 2020, Asher emailed. Hunting impala rams with a tracker on foot, he had seen something running through the bush. It was an aardvark, the first one he had ever seen in a lifetime of bush visits. He came across a rare white rhino. On the way back to the camp, he found an enormous pangolin walking across the road, his second. Few people see an aardvark, a pangolin and a white rhino in the wild in the space of a few hours. Asher's email ended: 'I realize how lucky I am.'

A few weeks later, Asher died suddenly of a heart attack. He was forty-five years old. Our last exchanges were about the pangolin. Seeing the animal, he had started to cry.

We still have a picture of Asher cradling the pangolin. Without him, we might have never seen that fabled creature.

In 2020, Australia adopted draconian border restrictions, transforming itself into a hermit kingdom in an ultimately futile attempt to stave off the virus. It brought a halt to our peregrinations. Even local travel within Australia became difficult due to internal restrictions on movement.

The global slowdown of travel and other human activity was christened the anthro-pause. Despite hopes that the hiatus would reduce emissions and pollution, even if temporarily, atmospheric carbon dioxide kept setting new records. A massive amount of plastic waste, discarded protective equipment and disposable medical supplies piled up. The elastic of cast-off face masks proved deadly to wild animals. When masks were used as nesting materials, birds or their chicks became entangled in the elastic and died.

Annual global tourism activity halved. Experts suggested that it could take up to five years for activity to recover if Covid-19 or variants were brought under control and no new disruption occurred. For nations and communities dependent on tourism, the consequences were devastating. By 2022, vaccines and treatments offered the prospect of a return of normality.

It wasn't only the pandemic. Events seemed to follow the Book of Revelation. Alongside the Covid-19 pestilence, war and famine emerged. Non-biblical problems, such as debt, rapidly rising prices, sharp increases in interest costs for the first time in a decade and financial calamity appeared. Concerns about the environment receded, replaced by alarm about unemployment, the cost of living, healthcare and security. Governments prioritised economic recovery and restoration of living standards, rolling back environmental protections to fast-track projects to provide employment or lower food and energy costs. Treasuries exhausted from spending to fight the pandemic and support the economy had less money for conservation initiatives.

In 2022, the Ukraine conflict and sanctions meant that foreign access to the Russian Far East, which Jade and I had hoped to revisit, was suspended. Environmentalists warned that planned militarisation of the region would pose problems for the fragile ecosystem. Thomas Dance, a columnist for *The Wall Street Journal*, urged the United States to reclaim Wrangel Island, which Lenin's gunboat *Krasny Oktyabr* (*Red October*) had seized in 1924.

The prospects for wilderness and wild animals were grim.

In lockdown, with our mobility restricted, we watched the birds near our home, who we know and who we suspect know us as well. The noisy minors squabbled, the magpies carolled and the butcherbird's beautiful flute-like song woke us some mornings. Possums scurried noisily across our metal roof. Orb spiders spun their delicate webs, large huntsman spiders stalked prey in our apartment. They all went about their lives.

Coronavirus trapped us at home in endless Zoom calls and streamed entertainment. But migratory birds continued their annual pilgrimages. We watched visitors from the Indonesian archipelago flying overhead – large channel-billed cuckoos, sometimes called storm birds, with their massive down-curved bills, their long tails and large wings forming a familiar crucifix-like silhouette. It was proof of the continuity of the natural world.

Our impingements – the inability to travel and endless fights with insurers and airlines over cancelled bookings – were insignificant middle-class entitlement meltdowns. People lost lives, loved ones and livelihoods. Many guides and drivers we knew struggled to earn any money at all. Without any prospect of work, life for them and their families became a struggle. We did what we could to assist.

Confined in the cement and glass shell of our apartment, without the ability to travel to see wildlife, our lives seemed flat and unmoored. Were we addicts?

In late 2022, as travel restrictions lifted, we resumed our journeys, with misgivings amid a boom in revenge travel. We rationalised the resumption on the grounds that the trips had been paid for but deferred due to the pandemic. There was much to see, but the accelerating deterioration of the planet's remaining natural ecosystems was striking.

Lack of visitors and loss of livelihoods during the pandemic meant increasing encroachment of humans into protected areas. Urban lockdowns and economic retrenchment forced many to return home to farms and villages, adding to pressures. Hunger and the need for income led to increased poaching. Local populations now had no incentive to protect the few vulnerable pockets of remaining habitat.

In Ghana, where we saw the legendary *Picathartes gymnocephalus* – white-necked rockfowl – damage from illegal hunting, logging and mining was plain. At Atewa Hills, a motorbike passed us with a dead duiker, a small antelope, tied to the back. On a trail, we came across a pile of feathers stripped from a dead long-tailed hawk, unique among birds of prey for its distinctive black-and-white striped tail. Used shotgun shells lay on the ground nearby. Our visibly upset guide, Paul, had seen the same bird alive days ago near the spot.

In Thailand, the use of bird hides and feeding stations had compounded the problem. With no visitors and a lack of funds, the absence of food meant that many birds had moved away. Some dependent birds hung around garbage dumps and kitchen waste, where we were forced to look for them. Other habituated ones suffered a more deadly fate. Locals left food to attract them, to allow capture either for the pet trade or to be slaughtered for food.

A trip to Brazil reinforced different changes. Wildlife photography now dominated. The abacus approach to wildlife had gained ground, with one global birding tour operator's website boasting that their trips have recorded over 10,600 bird species, far more than competitors. It was a none-too-subtle message for keen listers.

Many older, especially indigenous, guides are nearing the end of their working lives. Their knowledge gained over a lifetime spent in wilderness areas will soon be lost. Newer generations are not interested in guiding, choosing different futures, as is their right.

A new cohort of guides, many highly qualified biologists, speak incessantly about wildlife 'targets' and 'lifers'. There is an unhealthy reliance on technology – GPS co-ordinates of where the animal was last seen, excessive use of playback and powerful laser pointers. The panic on the face of guides when their smartphone fails or the internet coverage drops out is pitiful. Guides seem focused on generating images and videos of sightings to post online for self-promotion.

Last-chance-to-see ecotourism has an even greater poignancy. We travelled to a remote small town – Botumirim, located in the Brazilian state of Minas Gerais – in search of one bird. It provided perhaps the most bittersweet moment of our journey: a male blue-eyed ground dove. It was stunningly beautiful – cinnamon-coloured, with striking blue eyes and blue wing spots. Rediscovered in 2007 after being thought to be extinct, it was one of thirteen individuals left, based on the most recent census. Despite frantic efforts, it is unlikely that that the species can be saved. The sorrow we felt was immeasurable. Poet William Butler Yeats thought that humans most love what vanishes. It all seemed sordid, like necrophiliac tourism.

The animals do not want to see us, Nikita Ovsyanikov had suggested. Perhaps we should not try to see them. Reconciling the ever-present paradoxes of our journeys was impossible.

Jade and I have seen more of the Earth's surface and creatures than most humans, certainly more than two people from modest beginnings have any right to expect. Millions never have the opportunity to travel, take a holiday or enjoy the luxury of consuming wildlife spectacles. The inequality – our privilege and wealth compared to that of many in areas we have travelled – nags at us.

For a long time, we convinced ourselves that our pursuits had a worthy purpose. That some wild animals will be saved. That local people might benefit. We shared the experiences with fellow travellers, naturalists and guides, some who have become friends. It wasn't much, but it might make a small difference, we told ourselves.

Yet what we chose to believe turns out to be untrue. The damage to wilderness and wildlife is evident to even the casual return tourist. Alongside traditional threats, industrial ecotourism now cynically exploits the very things it pretends to protect. Words such as *ecology*, *environmentalism*, *conservation*, *preservation* and *activism* have lost meaning. They are hollow formulations, used to justify certain behaviours. There is no community of interest in preserving the Earth in anything close to its natural state. The focus is on short-term priorities, self-gratification and pursuing petty individual interests without regard for cost.

Rapacious desire is destroying the planet's natural history. And we are complicit. Delight has been replaced by dread and helplessness at the destruction. Much of what we have seen and once hoped to see will soon be lost, despite the best efforts of the dedicated few, beyond the next few decades.

The planet was once a place where wilderness and animals surrounded pockets of people. The future is one in which shrinking pockets of nature will barely survive, encircled by an ever-expanding human population. Much of what are now considered wild places will become little more than outdoor menageries. These state and private reserves are oases. Sometimes, the number of species seen can be high, a reflection of the lack of suitable habitat and threats elsewhere. But the number of individuals is low, and frequently insufficient to sustain a breeding population. The animals are at constant risk of dying off, leaving biological deserts.

While some species will adapt to human incursions, many animals, marginalised in these zoo-like areas, are increasingly living monuments to their own passing. They exist only for the pleasure of humankind, at whose mercy and whim they continue their precarious existence. With so many species now under threat of extinction, humans play god, deciding the fate of individual animals or species – who lives, who dies.

In a 1980 essay 'Why Look at Animals?', John Berger describes a captive animal's gaze, which briefly fixes on but quickly passes beyond the human spectator in its hopeless search to exist freely. This loss of connection diminishes us and symbolises human degeneration. All our exploring, T.S. Eliot thought, ends in us arriving back at the start and, for the first time, understanding the place.

It is perhaps mad to love animals and wild places, and there are penalties to that choice. Their beauty and attributes are testament to the complexity of the planet and our insignificance. But they are also proof of humanity's unspeakable violence towards nature. Environmental devastation is a marker of ignorance, stupidity and hypocrisy. It anticipates our own species' end, even if we choose to believe that all is well and ignore information to the contrary.

Our wild quests now seem to be little more than records of the passing of the natural world. We watch, trying to understand, unable to look away. We can only bear witness to the loss of the sublime.

The late natural historian Barry Lopez once found himself bowing to a horned lark, a common bird, while walking in the Arctic tundra.

It became a lifelong habit with the wild creatures he came across. It was a gesture of respect for different life forms. Perhaps we should have done the same.

ACKNOWLEDGEMENTS

I would like to thank Monash University Publishing for publishing *Wild Quests*. Thanks to Kate Morgan for her project management to ensure timely publication, Peter Long for the cover, Duncan Blachford for the typesetting, and Deb McInnes and her team for their hard and diligent work on promoting the book. I am particularly grateful to Julia Carlomagno, the publisher, for her enthusiastic support and strong belief in the work and its subject.

IMAGE CREDITS

p. 9, Polar bear: Orla / Shutterstock
p. 24, Platypus: Imagebroker / Alamy Stock Photo
p. 34, Proboscis monkey: blickwinkel / Alamy Stock Photo
p. 35, Bird-of-paradise: YouTube, John3028marsh
p. 61, Jaguar: kwiktor
p. 63, Sifaka: Survival photos / Alamy Stock Photo
p. 64, Mandrill: Anna Kucherova / Alamy Stock Photo
p. 66, Woolly spider monkey: BrazilPhotos / Alamy Stock Photo
p. 72, Wildebeest: iStock / adogslifephoto
p. 74, Shoebill stork: Mark Boulton / Alamy Stock Photo
p. 76, Giant anteater: Cavan Images / Alamy Stock Photo
p. 80, Silverback mountain gorilla: simoneemanphotography
p. 85, Japanese macaque: sepavo
p. 88, Harpy eagle: photogallet
p. 94, Stygian owl: AGAMI Photo Agency / Alamy Stock Photo
p. 103, Riflebird: Ray Wilson / Alamy Stock Photo
p. 105, Blue whale: Nature Picture Library / Alamy Stock Photo
p. 115, Gray whale eye: Andrea Izzotti / Alamy Stock Photo
p. 120, Anglerfish: Helmut Corneli / Alamy Stock Photo
p. 136, Ribbon seal: Nature and Science / Alamy Stock Photo
p. 146, Common buzzard: Les Gibbon / Alamy Stock Photo
p. 159, Tourist photographing giraffe: Andy Selinger / Alamy Stock Photo
p. 177, Crocodile: someman
p. 189, Helmeted hornbill: Tim Plowden / Alamy Stock Photo

p. 211, Douc langur: Nature Picture Library / Alamy Stock Photo
p. 213, Steller's sea cow: Universal Images Group North America LLC / Alamy Stock Photo
p. 226, Emperor penguin and chicks: vladsilver
p. 250, Sea coral: stephankerkhofs
p. 255, Pangolin: RooM the Agency / Alamy Stock Photo
p. 262, Channel-billed cuckoo: Rick & Nora Bowers / Alamy Stock Photo

FURTHER READING

CLIMATE CHANGE

Jonathan Franzen, *The End of the End of the Earth*, Farrer, Straus and Giroux, 2018.

Dale Jamieson, *Reason in a Dark Time: Why the Struggle Against Climate Change Failed – And What It Means for Our Future*, Oxford University Press, 2017.

Elizabeth Kolbert, *Field Notes from a Catastrophe: Man, Nature and Climate Change*, Bloomsbury, 2015.

Elizabeth Kolbert, *The Sixth Extinction: An Unnatural History*, Henry Holt, 2014.

Kari Marie Norgaard, *Living in Denial: Climate Change, Emotions, and Everyday Life*, The MIT Press, 2011.

CONSERVATION

David Attenborough, *A Life on Our Planet: My Witness Statement and a Vision for the Future*, Witness Books, 2020.

Eric Becker, 'The Influence of Environmental NGOs in the Global Society', *Butler Journal of Undergraduate Research*, vol. 2, article 17, 2016.

Raymond L. Bryant, 'Born to Be Wild? Non-Governmental Organisations, Politics and the Environment', *Geography Compass* 3/4, 2009, pp. 1540–58.

Adrienne Buller, *The Value of a Whale: On the Illusions of Green Capitalism*, Manchester University Press, 2023.

Partha Dasgupta, *The Economics of Biodiversity: The Dasgupta Review*, HM Treasury, 2021.

Rosaleen Duffy, *A Trip Too Far: Ecotourism, Politics and Exploitation*, Earthscan, 2002.

Justin Farrell, *Billionaire Wilderness: The Ultra-Wealthy and the Remaking of the American West*, Princeton University Press, 2020.

Edward Humes, *Eco Barons: The New Heroes of Environmental Activism*, Ecco, 2010.

Christine MacDonald, *Green Inc.: An Environmental Insider Reveals How a Good Cause Has Gone Bad*, The Lyons Press, 2009.

McKinsey Global Institute, *Valuing Nature Conservation: A Methodology for Quantifying the Benefits of Protecting the Planet's Natural Capital*, 2020.

Rex Weyler, *Greenpeace: How a Group of Ecologists, Journalists and Visionaries Changed the World*, Rodale, 2004.

ENVIRONMENTALISM

Edward Abbey, *Desert Solitaire: A Season in the Wilderness*, Simon and Schuster, 1968.

Rachel Carson, *Silent Spring*, Houghton Mifflin, 2002.

Anne Dillard, *Pilgrim at Tinker Creek*, Harper Perennial, 1974.

Michael H. Graham, Joan Parker and Paul K. Dayton, *The Essential Naturalist: Timeless Readings in Natural History*, University of Chicago Press, 2011.

Justin Gregg, *If Nietzsche Were a Narwhal: What Animal Intelligence Reveals About Human Stupidity*, Little, Brown, 2022.

Ramchandra Guha, *Environmentalism: A Global History*, Longman, 2000.

Aldo Leopold, *Sand County Almanac*, Ballantine Books, 1986.

J.R. McNeil, *An Environmental History of the Twentieth-Century World*, W.W. Norton, 2000.

David Petersen del Mar, *Environmentalism*, Pearson Longman, 2006.

Timothy Morton, *Being Ecological*, Pelican, 2018.

David Quammen, *The Song of the Dodo*, Scribner, 1996.

John W. Reid and Thomas E. Lovejoy, *Ever Green: Saving Big Forests to Save the Planet*, W.W. Norton, 2022.

Alan Weisman, *The World Without Us*, Picador, 2007.

Edward O. Wilson, *Half-Earth: Our Planet's Fight for Life*, W.W. Norton, 2016.

Edward O. Wilson, *The Creation: An Appeal to Save Life on Earth*, W.W. Norton, 2006.

Edward O. Wilson, *The Diversity of Life*, W.W. Norton, 1992.

Edward O. Wilson, *The Future of Life*, Vintage, 2002.

EXPLORATION

Benedict Allen, *Exploration*, Faber and Faber, 2004.

Charles Darwin, *The Origin of Species*, Signet, 2003.

Alexander von Humboldt, *Personal Narrative of a Journey to the Equinoctial Regions of the New Continent: Abridged Edition*, Penguin Classics, 1996.

Alexander von Humboldt, *Views of Nature*, University of Chicago Press, 2016.

Alfred Russel Wallace, *The Malay Archipelago*, John Beaufoy Publishing, 2016.

Andrea Wulf, *The Invention of Nature: Alexander von Humboldt's New World*, Vintage, 2016.

TRAVEL

Douglas Adams and Mark Carwardine, *Last Chance to See*, Ballantine Books, 1990.

Ismar Borges De Lima & Ronda J. Green, *Wildlife Tourism, Environmental Learning and Ethical Encounters – Ecological and Conservation Aspects*, Springer-Verlag, 2017.

Alain de Botton, *The Art of Travel*, Hamish Hamilton, 2002.

Marco D'Eramo, *The World in a Selfie: An Inquiry into the Tourist Age*, Verso, 2021.

David A. Fennell, *Ecotourism*, Routledge, 2017.

Jennifer Hill & Tim Gale, *Ecotourism and Environmental Sustainability*, Ashgate, 2009.

Martha Honey, *Ecotourism and Sustainable Development*, Oxford University Press, 2008.

John Keay (ed.), *Travel in Dangerous Places,* Constable & Robinson, 1993.

Eric J. Leed, *The Mind of the Traveller: From Gilgamesh to Global Tourism*, Basic Books, 1992.

Nicholas T. Parsons, *Worth the Detour: A History of the Guidebook*, Sutton Publishing, 2007.

Peter Whitfield, *Travel: A Literary History*, Bodelian Library, 2011.

Eric Zuelow, *A History of Modern Tourism*, Palgrave Macmillan, 2015.

WILDLIFE AND DESTINATIONS

Simon Barnes, *How to Be a Bad Birdwatcher: To the Greater Glory of Life*, Short Books, 2004.

Stanley Breeden and Belinda Wright, *Through the Tiger's Eyes: A Chronicle of India's Wildlife*, Ten Speed Press, 1996.

D. Graham Burnett, *The Sounding of the Whale: Science and Cetaceans in the Twentieth Century*, University of Chicago Press, 2012.

David G. Campbell, *The Crystal Desert: Summers in Antarctica*, Mariner Books, 2002.

Catherine Caulfield, *In the Rainforest*, Picador, 1986.

Mark Cocker, *Birders: Tales of a Tribe*, Vintage, 2002.

Gretchen Ehrlich, *This Cold Heaven: Seven Seasons in Greenland*, Fourth Estate, 2003.

Charlie Elder, *While the Flocks Last*, Corgi Books, 2009.

Richard Ellis, *The Empty Ocean*, Island Press, 2003.

Donna J. Haraway, *Primate Visions: Gender, Race, and Nature in the World of Modern Science*, Routledge, 1990.

Karen Higginbottom (ed.) *Wildlife Tourism: Impacts, Management and Planning*, Common Ground Publishing, 2004.

Robert Kunzig, *Mapping the Deep: The Extraordinary Story of Ocean Science*, Sort of Books, 2000.

Mark Kurlansky, *Cod: A Biography of the Fish That Changes the World*, Penguin, 1997.
Barry Lopez, *Arctic Dreams: Imagination and Desire in a Northern Landscape*, The Harvill Press, 1986.
Nancy Lord, *Beluga Days: Tracking a White Whale's Truths*, Counterpoint, 2004.
Stephen Moss, *A Bird in the Bush: A Social History of Birdwatching*, Aurum, 2004.
Peter Matthiessen, *African Silences*, Harvill, 1991.
Peter Matthiessen, *Ends of the Earth: Voyages to Antarctica*, Vintage, 2003.
Peter Matthiessen, *The Cloud Forest: A Chronicle of the South American Wilderness*, Vintage, 1978.
Peter Matthiessen, *The Snow Leopard*, Vintage, 2003.
Peter Matthiessen, *Tigers in the Snow*, North Point Press, 2000.
David R. Montgomery, *King of Fish: The Thousand-Year Run of Salmon*, Westview Press, 2003.
Bill Streever, *Cold: Adventures in the World's Frozen Place*, Back Bay Books, 2009.
Valmik Thapar, *The Last Tiger: Struggling for Survival*, Oxford University Press, 2006.
Sara Wheeler, *Terra Incognita: Travels in Antarctica*, Vintage, 1997.
Art Wolfe and Barbara Sleeper, *Primates: The Amazing World of Lemurs, Monkeys and Apes*, Chronicle Books, 1997.
Ed Yong, *An Immense World: How Animal Senses Reveal the Hidden Realms Around Us*, Random House, 2022.

WILDLIFE FILMMAKING

David Attenborough, *Life On Air*, BBC, 2002.
Nick Gordon, *In the Heart of the Amazon*, Metro Publishing, 2002.
Jan-Christopher Horak, 'Wildlife Documentaries: From Classical Forms to Reality TV', *Film History*, vol. 18, 2006, pp. 459–75.
Eleanor Macleod Louson, 'Never Before Seen: Spectacle, Staging, and Story in Wildlife Film's Blue-Chip Renaissance', PhD thesis, York University Toronto, Ontario, September 2018.
Gregg Mitman, *Reel Nature: America's Romance with Wildlife on Film*, University of Washington Press, 1999.
Chris Palmer, *Shooting in the Wild: An Insider's Account of Making Movies in the Animal Kingdom*, Sierra Book Club Books, 2010.
Alan Root, *Ivory, Apes & Peacocks: Animals, Adventures and Discovery in the Wild Places of Africa*, Vintage Books, 2012.